EARTHSONG

Volume I

Written and Illustrated
by Lady Yates

EARTHSONG

© Lady Yates 2004

First published online at www.earthsongsaga.com

Publisher: Seven Seas Entertainment

Visit us online at www.gomanga.com

ISBN: 1-933164-15-8

Printed in Canada

First printing: April, 2006

10 9 8 7 6 5 4 3 2 1

EARTHSONG

EARTHSONG

EARTHSONG

Volume I, Chapter I

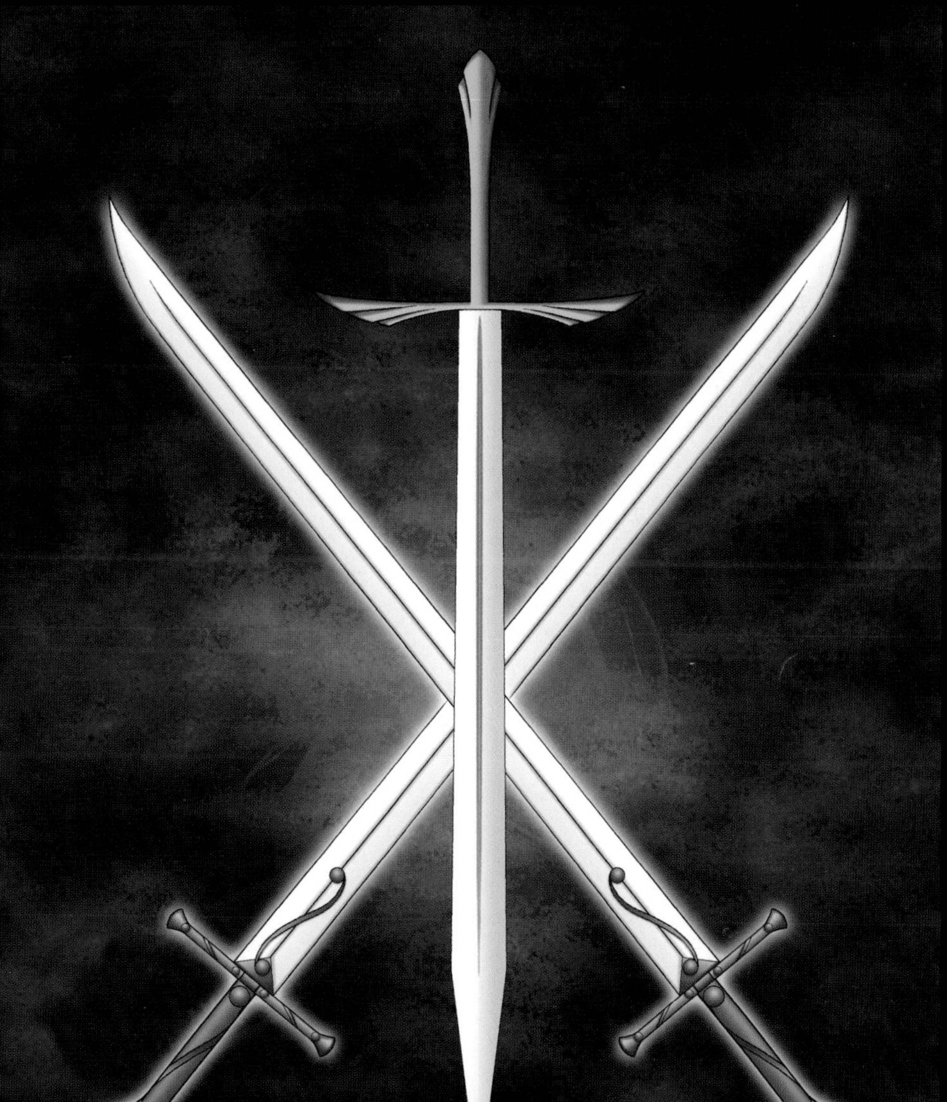

The Saga Begins...

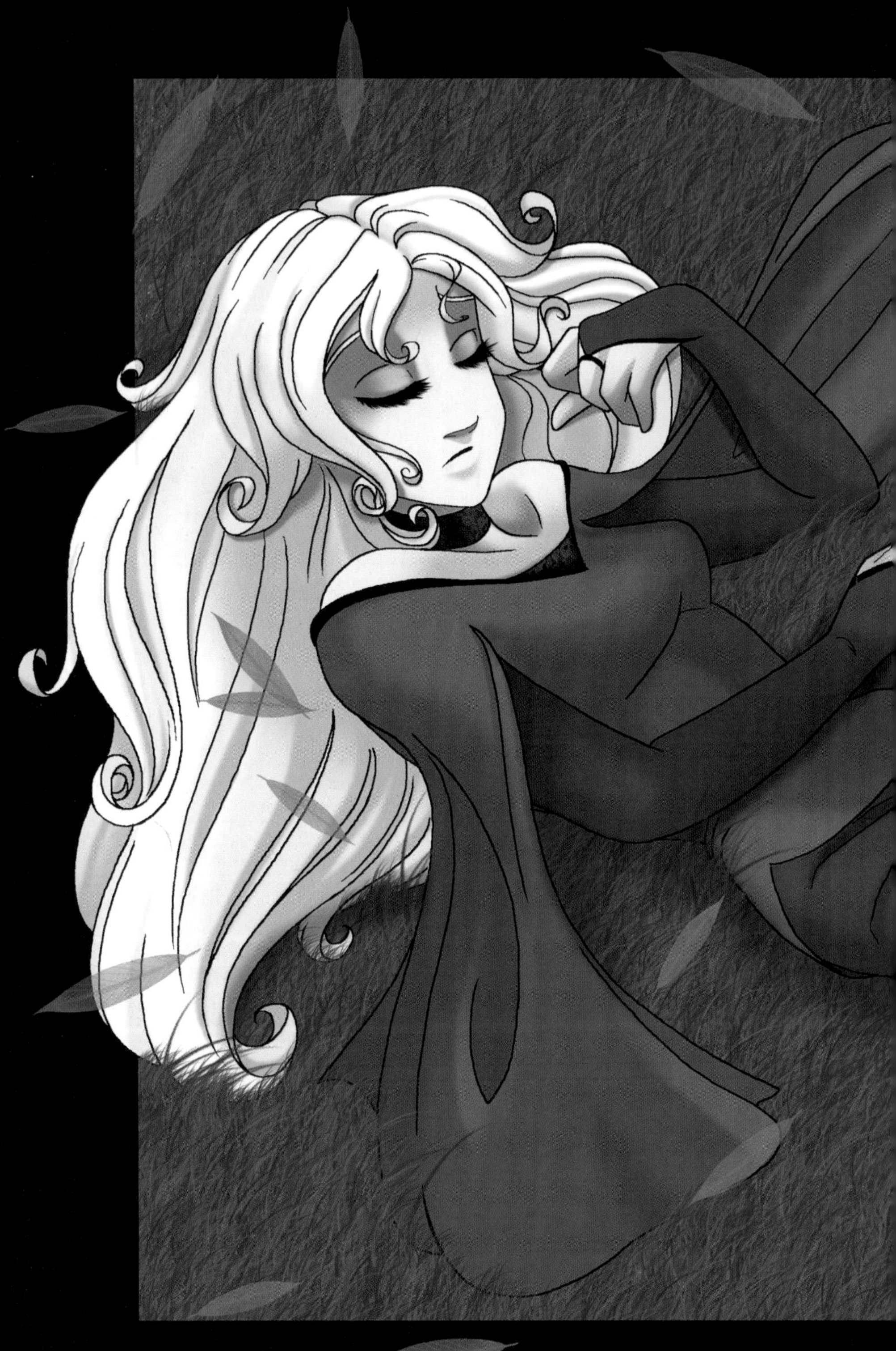

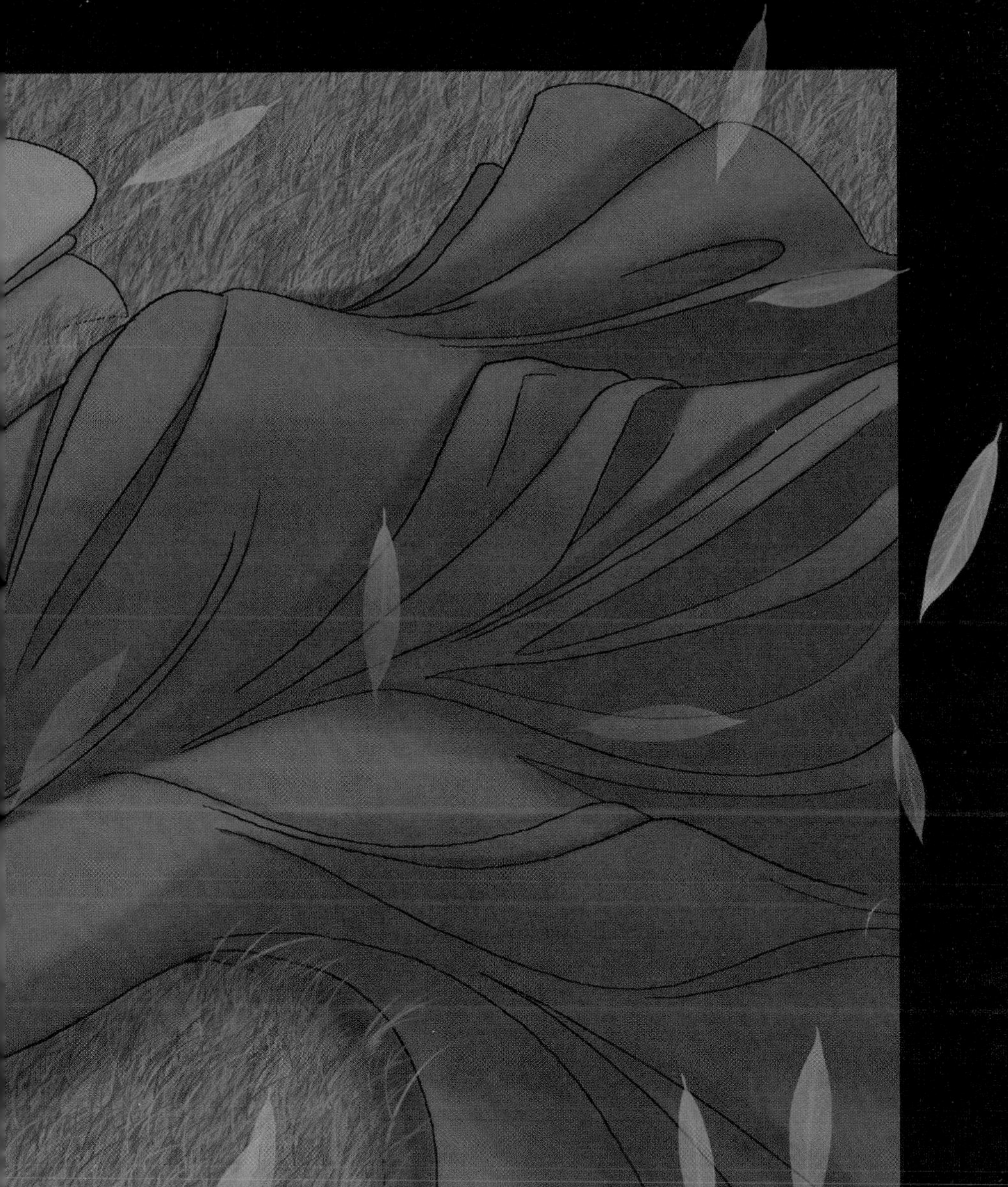

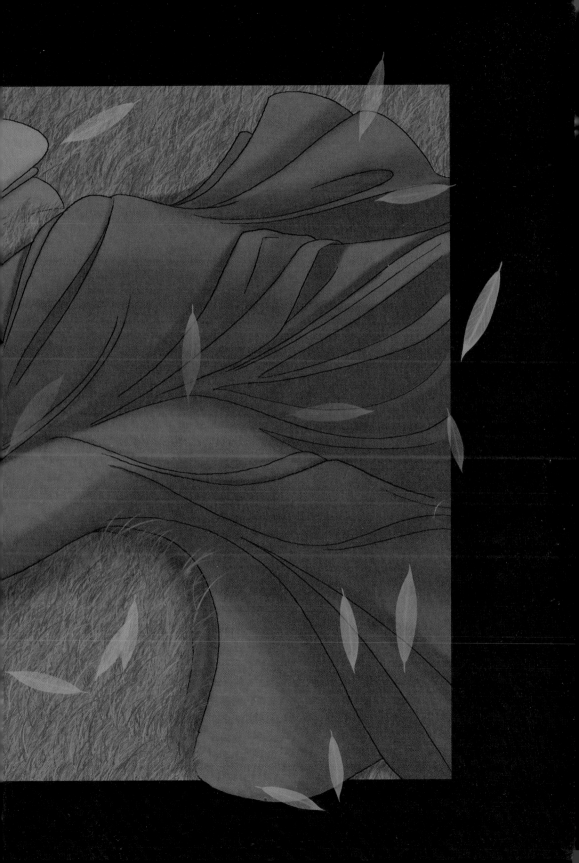

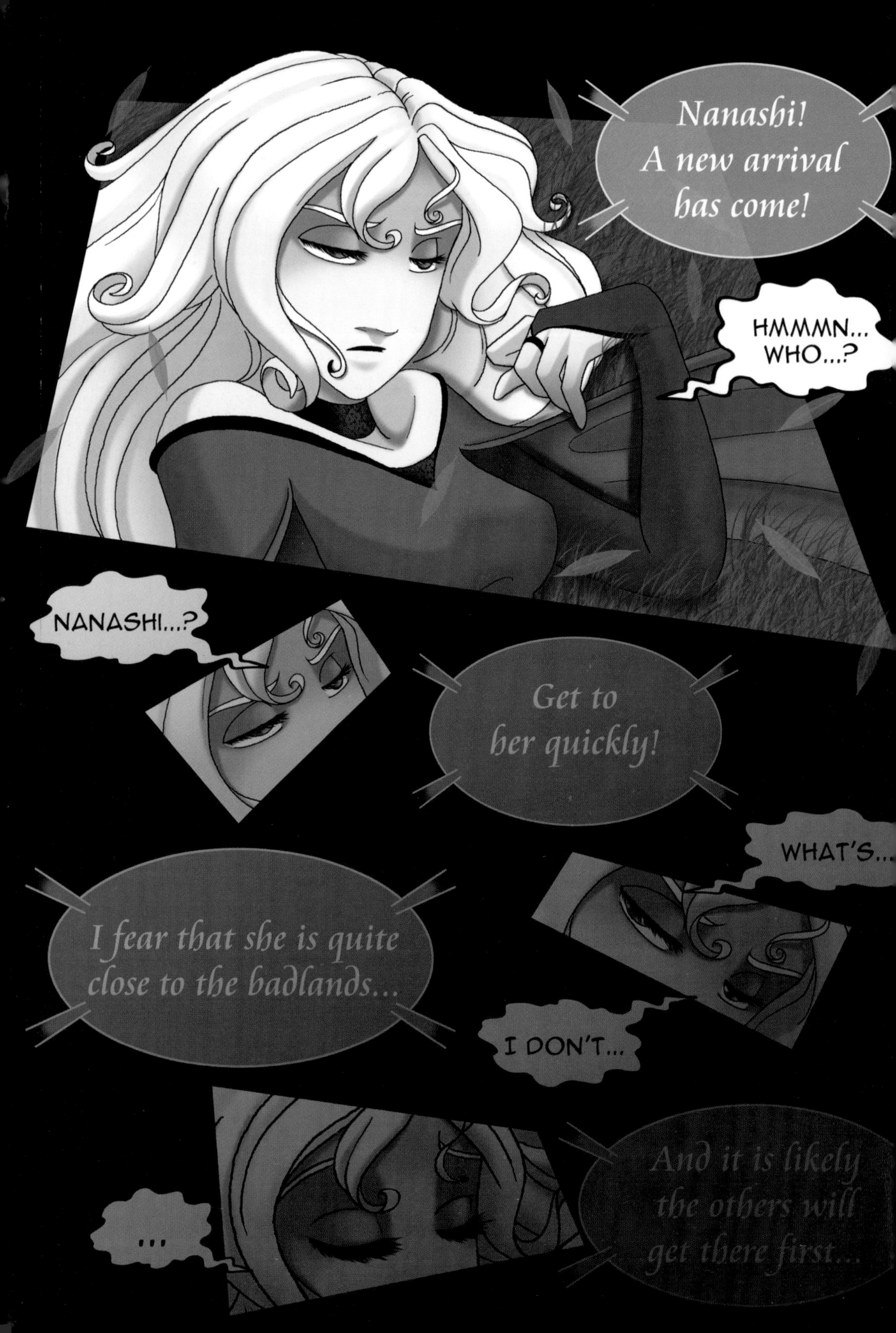
Nanashi! A new arrival has come!
HMMMN... WHO...?
NANASHI...?
Get to her quickly!
I fear that she is quite close to the badlands...
WHAT'S...
I DON'T...
...
And it is likely the others will get there first...

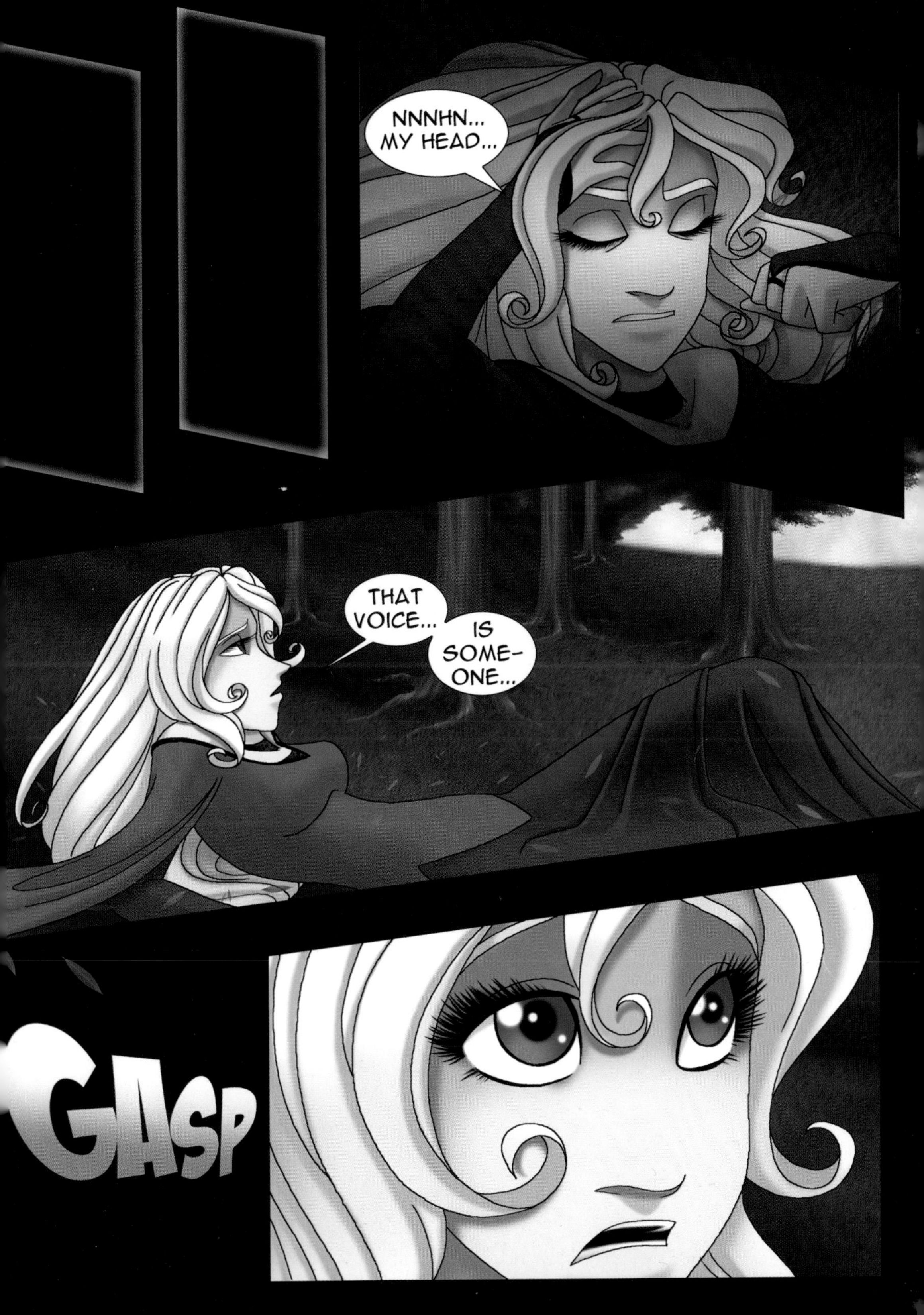
NNNHN... MY HEAD...
THAT VOICE...
IS SOME-ONE...
GASP

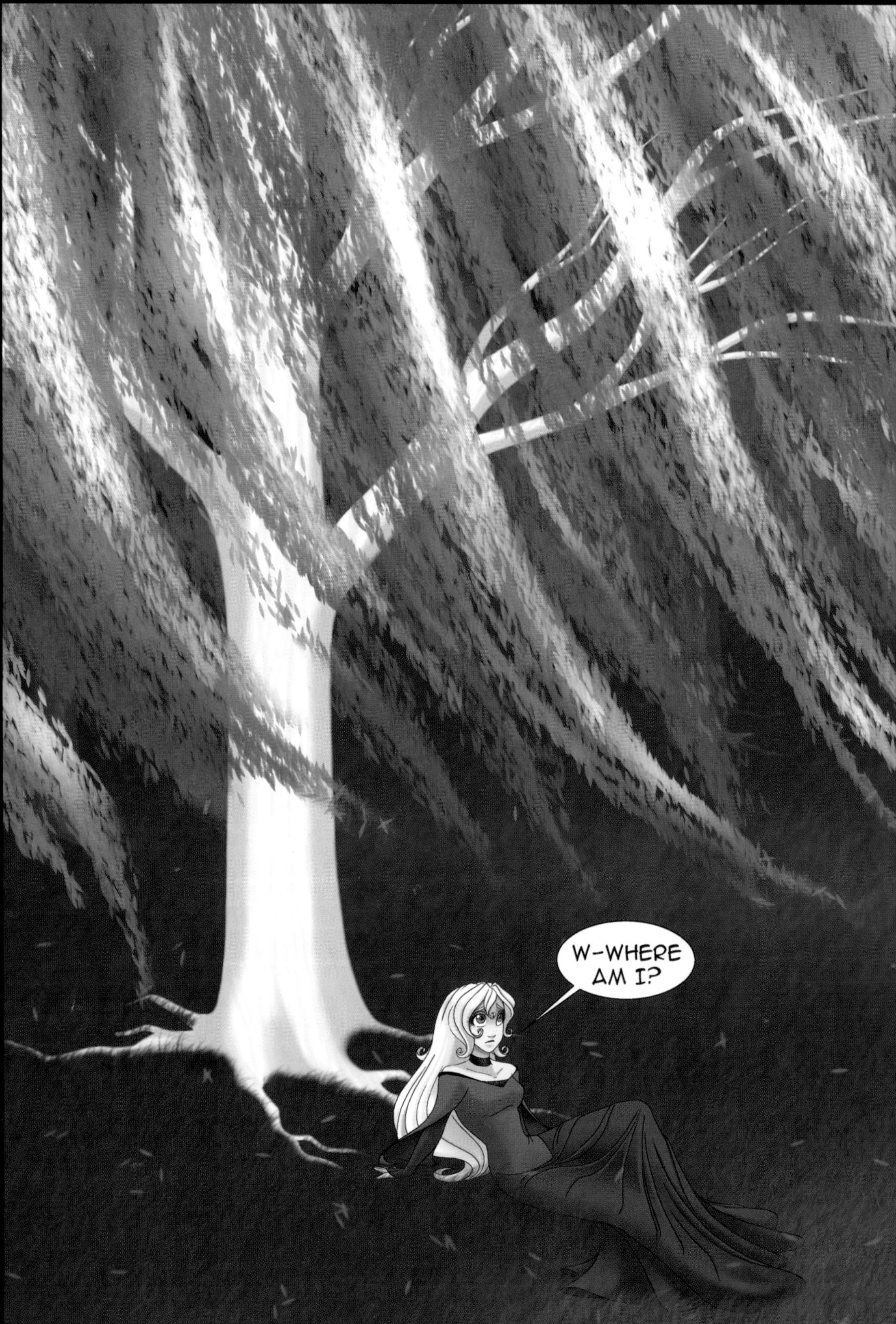
W-WHERE AM I?

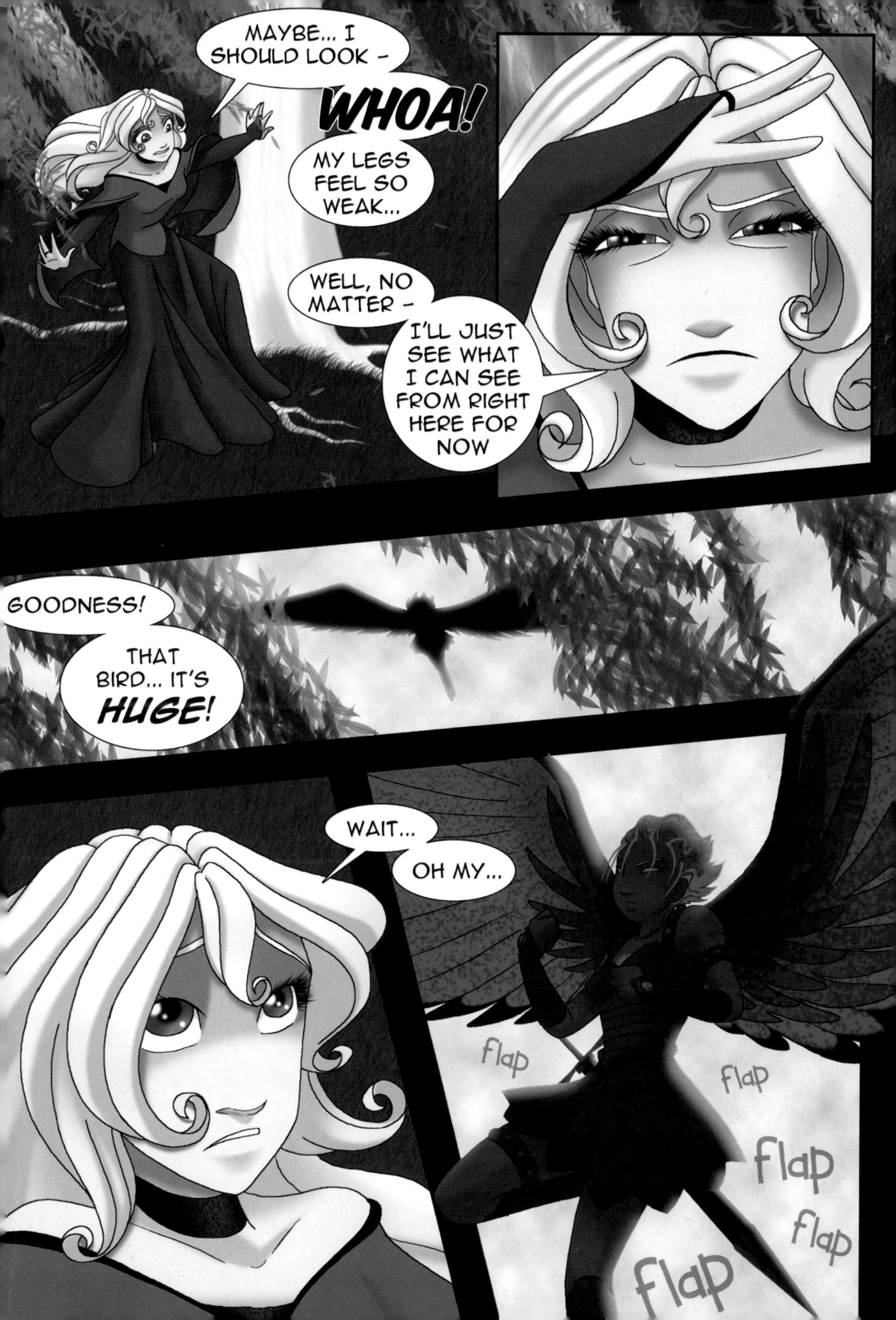
MAYBE... I SHOULD LOOK -
WHOA!
MY LEGS FEEL SO WEAK...
WELL, NO MATTER -
I'LL JUST SEE WHAT I CAN SEE FROM RIGHT HERE FOR NOW
GOODNESS!
THAT BIRD... IT'S HUGE!
WAIT...
OH MY...
flap
flap
flap
flap
flap

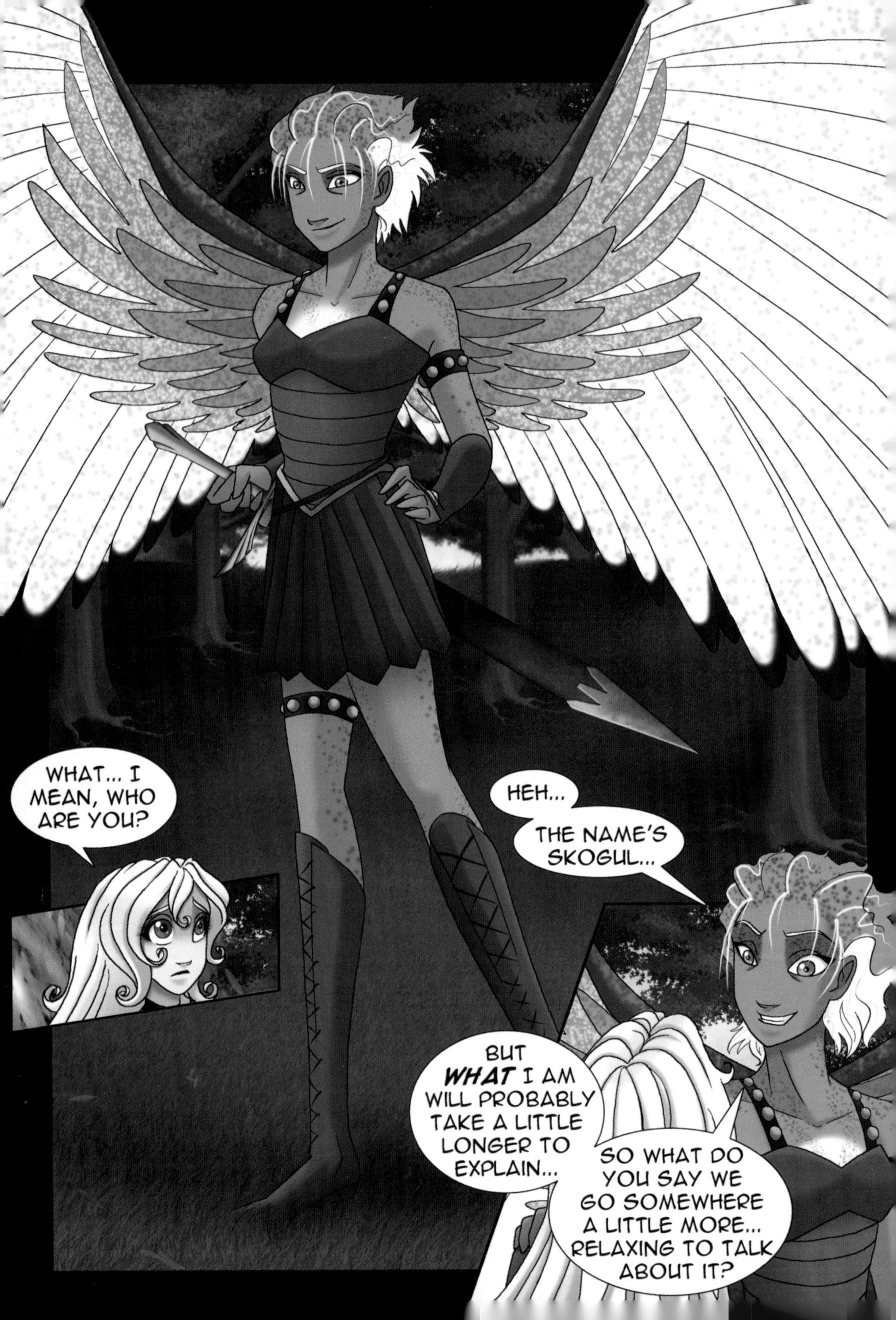
WHAT... I MEAN, WHO ARE YOU?
HEH...
THE NAME'S SKOGUL...
BUT ***WHAT*** I AM WILL PROBABLY TAKE A LITTLE LONGER TO EXPLAIN...
SO WHAT DO YOU SAY WE GO SOMEWHERE A LITTLE MORE... RELAXING TO TALK ABOUT IT?

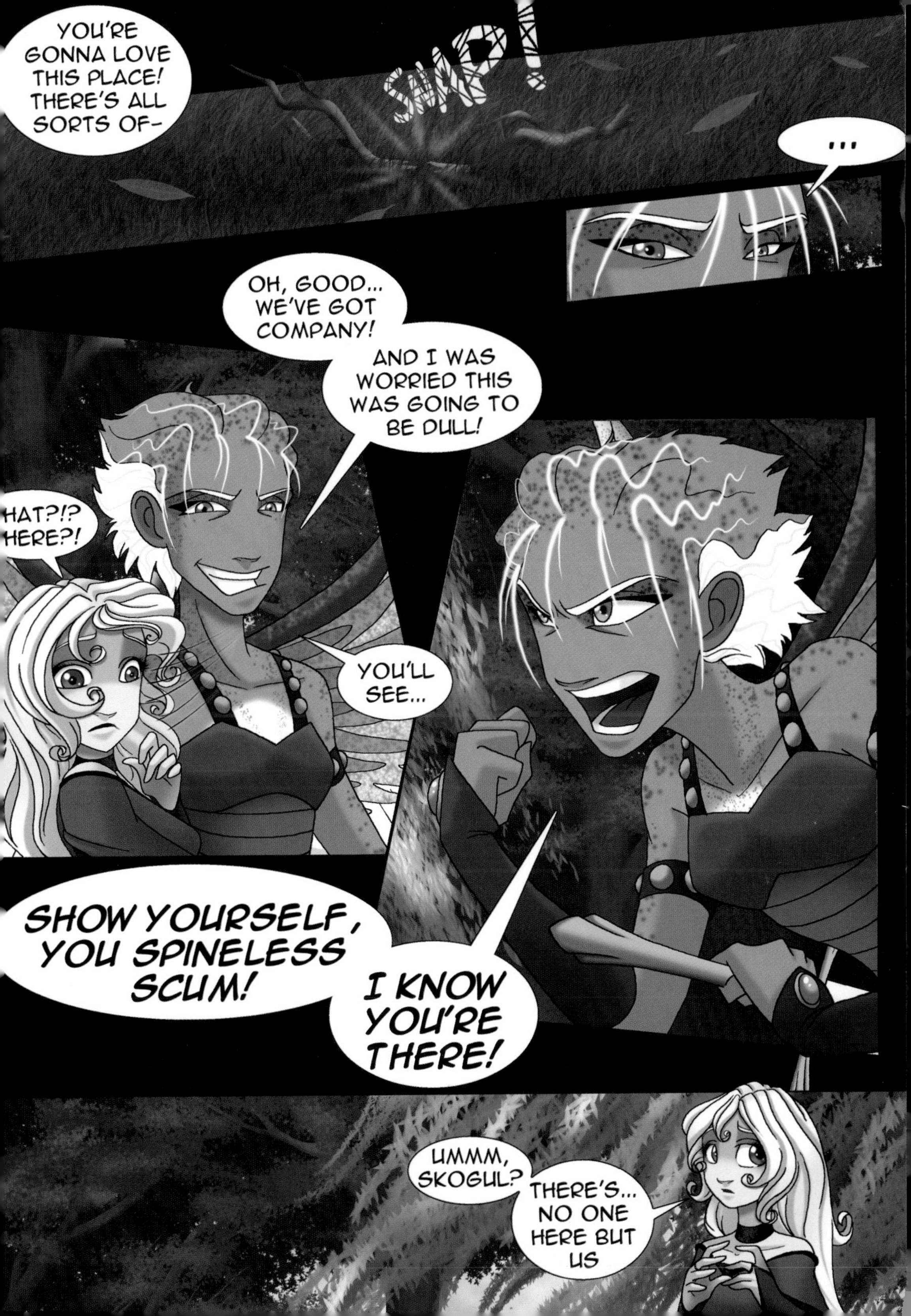
YOU'RE GONNA LOVE THIS PLACE! THERE'S ALL SORTS OF-
SNAP!
...
OH, GOOD... WE'VE GOT COMPANY!
AND I WAS WORRIED THIS WAS GOING TO BE DULL!
HAT?!? HERE?!
YOU'LL SEE...
SHOW YOURSELF, YOU SPINELESS SCUM!
I KNOW YOU'RE THERE!
UMMM, SKOGUL?
THERE'S... NO ONE HERE BUT US

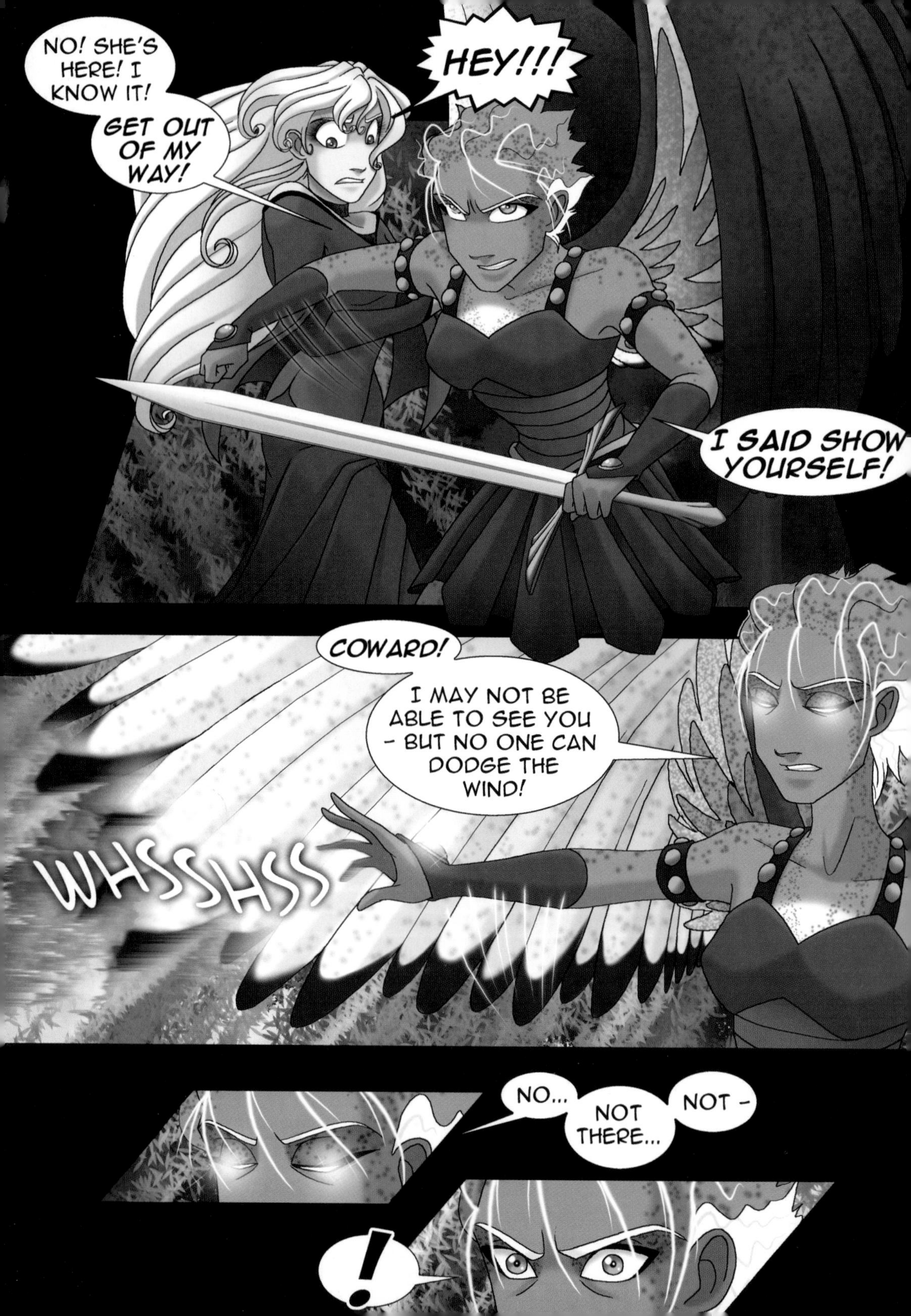
NO! SHE'S HERE! I KNOW IT!
GET OUT OF MY WAY!
HEY!!!
I SAID SHOW YOURSELF!
COWARD!
I MAY NOT BE ABLE TO SEE YOU - BUT NO ONE CAN DODGE THE WIND!
WHSSHSS
NO...
NOT THERE...
NOT -
!

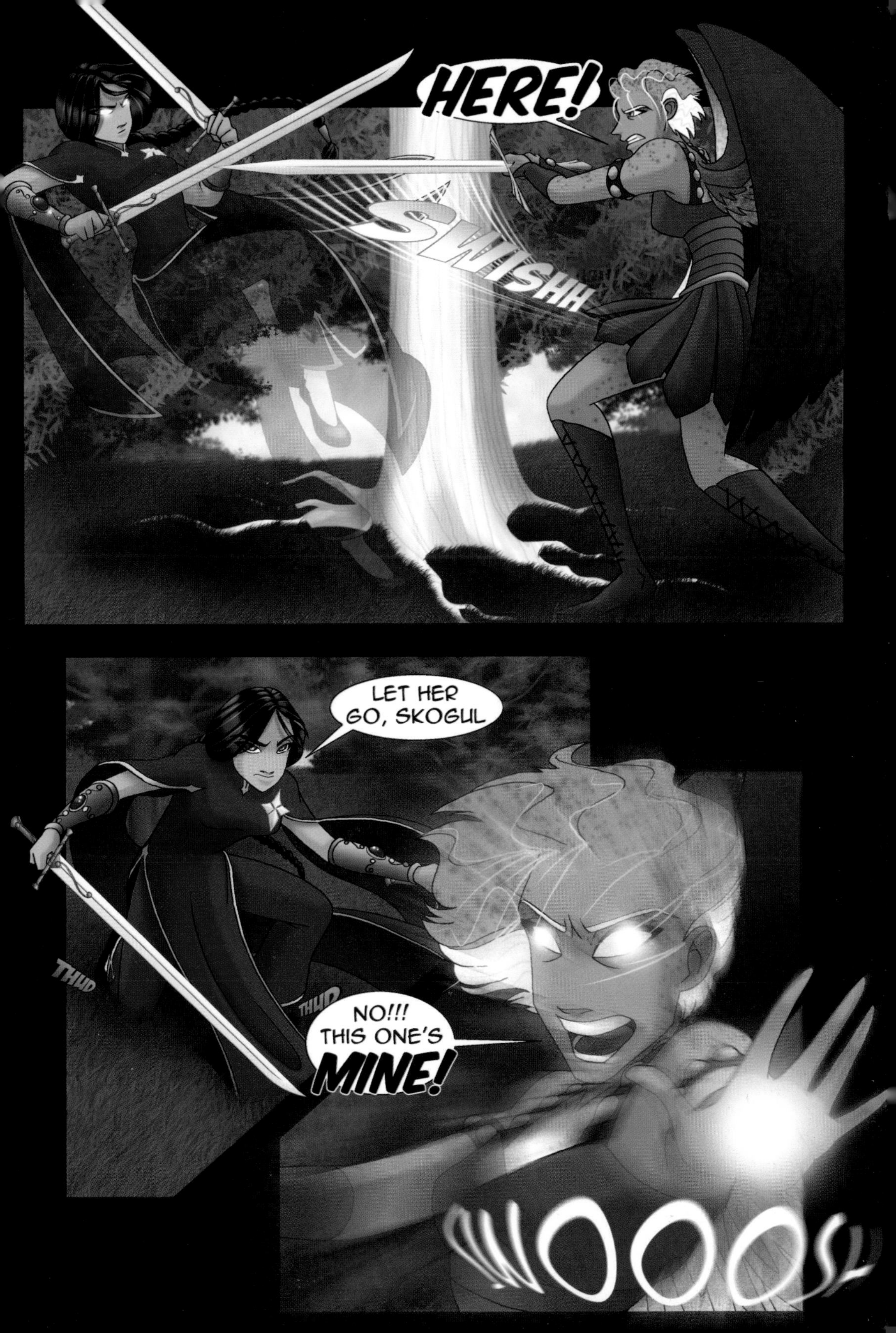
HERE!
SWISHH
LET HER GO, SKOGUL
THUD
THUD
NO!!! THIS ONE'S MINE!

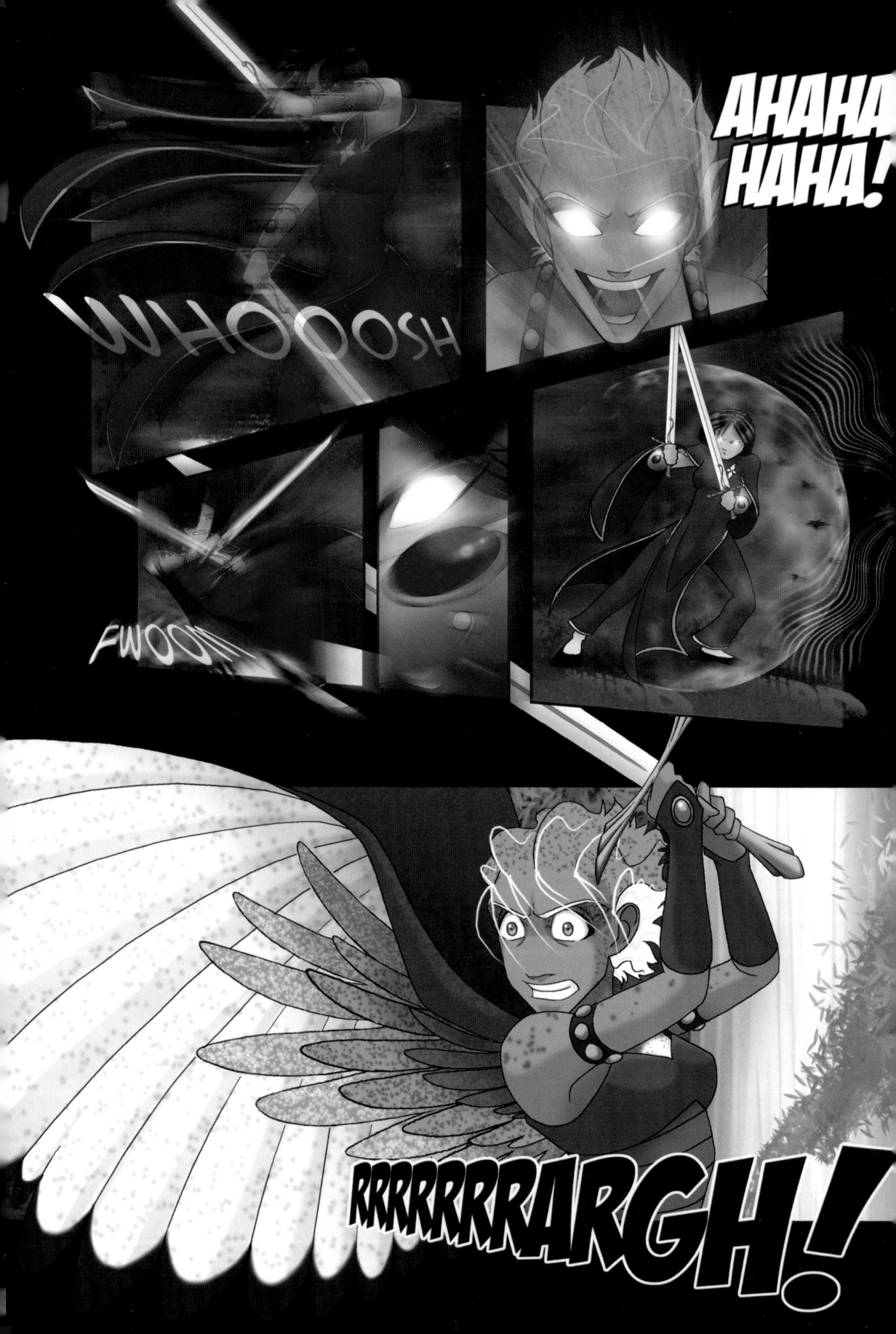
WHOOOSH
AHAHA HAHA!
FWOOM
RRRRRRRARGH!

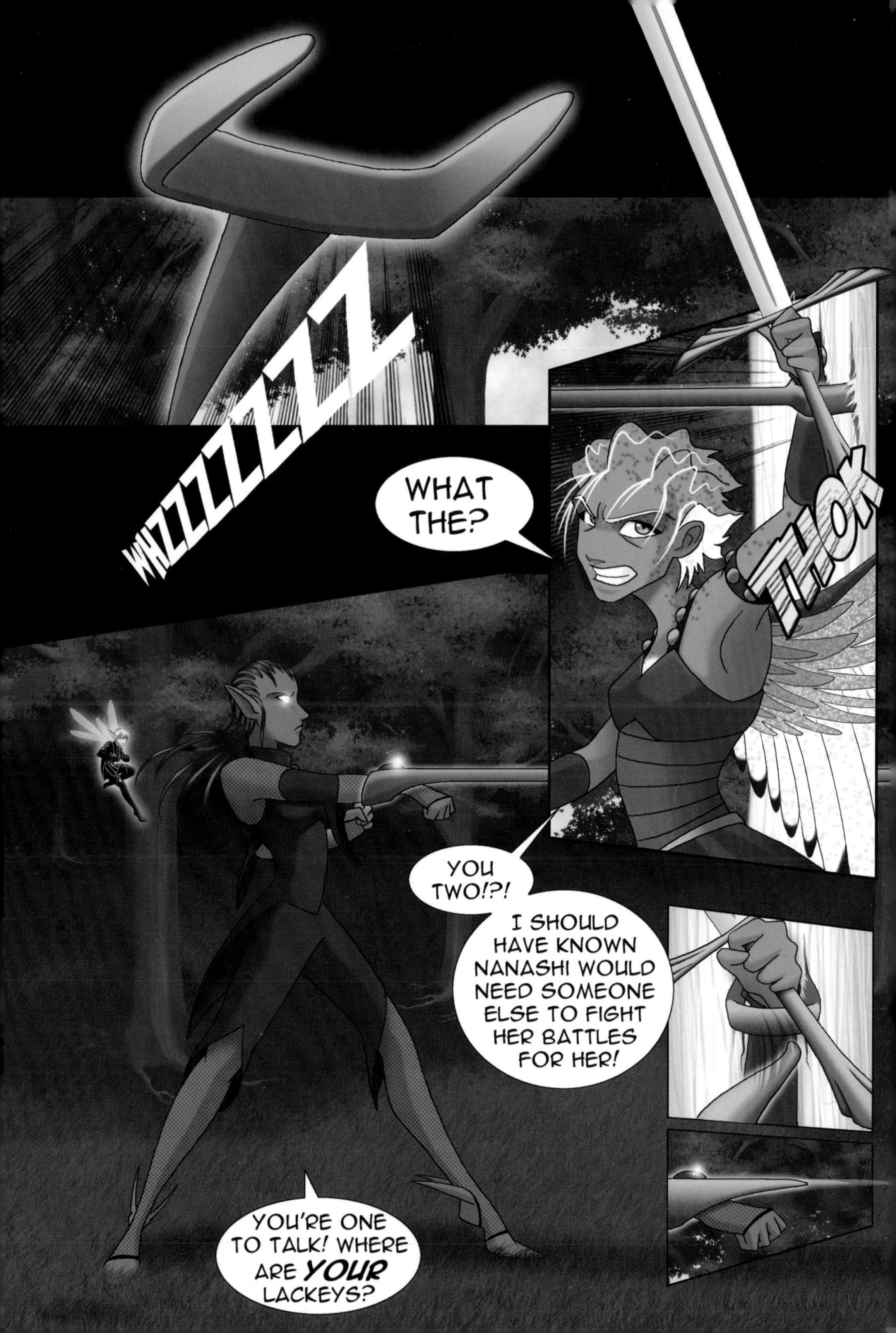
WHZZZZZZZZ
WHAT THE?
THOK
YOU TWO!?!
I SHOULD HAVE KNOWN NANASHI WOULD NEED SOMEONE ELSE TO FIGHT HER BATTLES FOR HER!
YOU'RE ONE TO TALK! WHERE ARE *YOUR* LACKEYS?

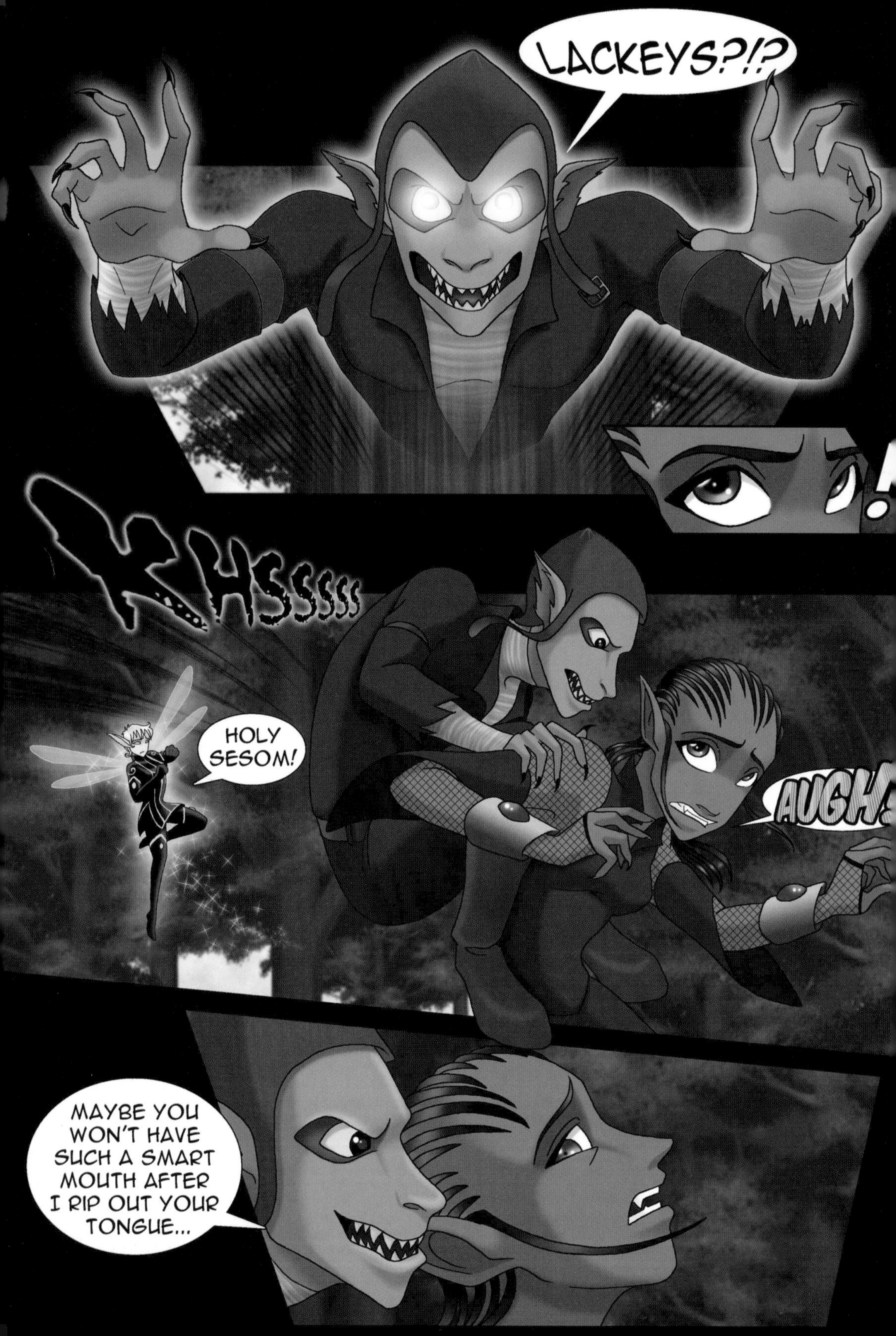
LACKEYS?!?
!
KHSSSSS
HOLY SESOM!
AUGH!
MAYBE YOU WON'T HAVE SUCH A SMART MOUTH AFTER I RIP OUT YOUR TONGUE...

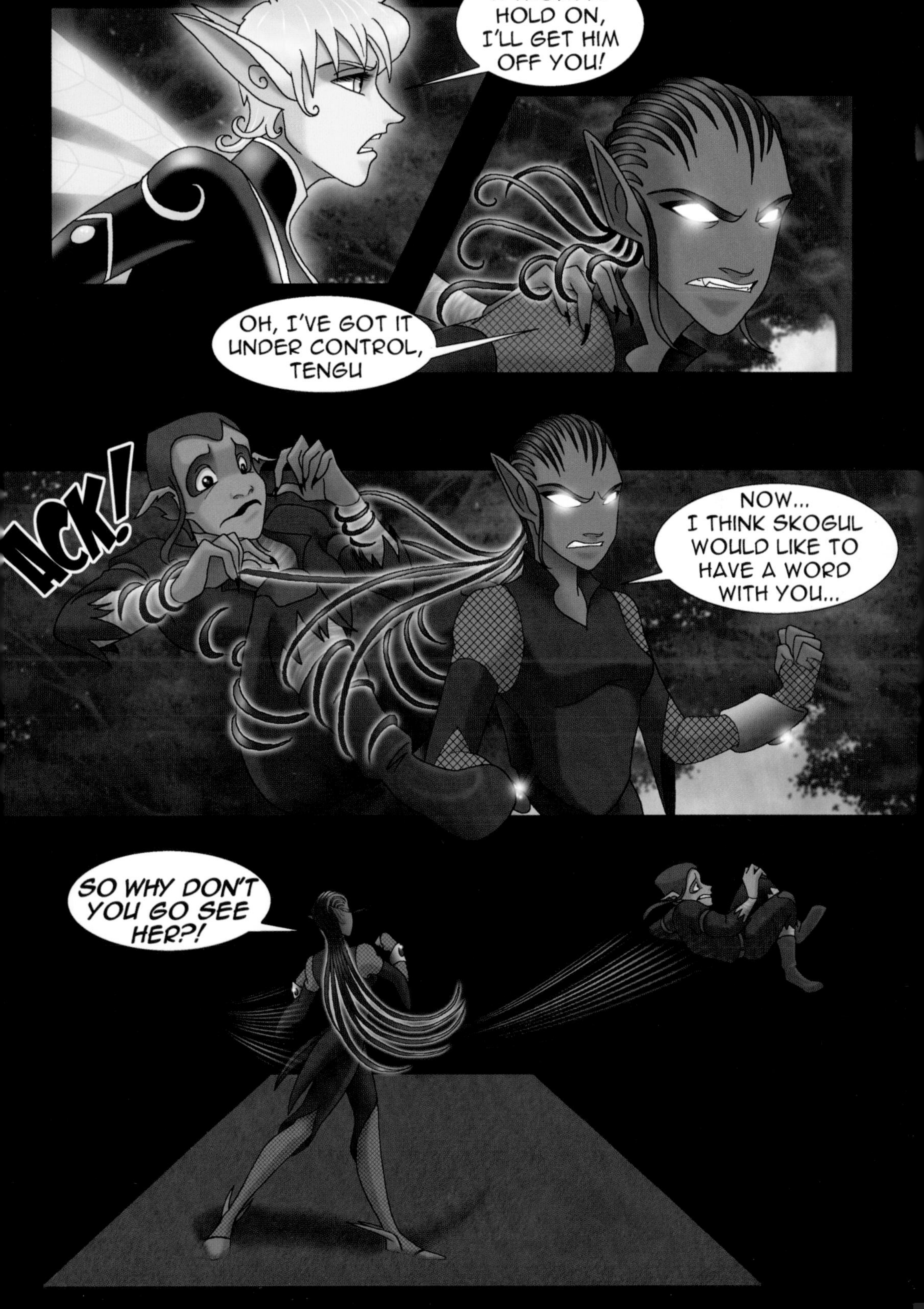
K'THONYA! HOLD ON, I'LL GET HIM OFF YOU!
OH, I'VE GOT IT UNDER CONTROL, TENGU
ACK!
NOW... I THINK SKOGUL WOULD LIKE TO HAVE A WORD WITH YOU...
SO WHY DON'T YOU GO SEE HER?!

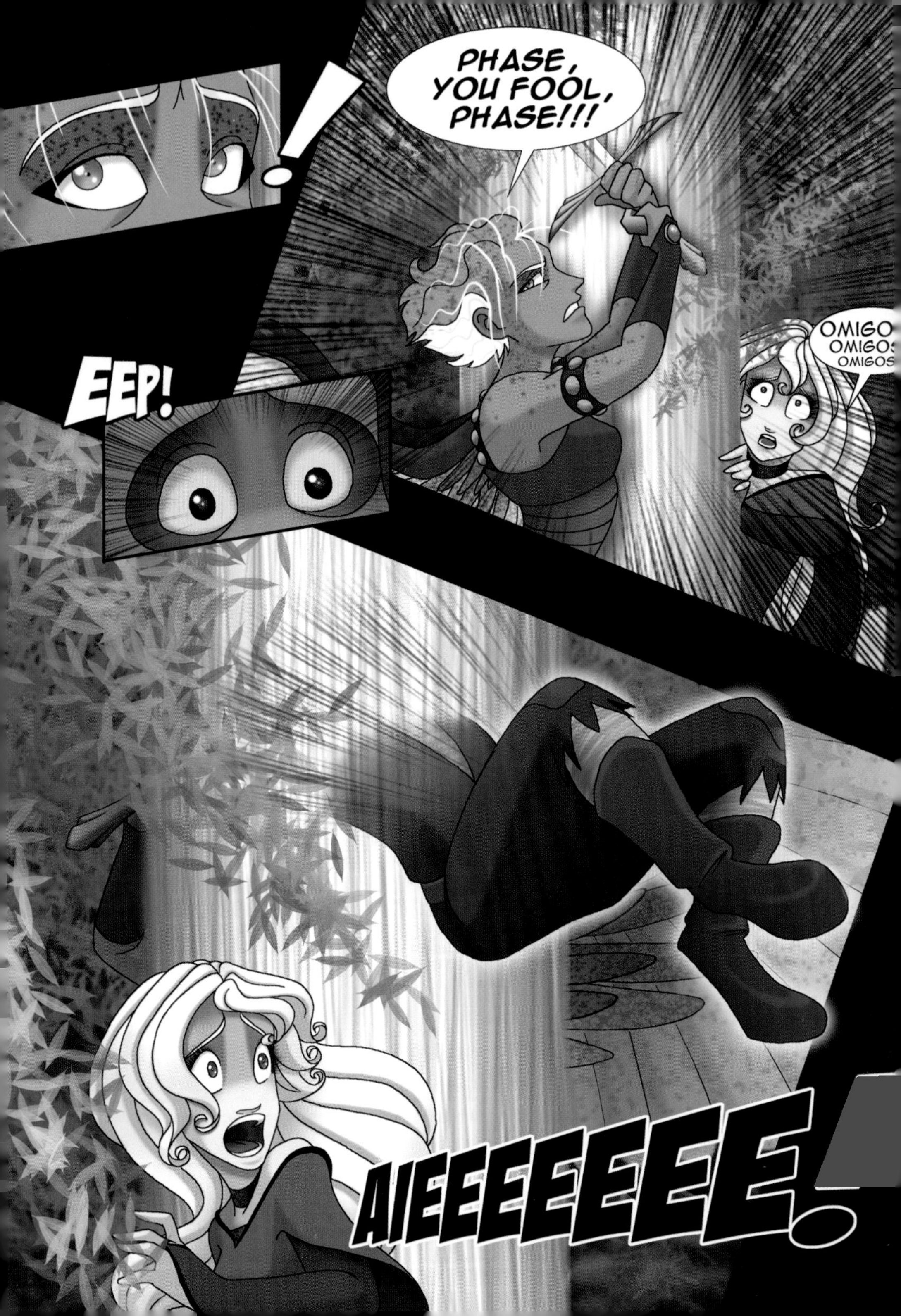
!
PHASE, YOU FOOL, PHASE!!!
OMIGO OMIGOS OMIGOS
EEP!
AIEEEEEEEE.

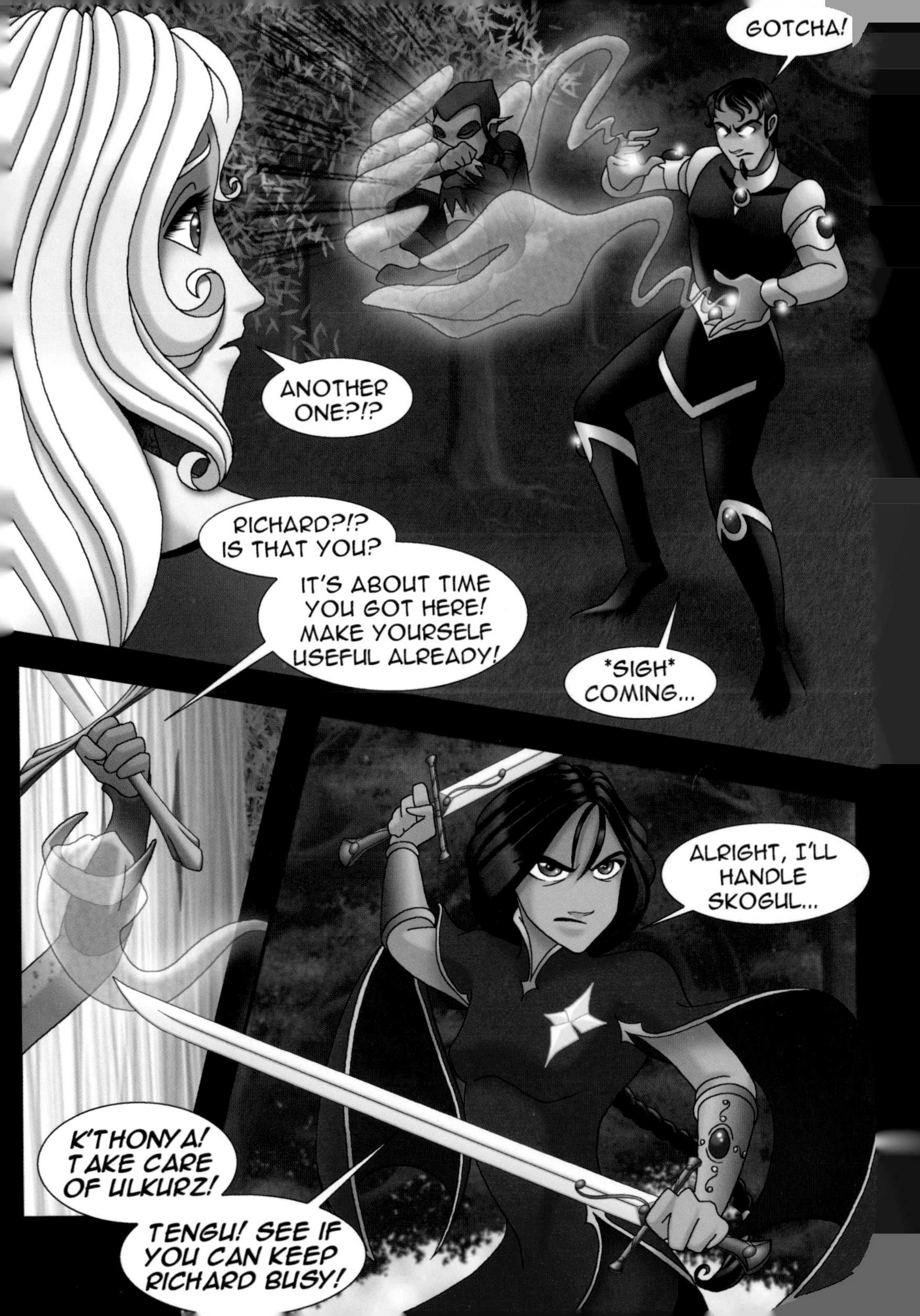
GOTCHA!
ANOTHER ONE?!?
RICHARD?!? IS THAT YOU?
IT'S ABOUT TIME YOU GOT HERE! MAKE YOURSELF USEFUL ALREADY!
SIGH COMING...
ALRIGHT, I'LL HANDLE SKOGUL...
K'THONYA! TAKE CARE OF ULKURZ!
TENGU! SEE IF YOU CAN KEEP RICHARD BUSY!

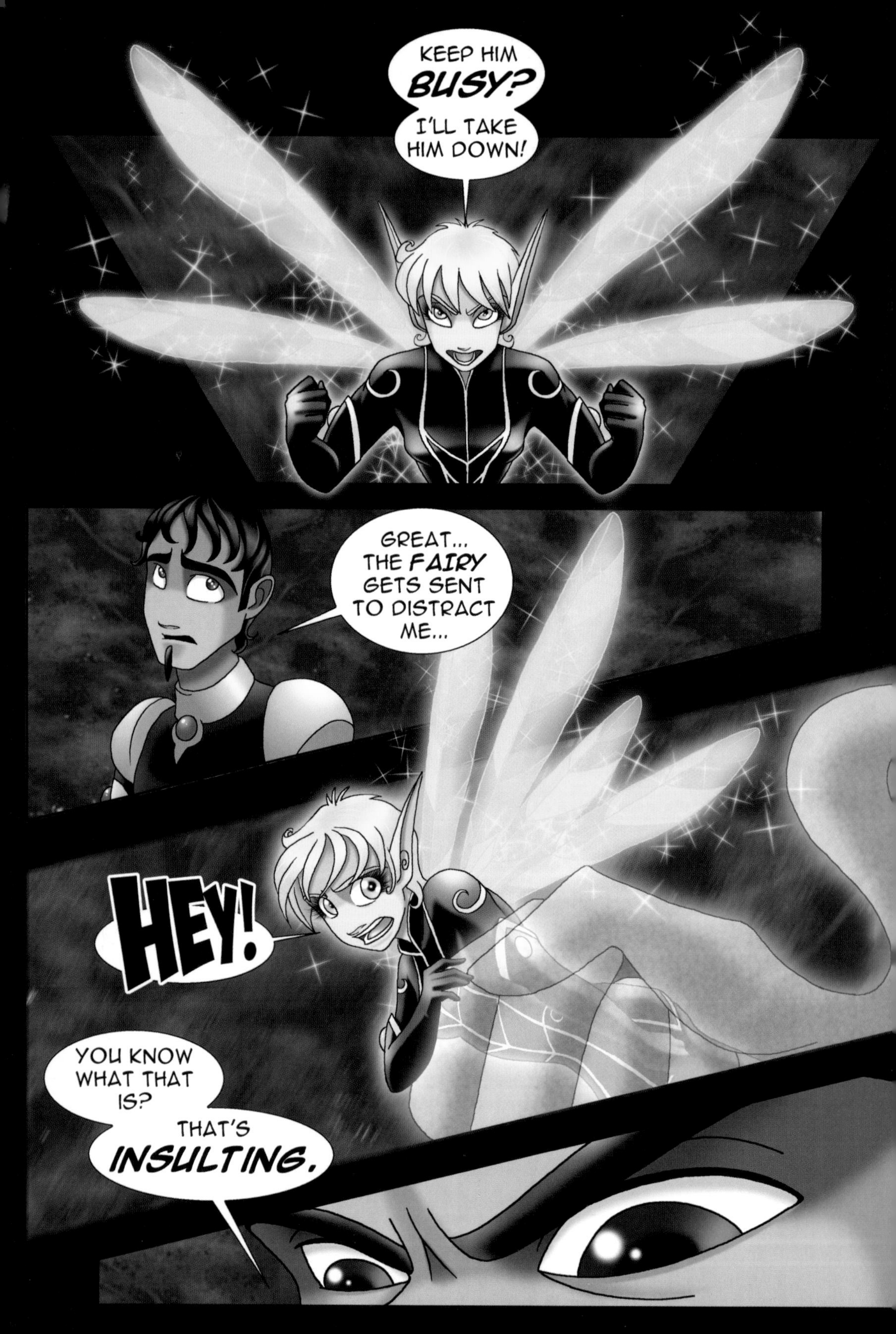
KEEP HIM BUSY?
I'LL TAKE HIM DOWN!
GREAT... THE FAIRY GETS SENT TO DISTRACT ME...
HEY!
YOU KNOW WHAT THAT IS?
THAT'S INSULTING.

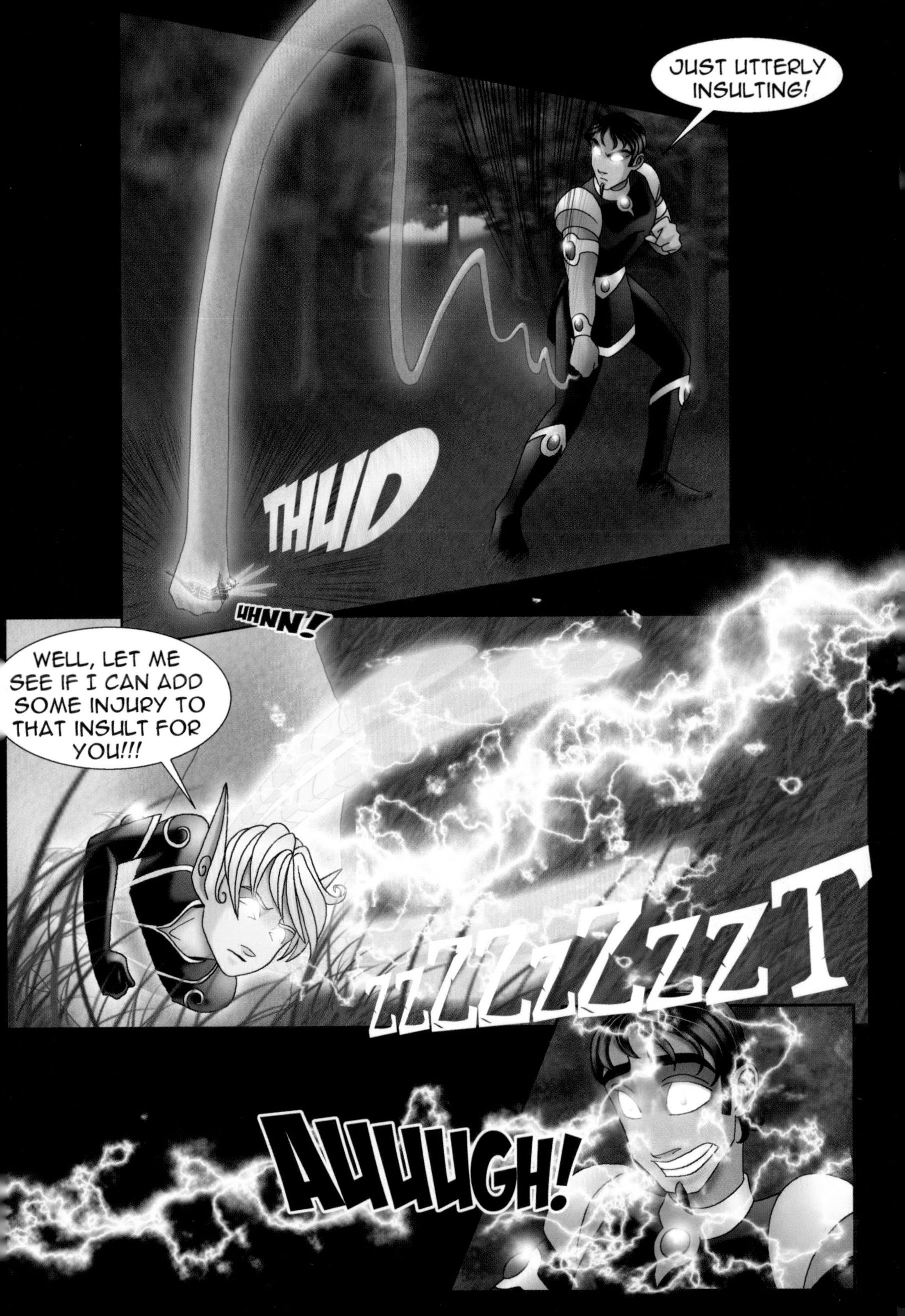
JUST UTTERLY INSULTING!
THUD
UHNN!
WELL, LET ME SEE IF I CAN ADD SOME INJURY TO THAT INSULT FOR YOU!!!
ZZZZZZZZZT
AUUUGH!

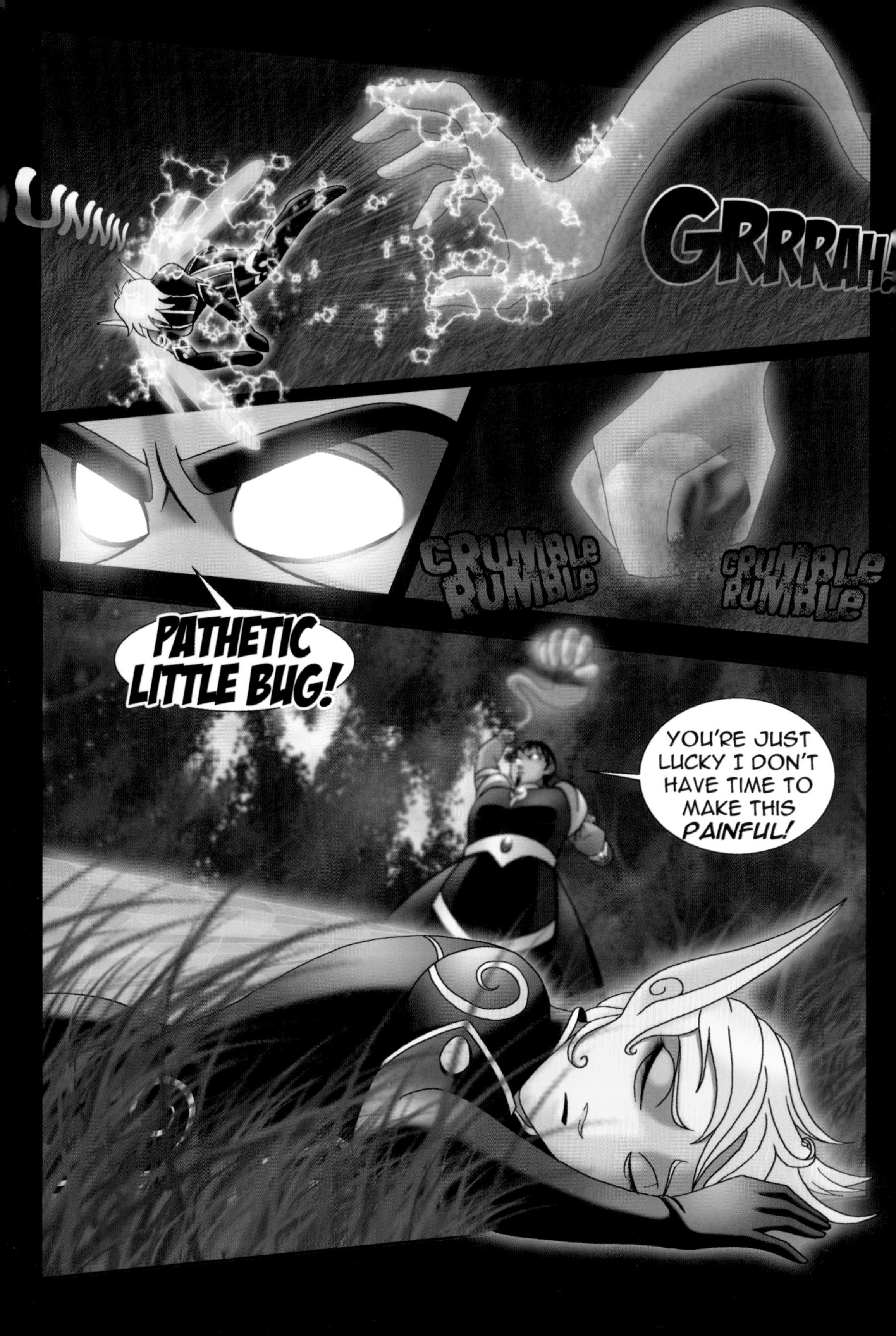
UNNN
GRRRAH!
CRUMBLE RUMBLE
CRUMBLE RUMBLE
PATHETIC LITTLE BUG!
YOU'RE JUST LUCKY I DON'T HAVE TIME TO MAKE THIS PAINFUL!

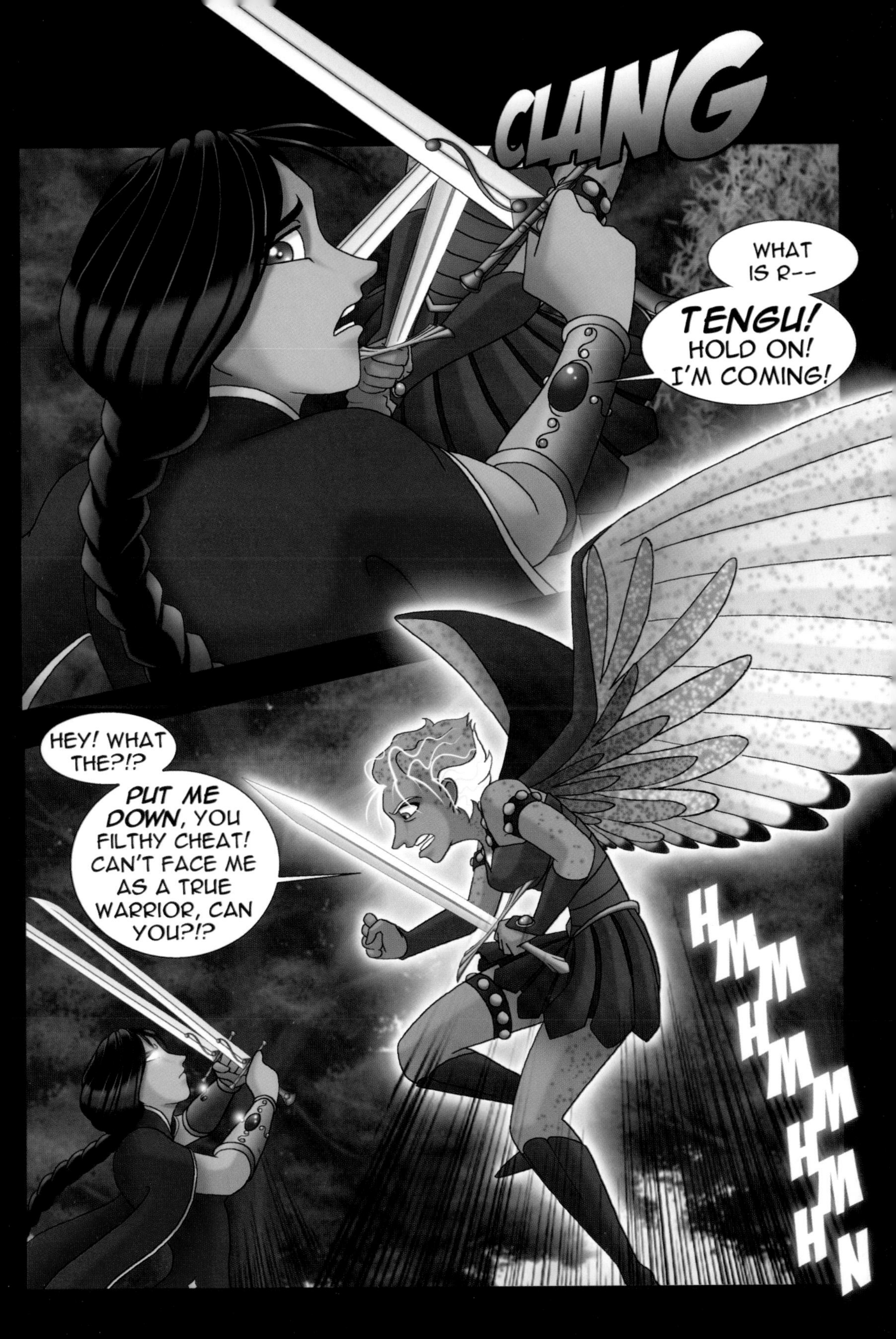
CLANG
WHAT IS R--
TENGU! HOLD ON! I'M COMING!
HEY! WHAT THE?!?
PUT ME DOWN, YOU FILTHY CHEAT! CAN'T FACE ME AS A TRUE WARRIOR, CAN YOU?!?
HMMMHMMMHMMMHMMN

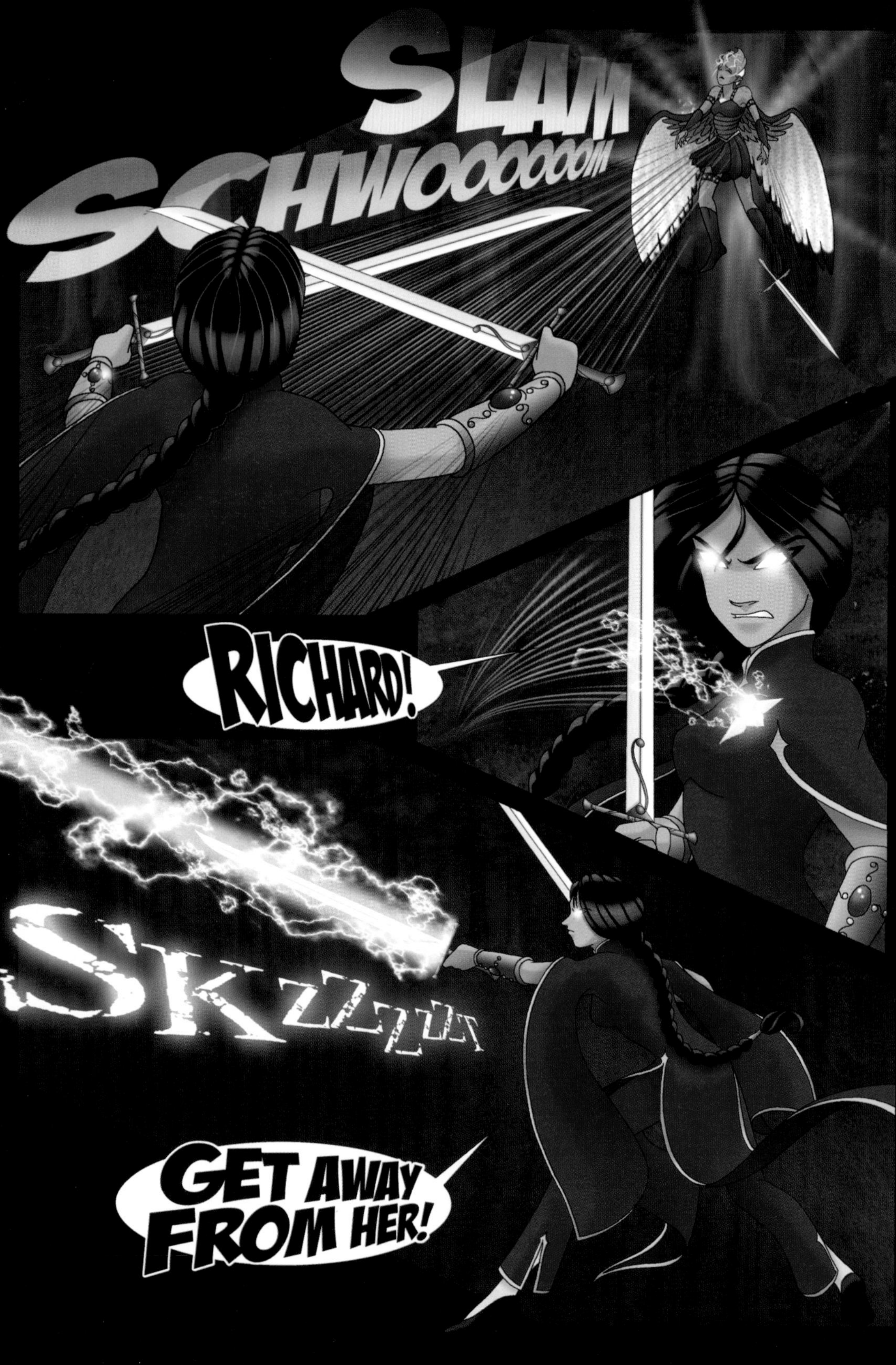
SLAM
SCHWOOOOOOM
RICHARD!
SKZZZZT
GET AWAY FROM HER!

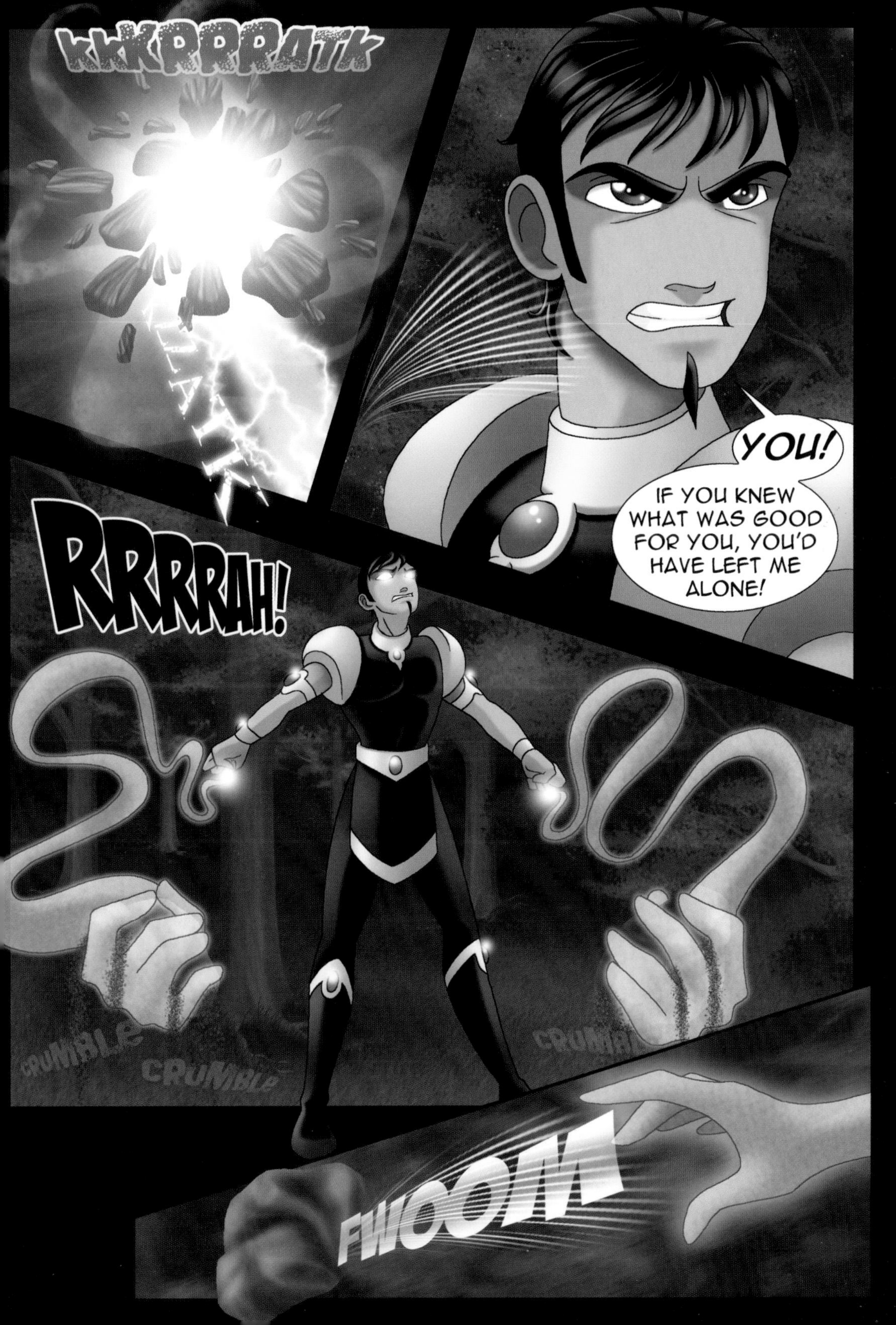
KKKRRRATK
YOU!
IF YOU KNEW WHAT WAS GOOD FOR YOU, YOU'D HAVE LEFT ME ALONE!
RRRRAH!
CRUMBLE
CRUMBLE
FWOOM

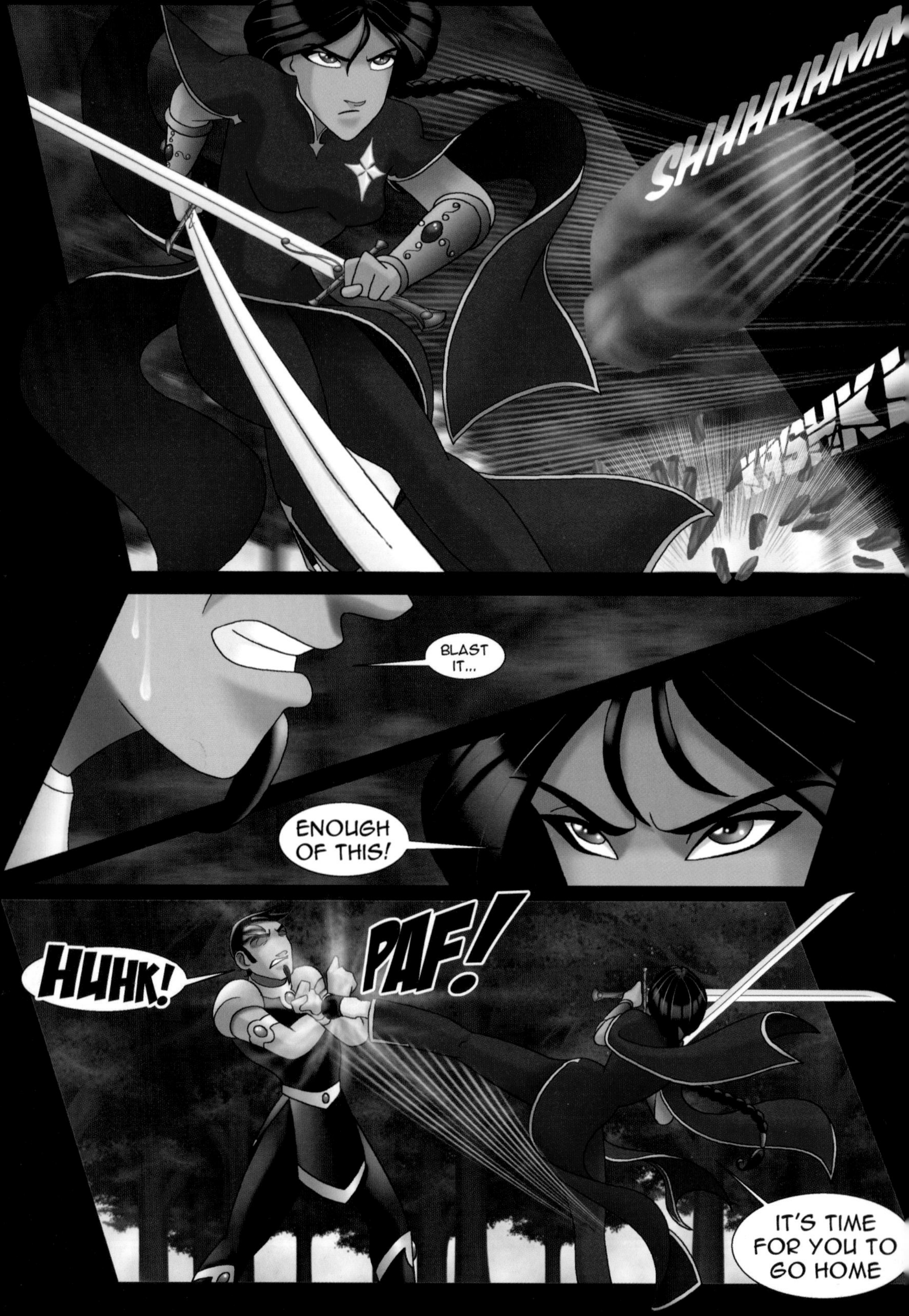
SHHHHHMM
BLAST IT...
ENOUGH OF THIS!
HUHK!
PAF!
IT'S TIME FOR YOU TO GO HOME

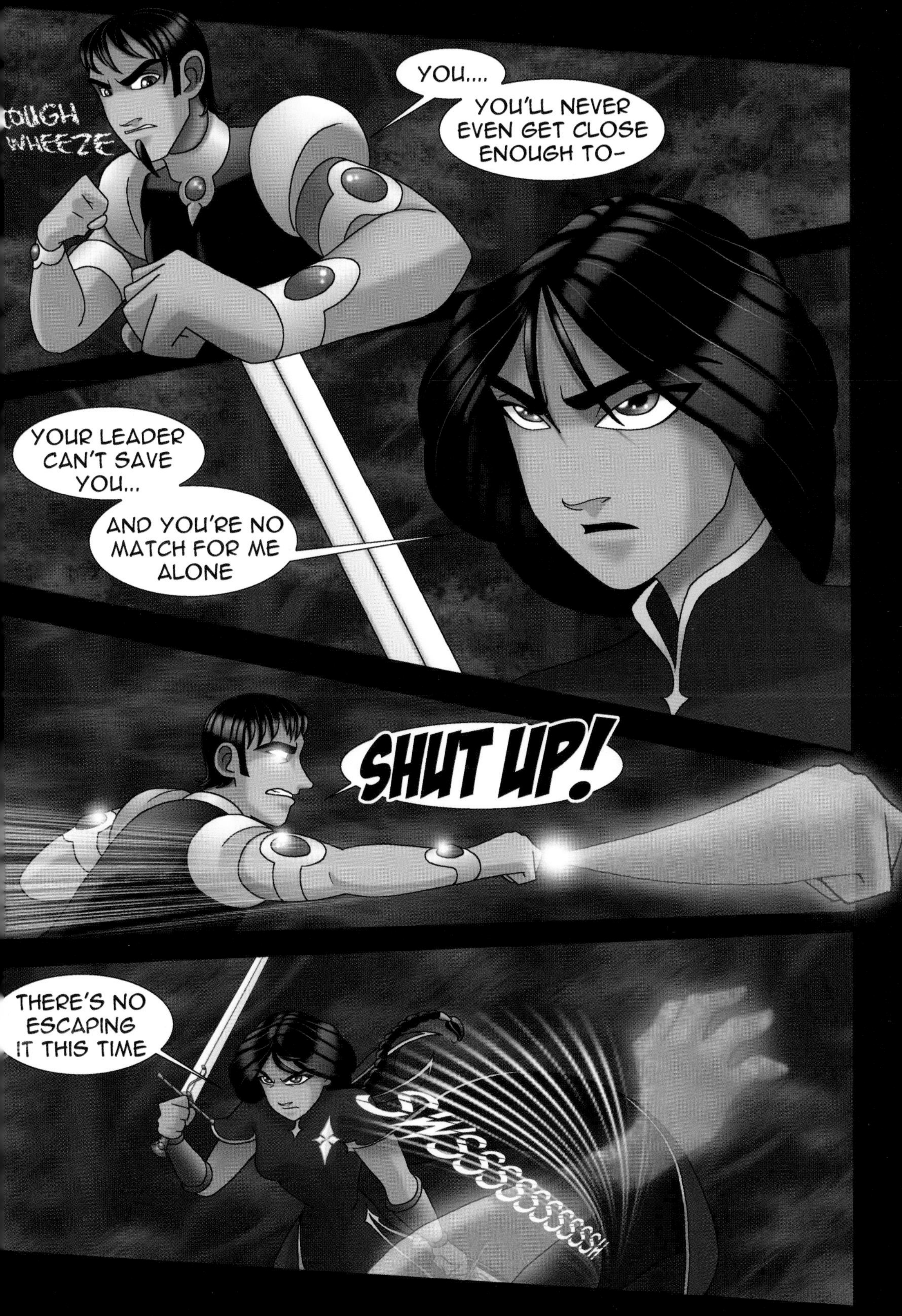
OUGH
WHEEZE
YOU....
YOU'LL NEVER EVEN GET CLOSE ENOUGH TO-
YOUR LEADER CAN'T SAVE YOU...
AND YOU'RE NO MATCH FOR ME ALONE
SHUT UP!
THERE'S NO ESCAPING IT THIS TIME
SWSSSSSSSSSSSH

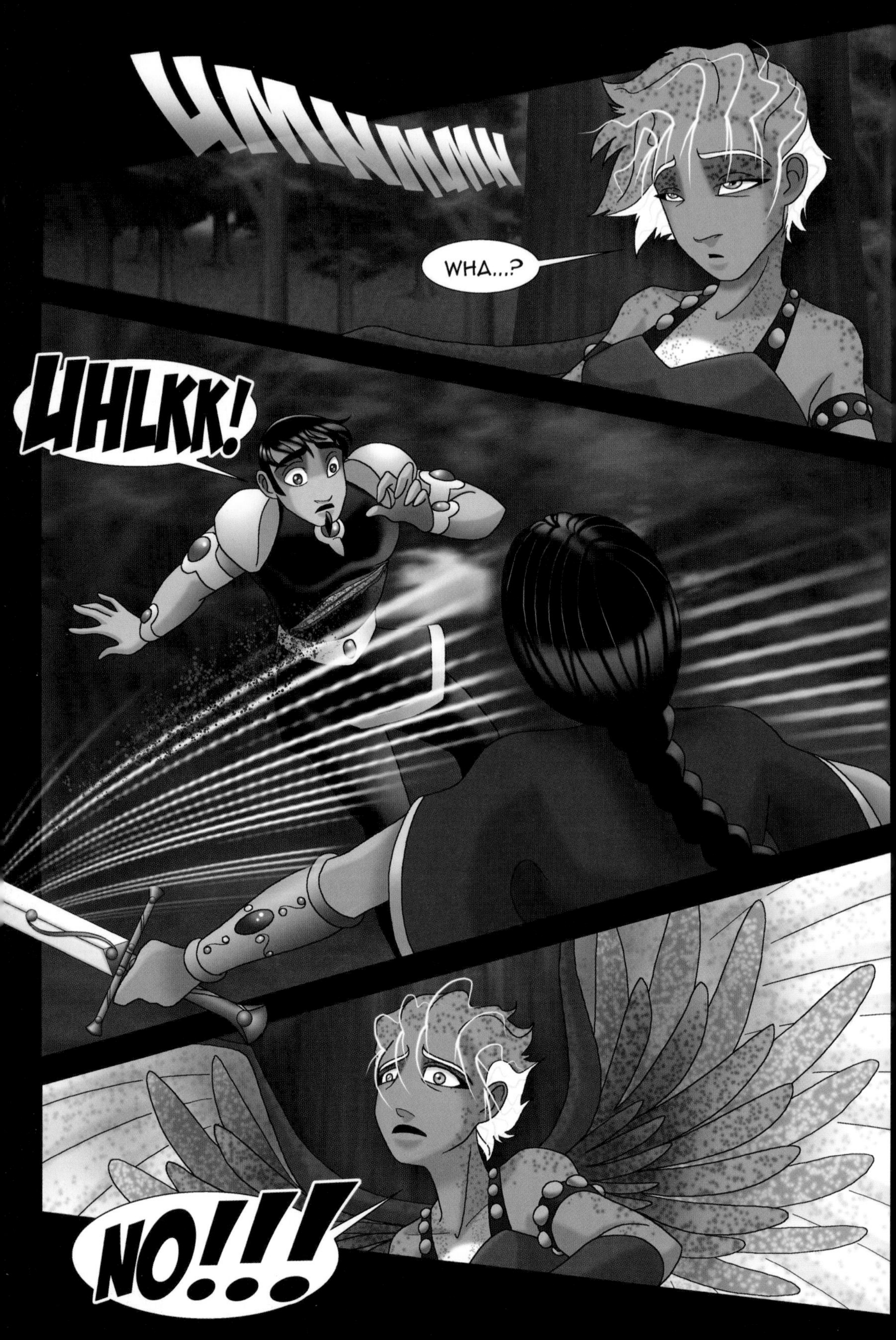
UMMMMMN
WHA...?
UHLKK!
NO!!!

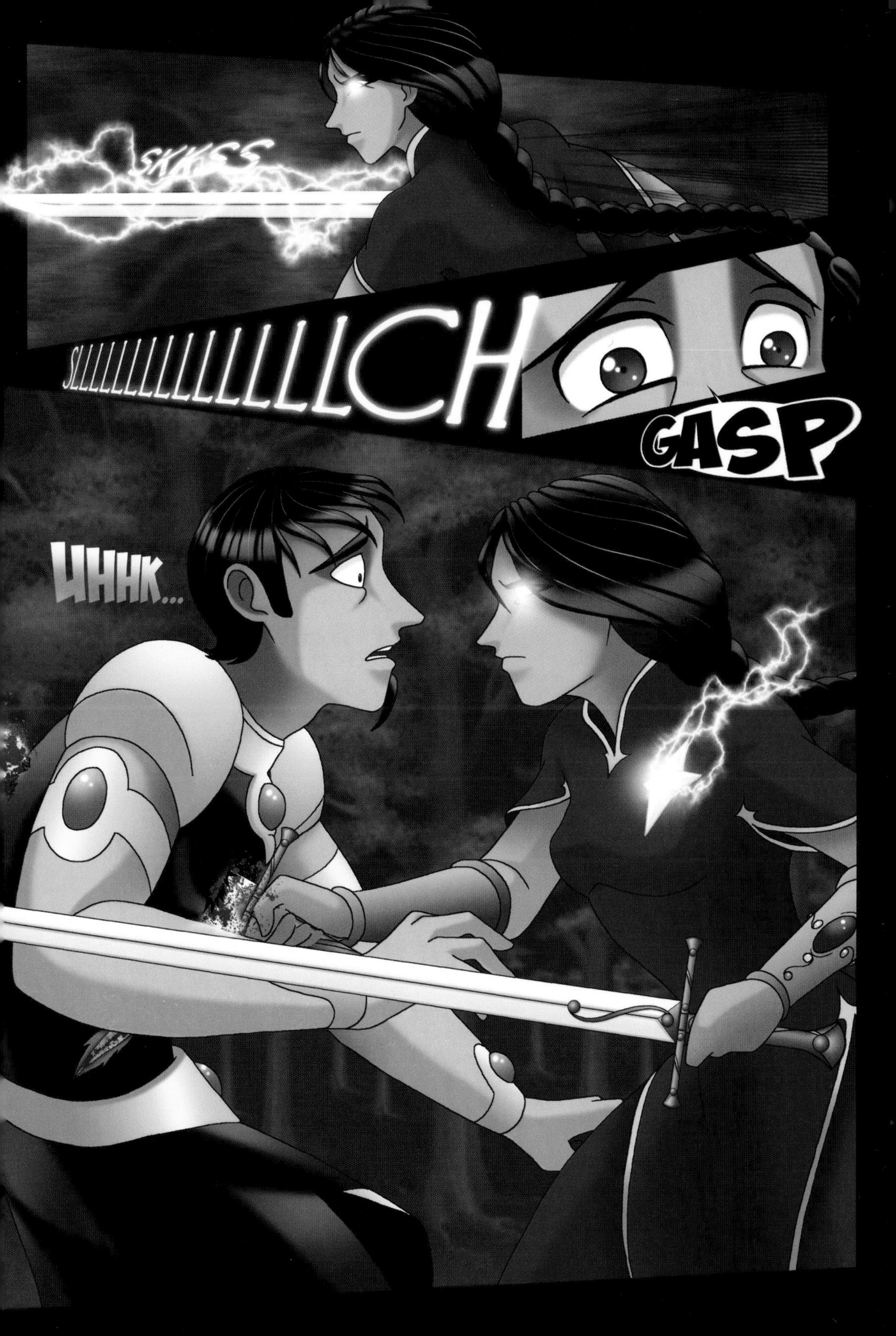
SKKSS
SLLLLLLLLLLLLLCH
GASP
UHHK...

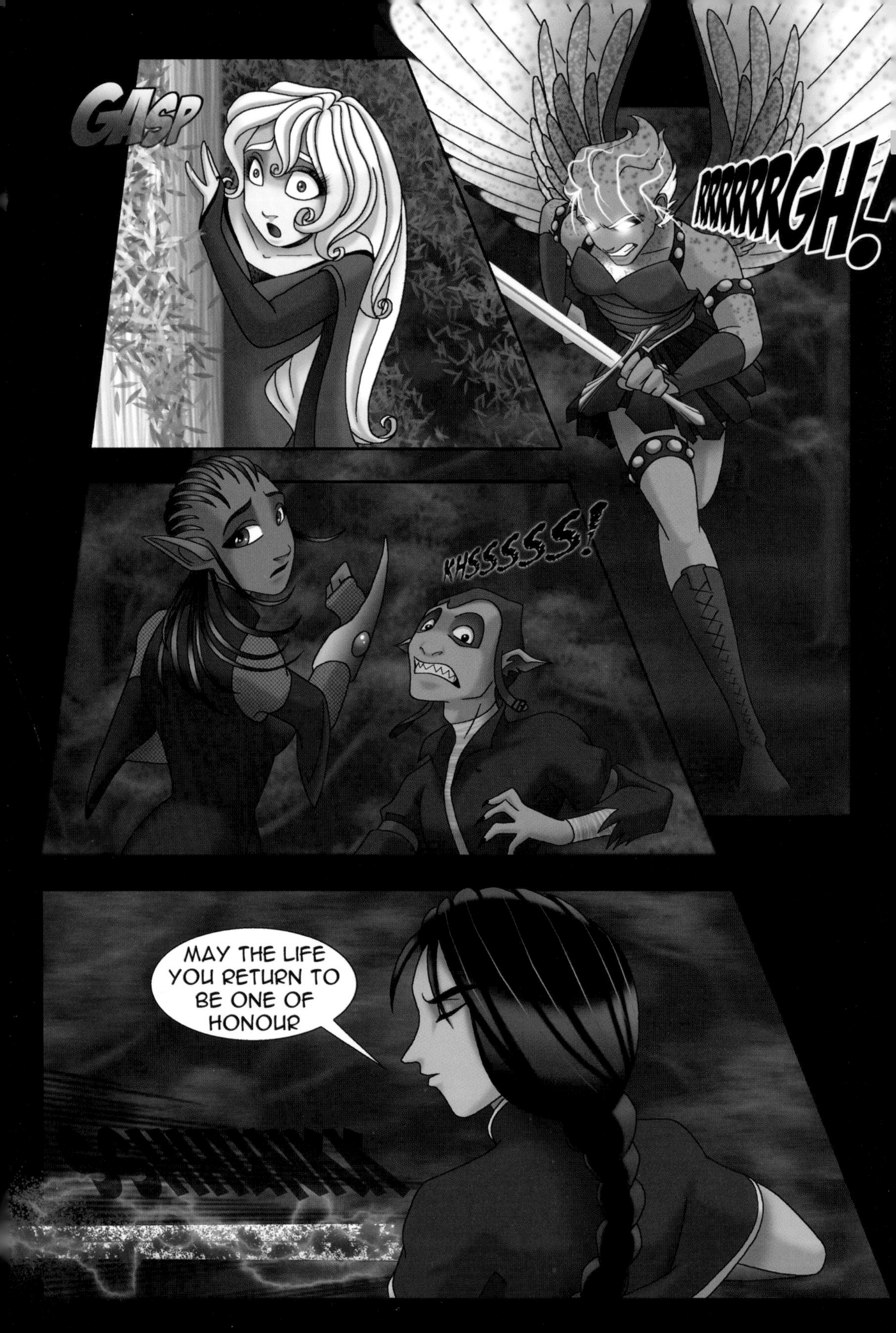
GASP
RRRRRRRGH!
KHSSSSSS!
MAY THE LIFE YOU RETURN TO BE ONE OF HONOUR

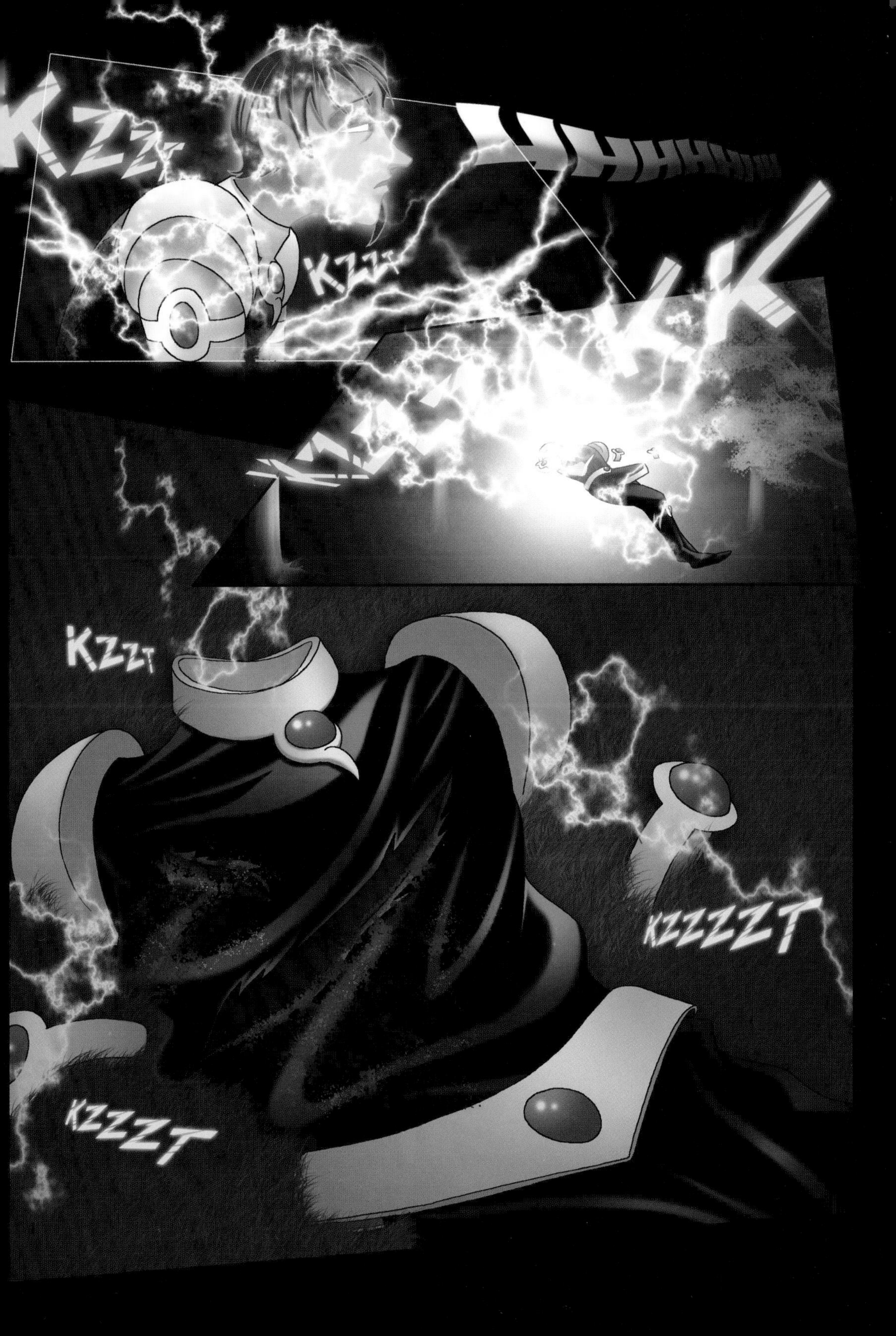
KZZT
KZZT
KZZT
KZZZZT
KZZZT

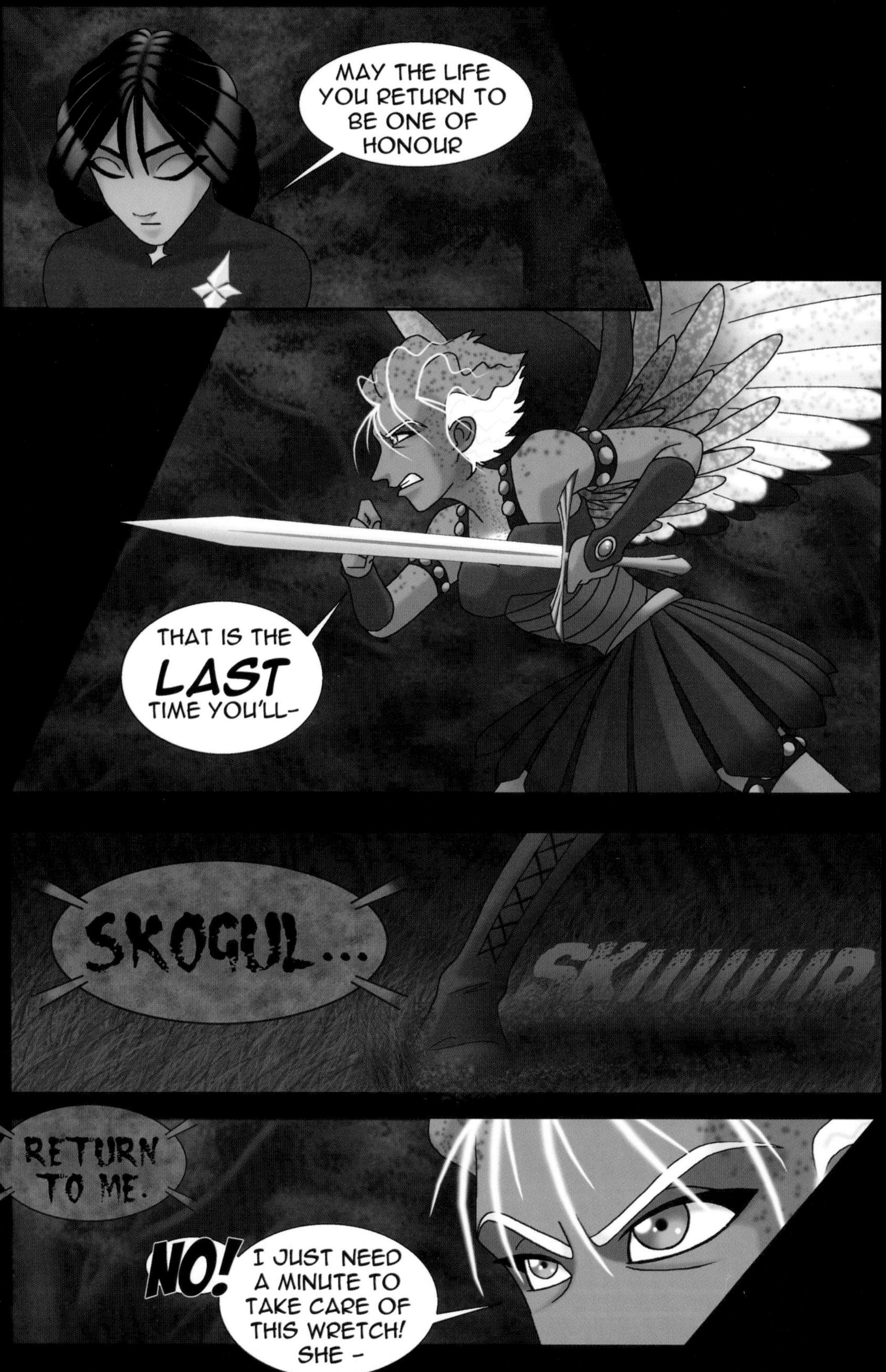
MAY THE LIFE YOU RETURN TO BE ONE OF HONOUR
THAT IS THE LAST TIME YOU'LL-
SKOGUL...
SKUUUUR
RETURN TO ME.
NO!
I JUST NEED A MINUTE TO TAKE CARE OF THIS WRETCH! SHE -

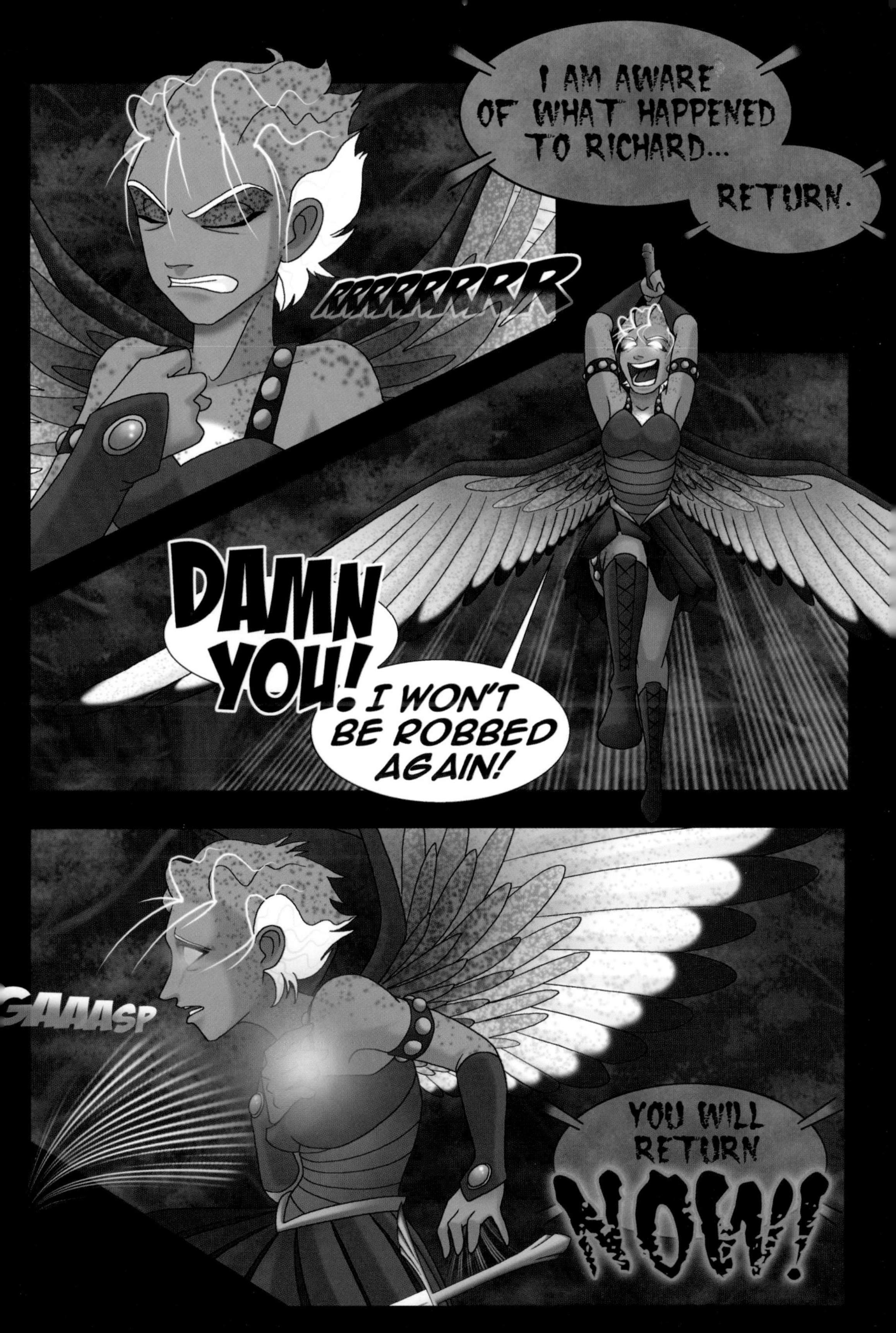
I AM AWARE OF WHAT HAPPENED TO RICHARD...
RETURN.
RRRRRRRR
DAMN YOU!
I WON'T BE ROBBED AGAIN!
GAAASP
YOU WILL RETURN NOW!

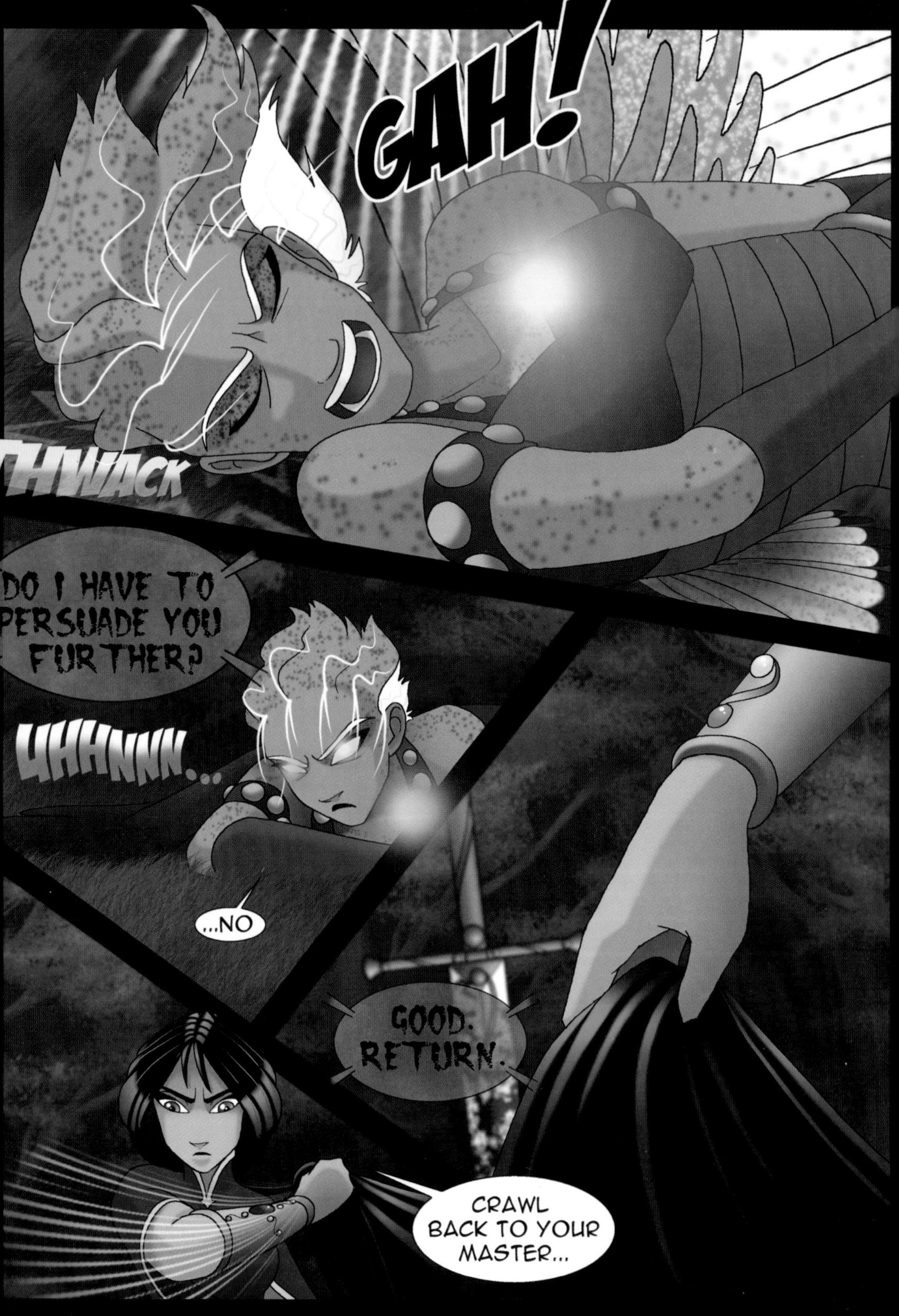
GAH!
THWACK
DO I HAVE TO PERSUADE YOU FURTHER?
UHHNNN...
...NO
GOOD. RETURN.
CRAWL BACK TO YOUR MASTER...

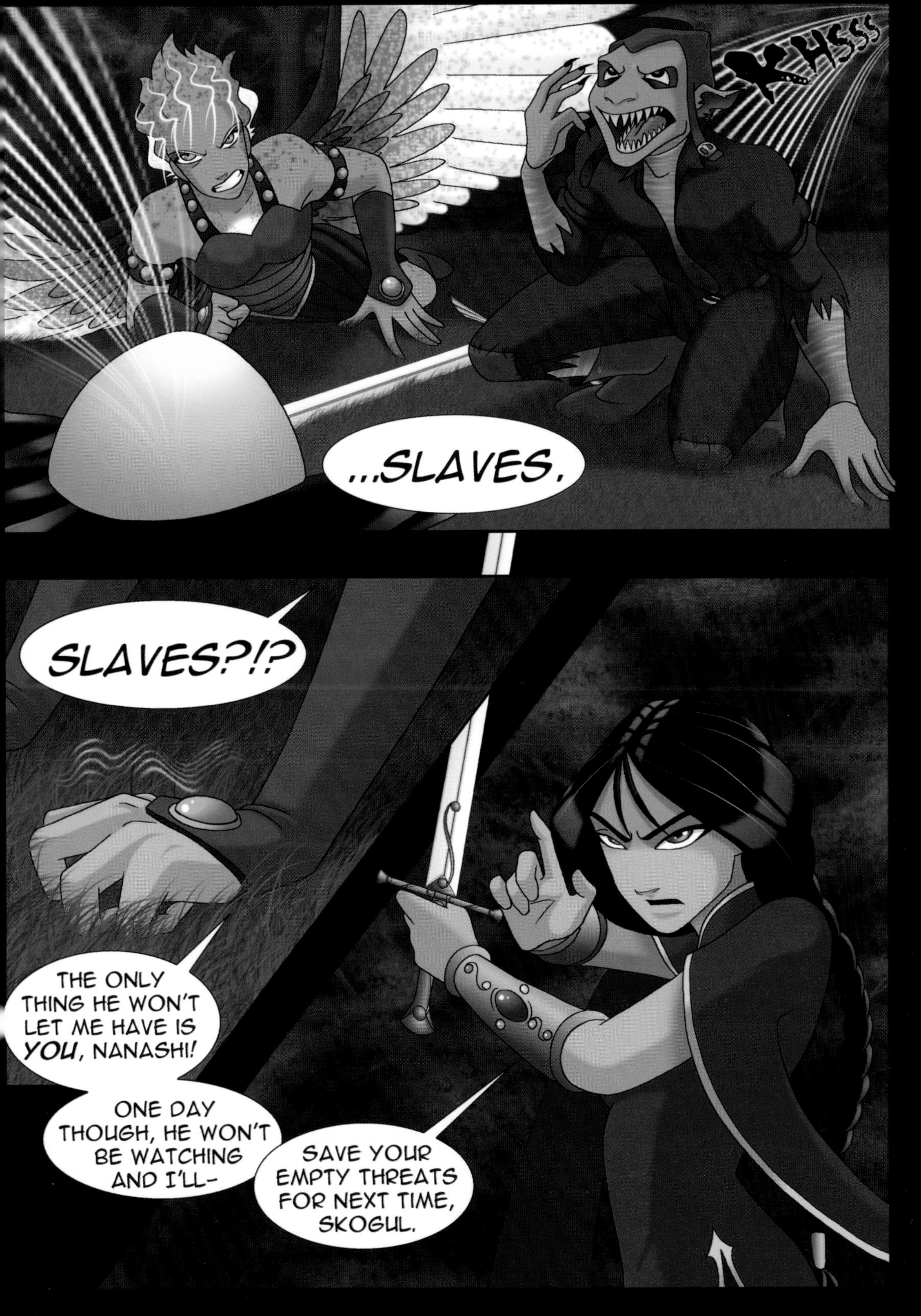
KHSSS
...SLAVES.
SLAVES?!?
THE ONLY THING HE WON'T LET ME HAVE IS *YOU*, NANASHI!
ONE DAY THOUGH, HE WON'T BE WATCHING AND I'LL-
SAVE YOUR EMPTY THREATS FOR NEXT TIME, SKOGUL.

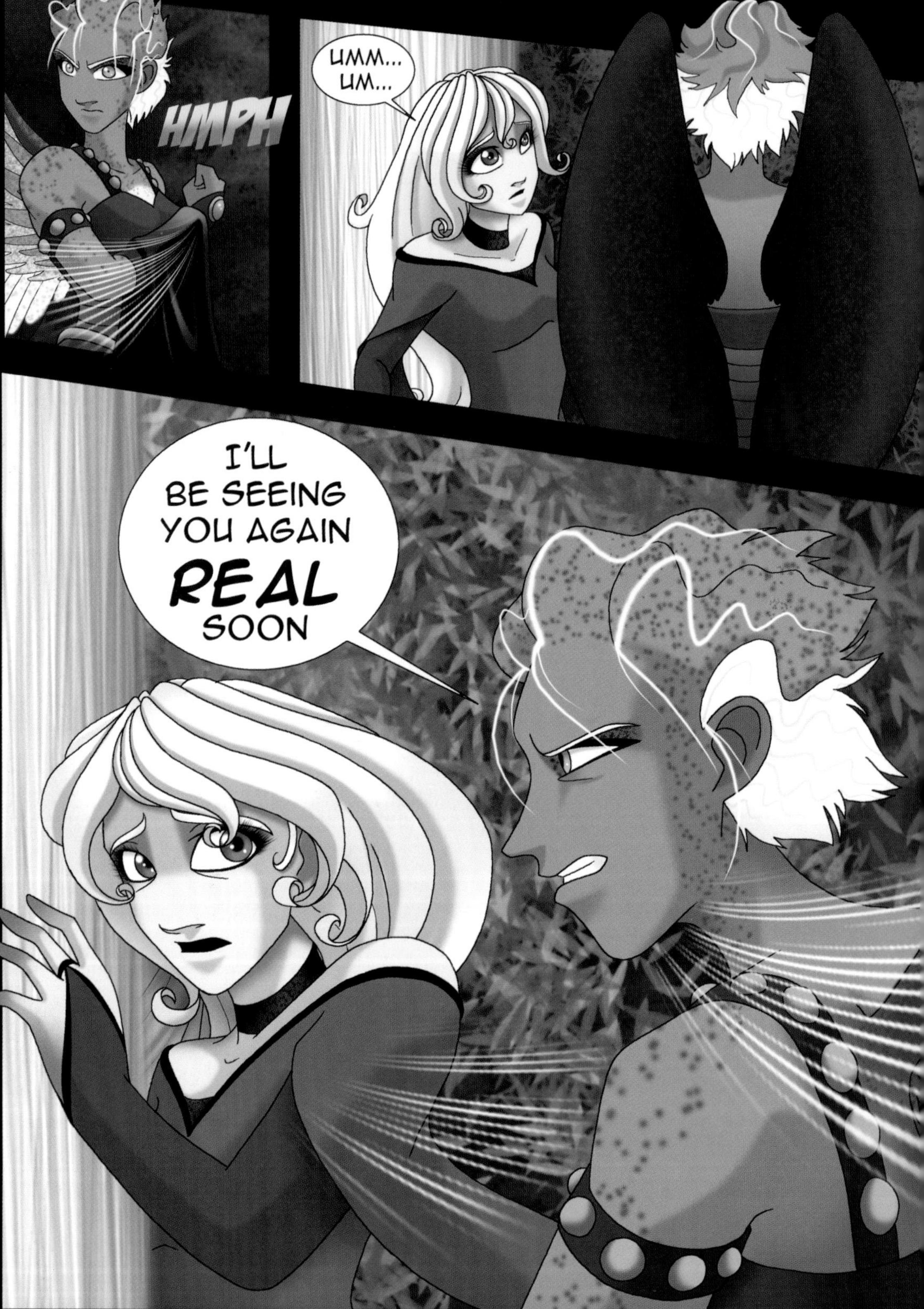
HMPH
UMM... UM...
I'LL BE SEEING YOU AGAIN REAL SOON

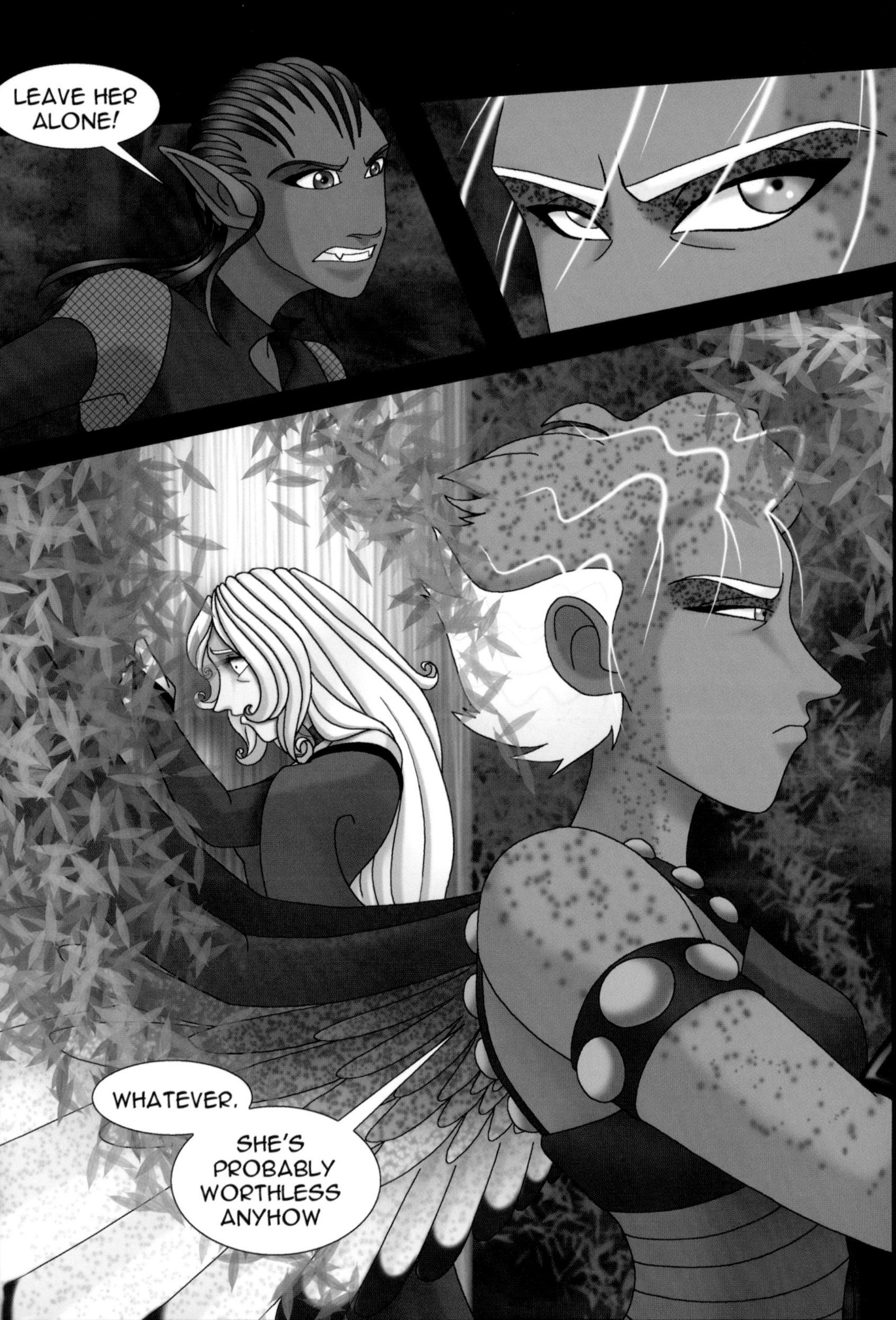
LEAVE HER ALONE!
WHATEVER.
SHE'S PROBABLY WORTHLESS ANYHOW

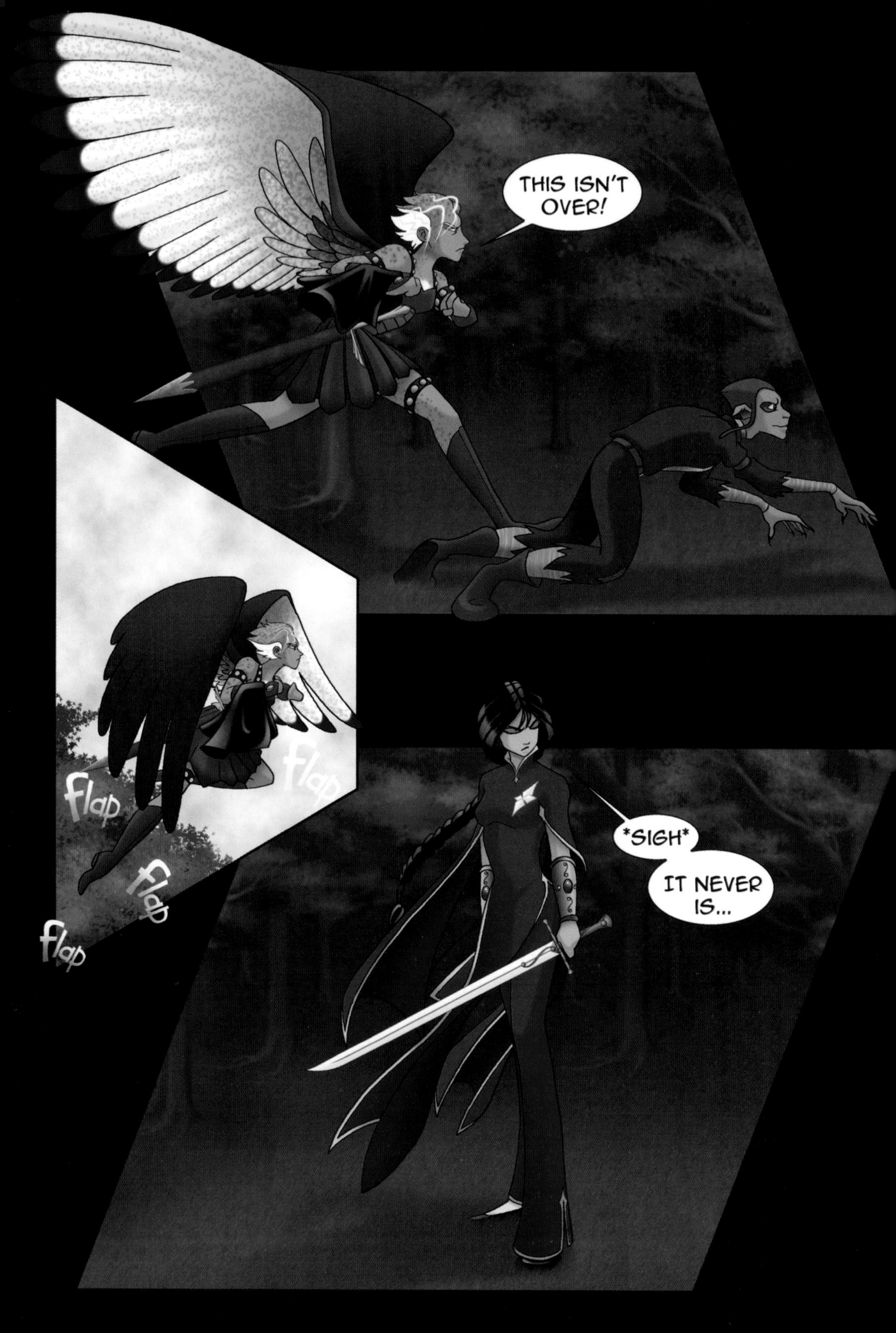
THIS ISN'T OVER!
flap
flap
flap
flap
SIGH
IT NEVER IS...

EARTHSONG

Volume I, Chapter II

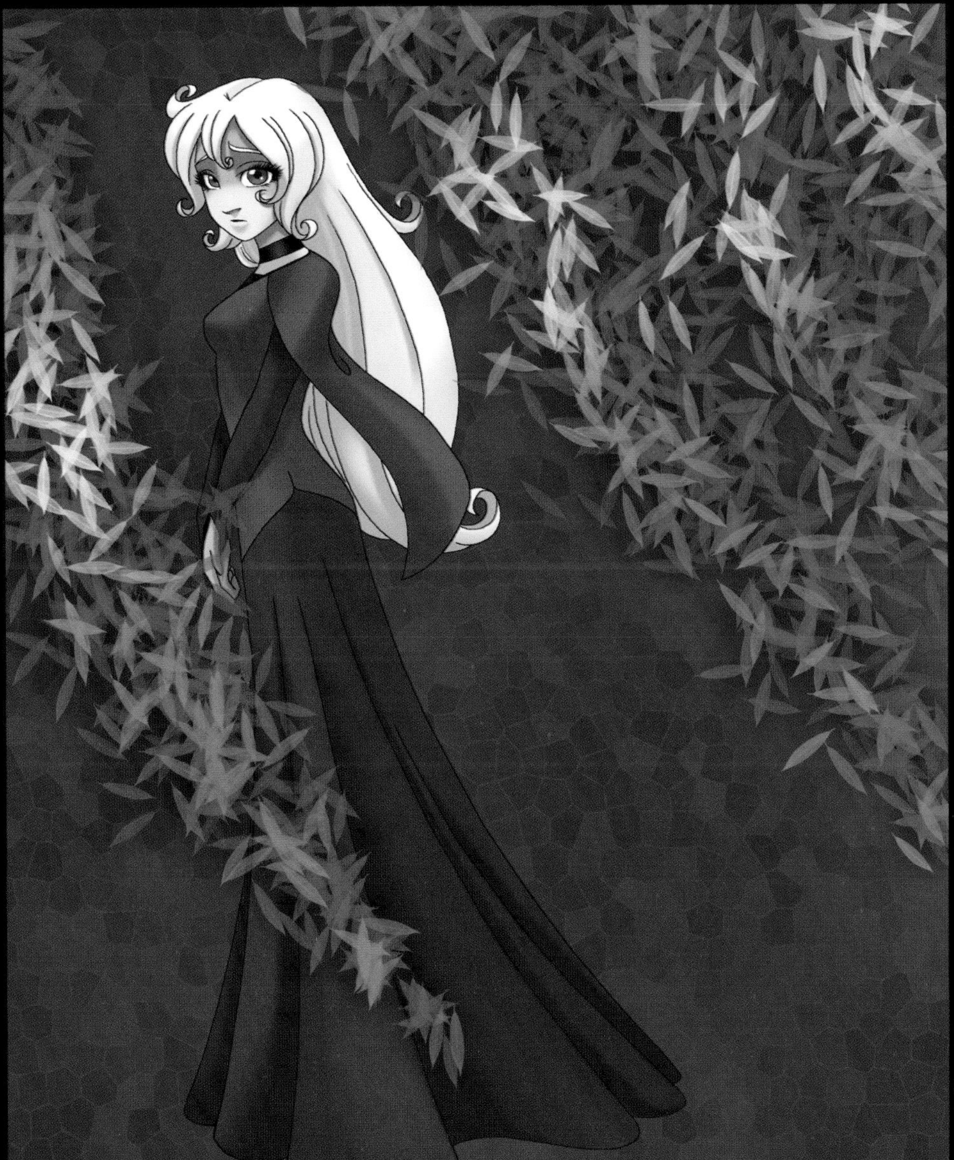

Willow

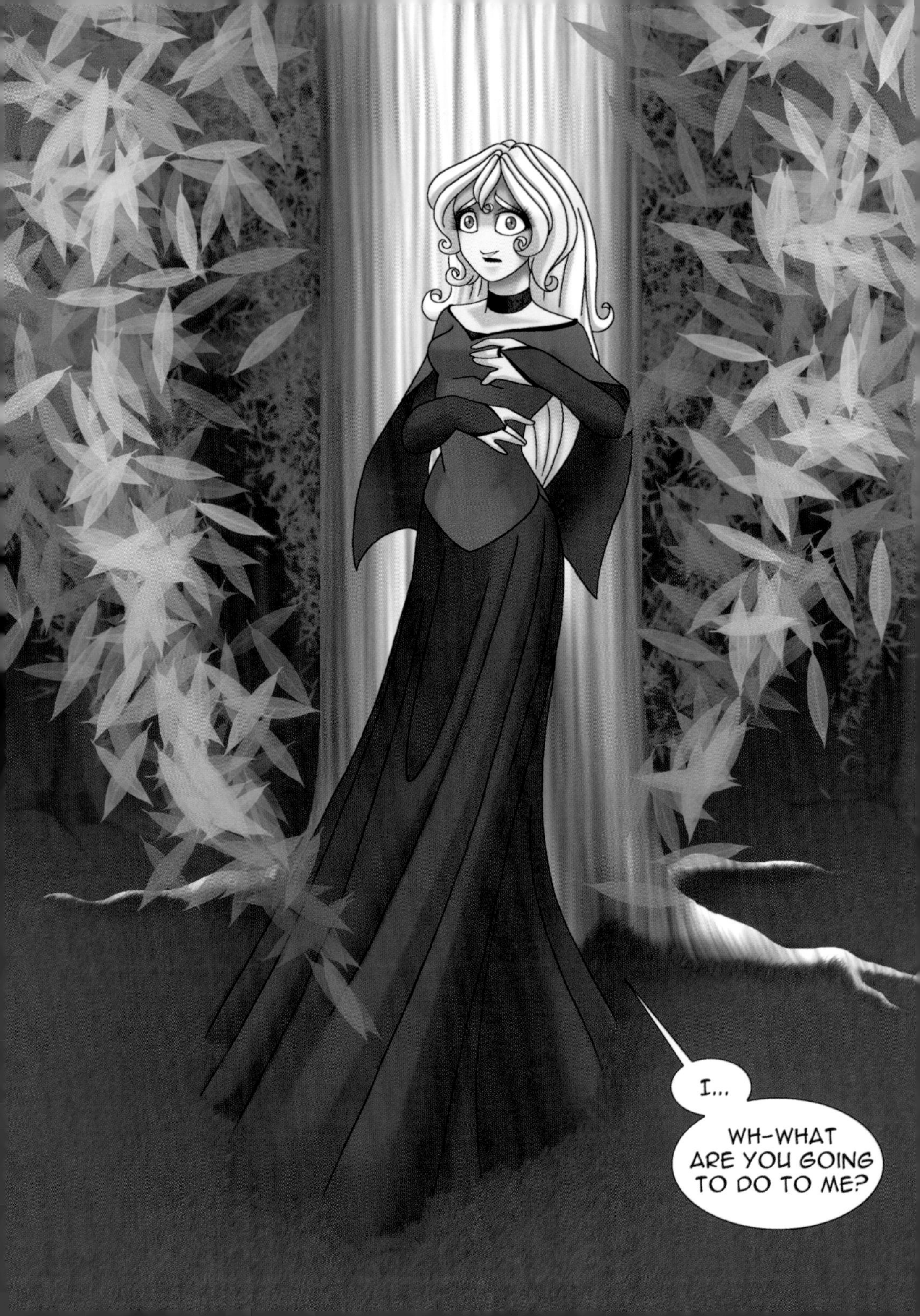
I...
WH-WHAT ARE YOU GOING TO DO TO ME?

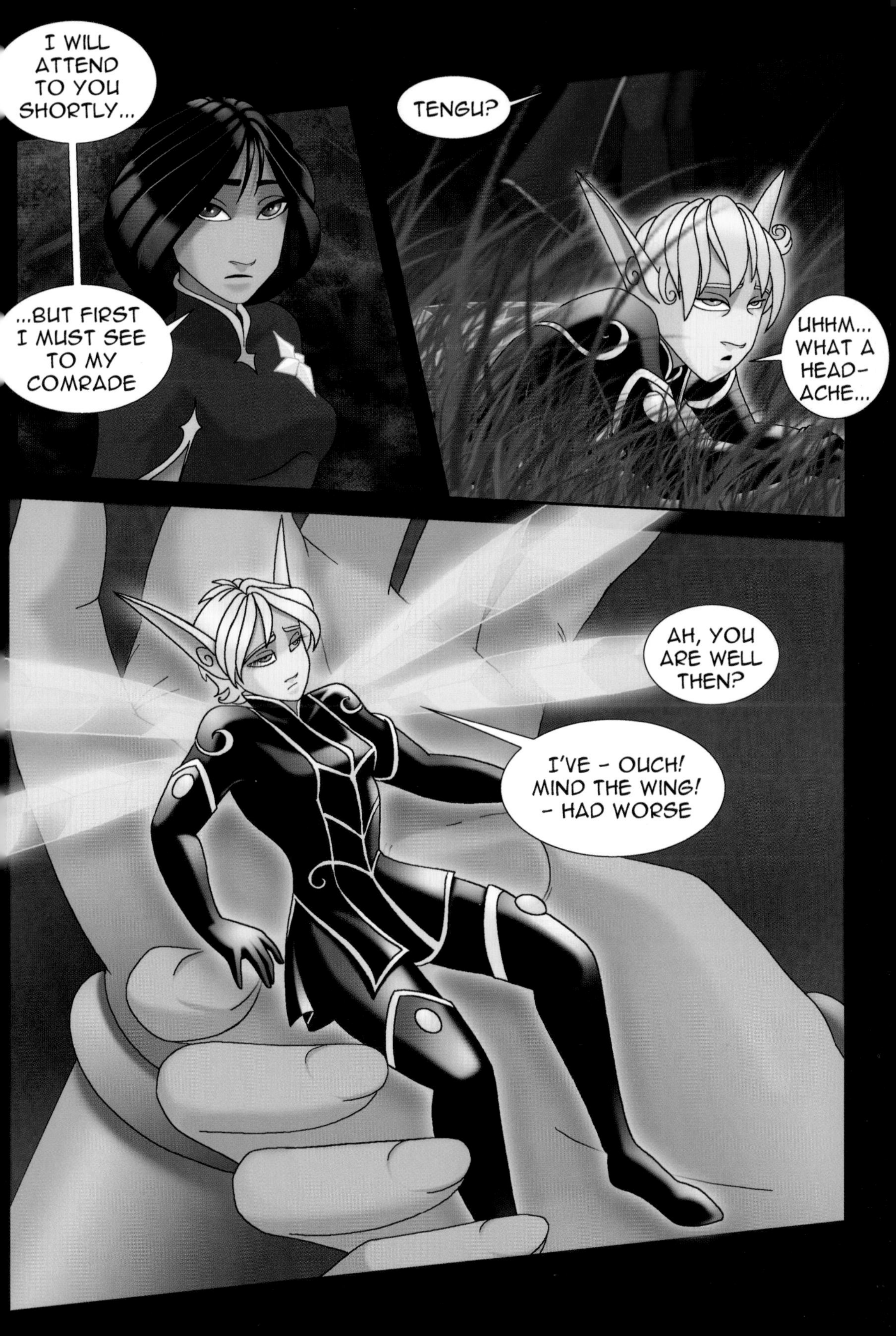
I WILL ATTEND TO YOU SHORTLY...
...BUT FIRST I MUST SEE TO MY COMRADE
TENGU?
UHHM... WHAT A HEAD-ACHE...
AH, YOU ARE WELL THEN?
I'VE - OUCH! MIND THE WING! - HAD WORSE

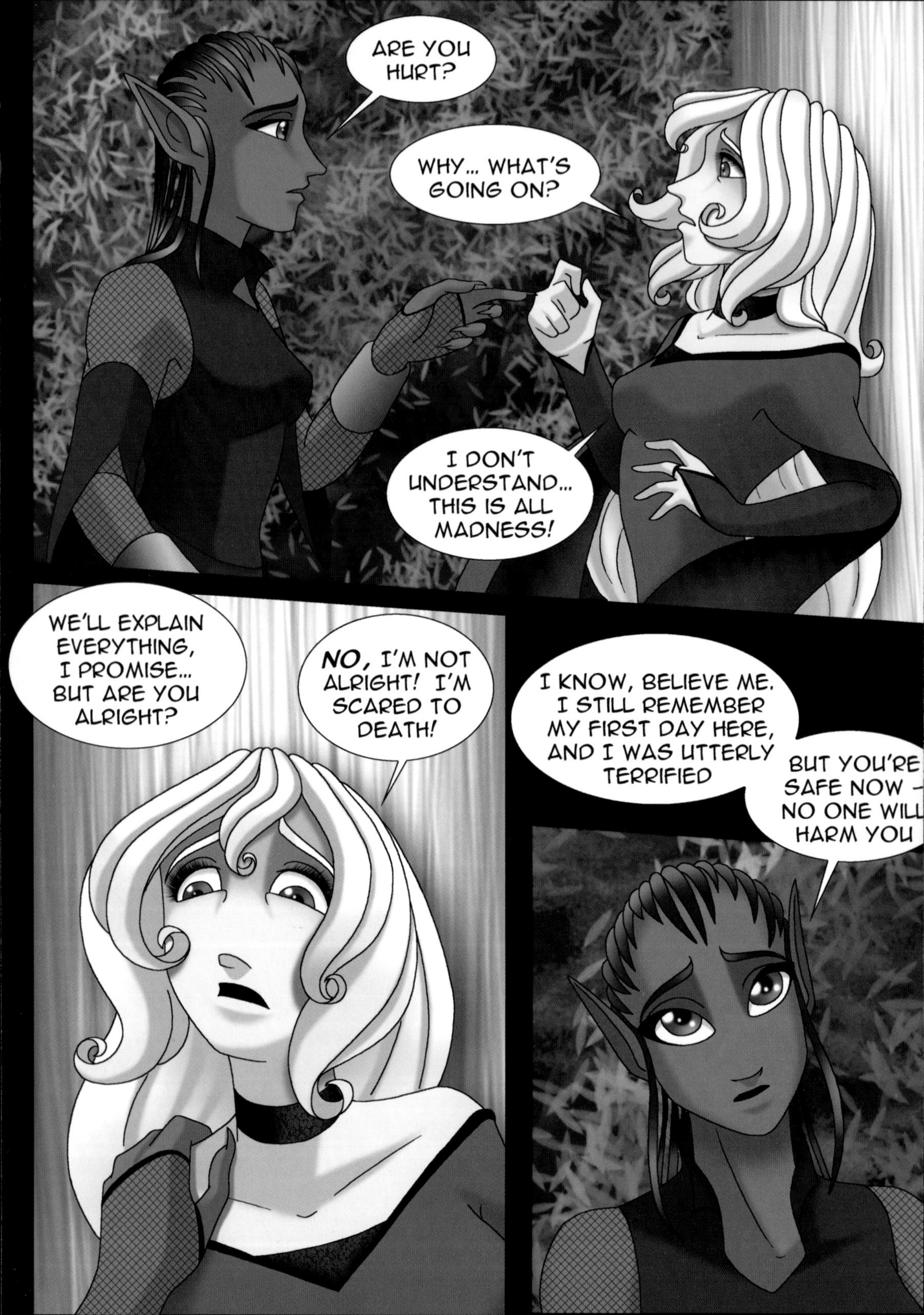
ARE YOU HURT?
WHY... WHAT'S GOING ON?
I DON'T UNDERSTAND... THIS IS ALL MADNESS!
WE'LL EXPLAIN EVERYTHING, I PROMISE... BUT ARE YOU ALRIGHT?
NO, I'M NOT ALRIGHT! I'M SCARED TO DEATH!
I KNOW, BELIEVE ME. I STILL REMEMBER MY FIRST DAY HERE, AND I WAS UTTERLY TERRIFIED
BUT YOU'RE SAFE NOW – NO ONE WILL HARM YOU

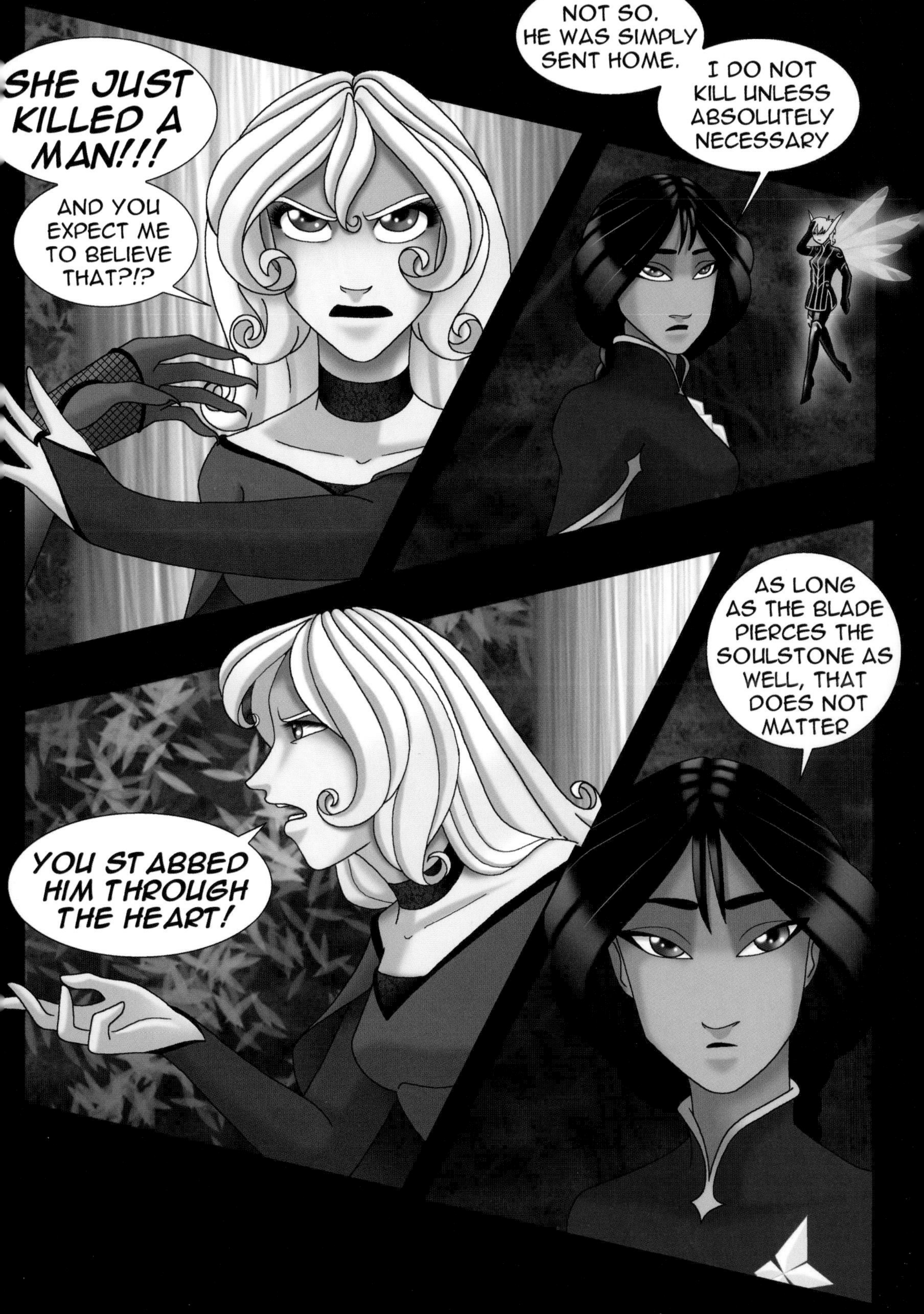
SHE JUST KILLED A MAN!!!
AND YOU EXPECT ME TO BELIEVE THAT?!?
NOT SO. HE WAS SIMPLY SENT HOME.
I DO NOT KILL UNLESS ABSOLUTELY NECESSARY
YOU STABBED HIM THROUGH THE HEART!
AS LONG AS THE BLADE PIERCES THE SOULSTONE AS WELL, THAT DOES NOT MATTER

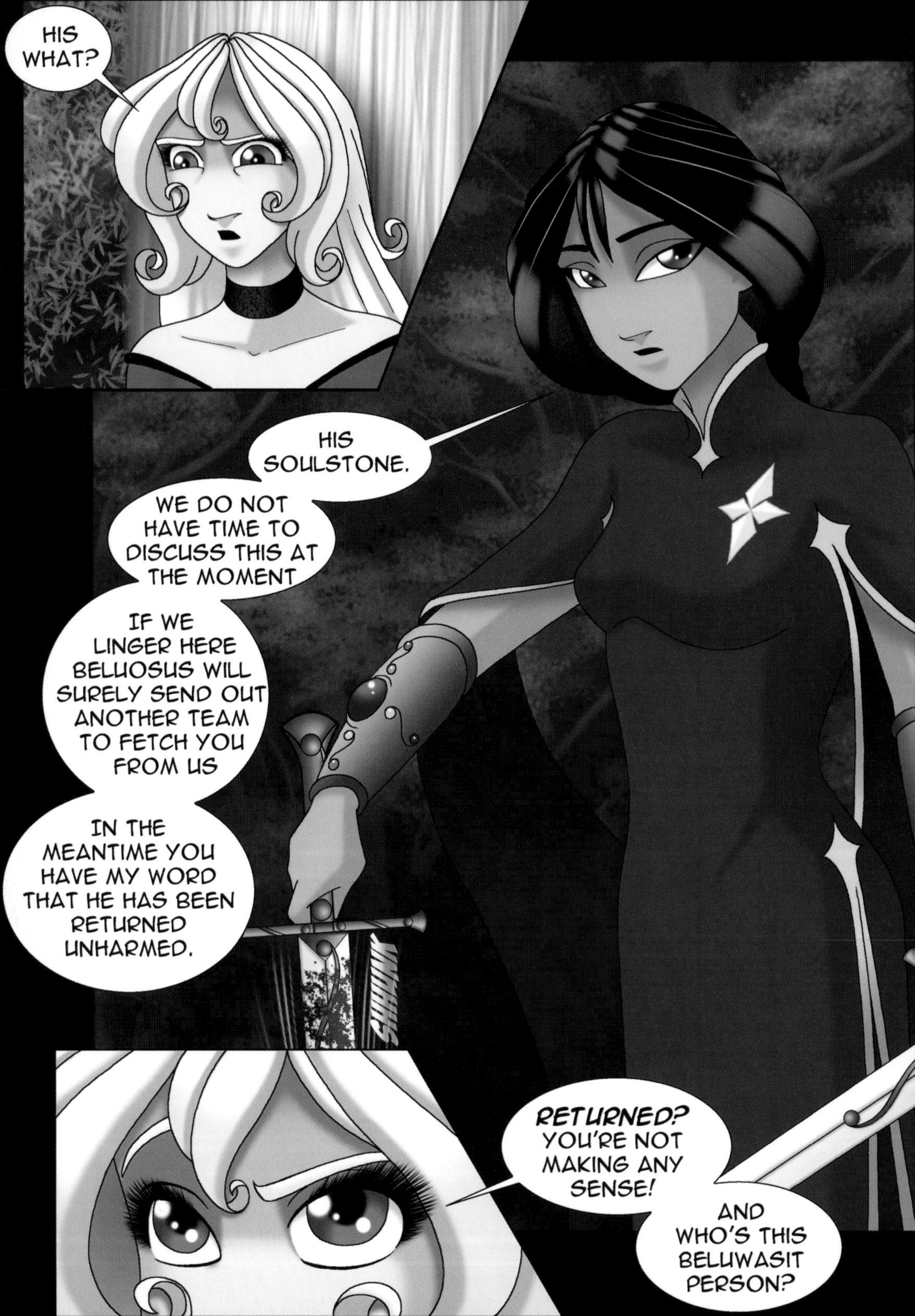
HIS WHAT?
HIS SOULSTONE.
WE DO NOT HAVE TIME TO DISCUSS THIS AT THE MOMENT
IF WE LINGER HERE BELUOSUS WILL SURELY SEND OUT ANOTHER TEAM TO FETCH YOU FROM US
IN THE MEANTIME YOU HAVE MY WORD THAT HE HAS BEEN RETURNED UNHARMED.
RETURNED? YOU'RE NOT MAKING ANY SENSE!
AND WHO'S THIS BELUWASIT PERSON?

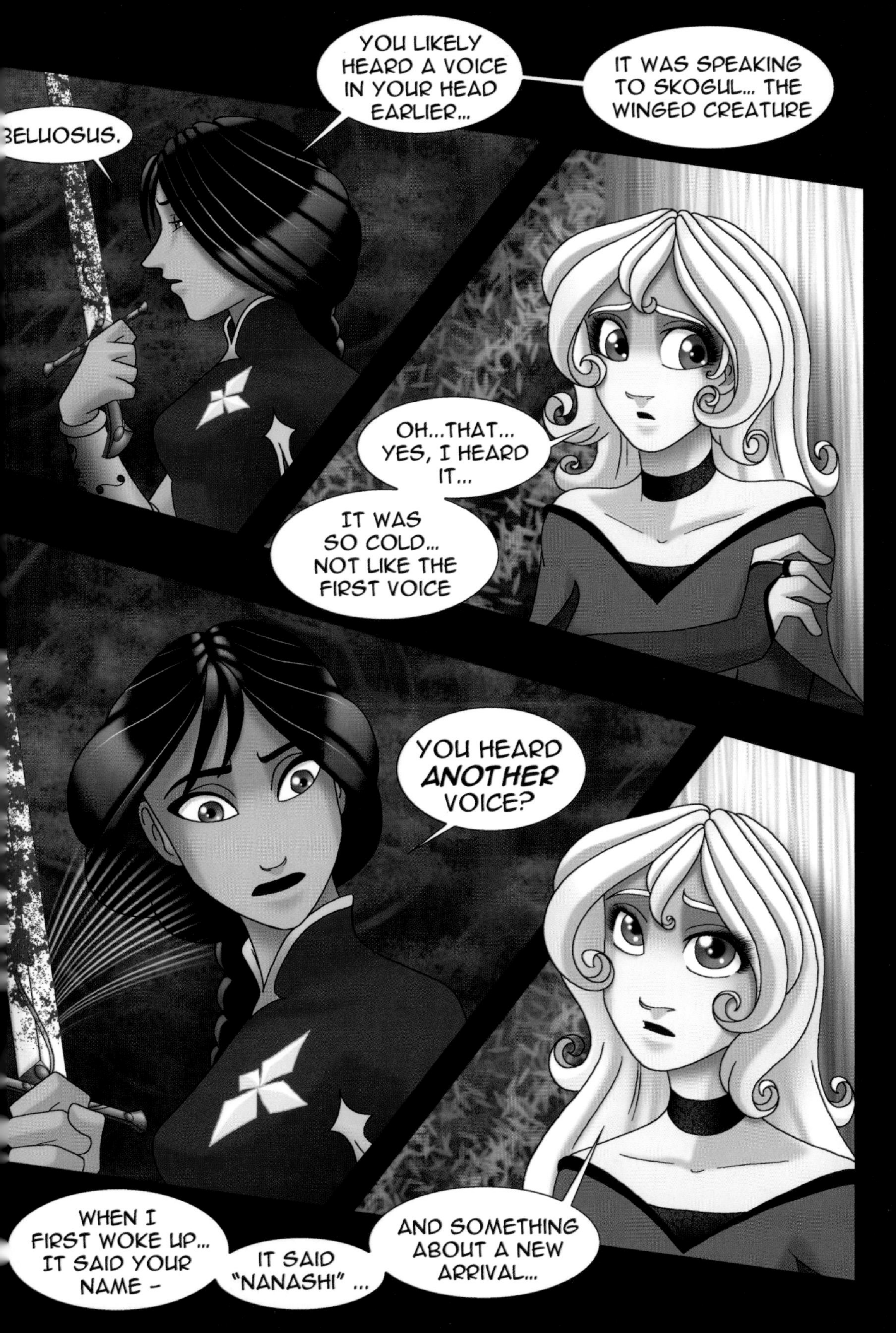
BELUOSUS.
YOU LIKELY HEARD A VOICE IN YOUR HEAD EARLIER...
IT WAS SPEAKING TO SKOGUL... THE WINGED CREATURE
OH...THAT... YES, I HEARD IT...
IT WAS SO COLD... NOT LIKE THE FIRST VOICE
YOU HEARD ANOTHER VOICE?
WHEN I FIRST WOKE UP... IT SAID YOUR NAME -
IT SAID "NANASHI" ...
AND SOMETHING ABOUT A NEW ARRIVAL...

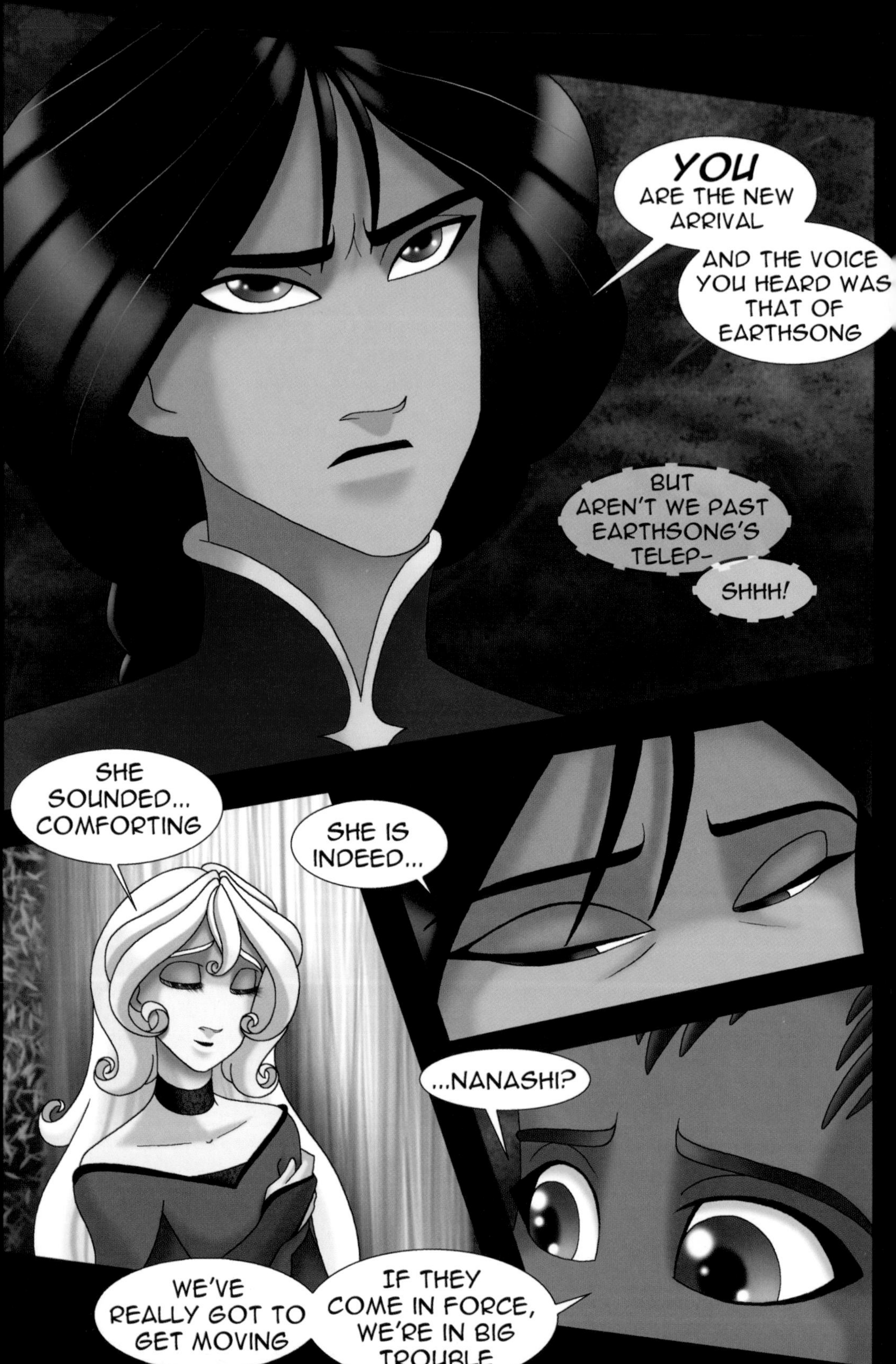
YOU ARE THE NEW ARRIVAL
AND THE VOICE YOU HEARD WAS THAT OF EARTHSONG
BUT AREN'T WE PAST EARTHSONG'S TELEP-
SHHH!
SHE SOUNDED... COMFORTING
SHE IS INDEED...
...NANASHI?
WE'VE REALLY GOT TO GET MOVING
IF THEY COME IN FORCE, WE'RE IN BIG TROUBLE

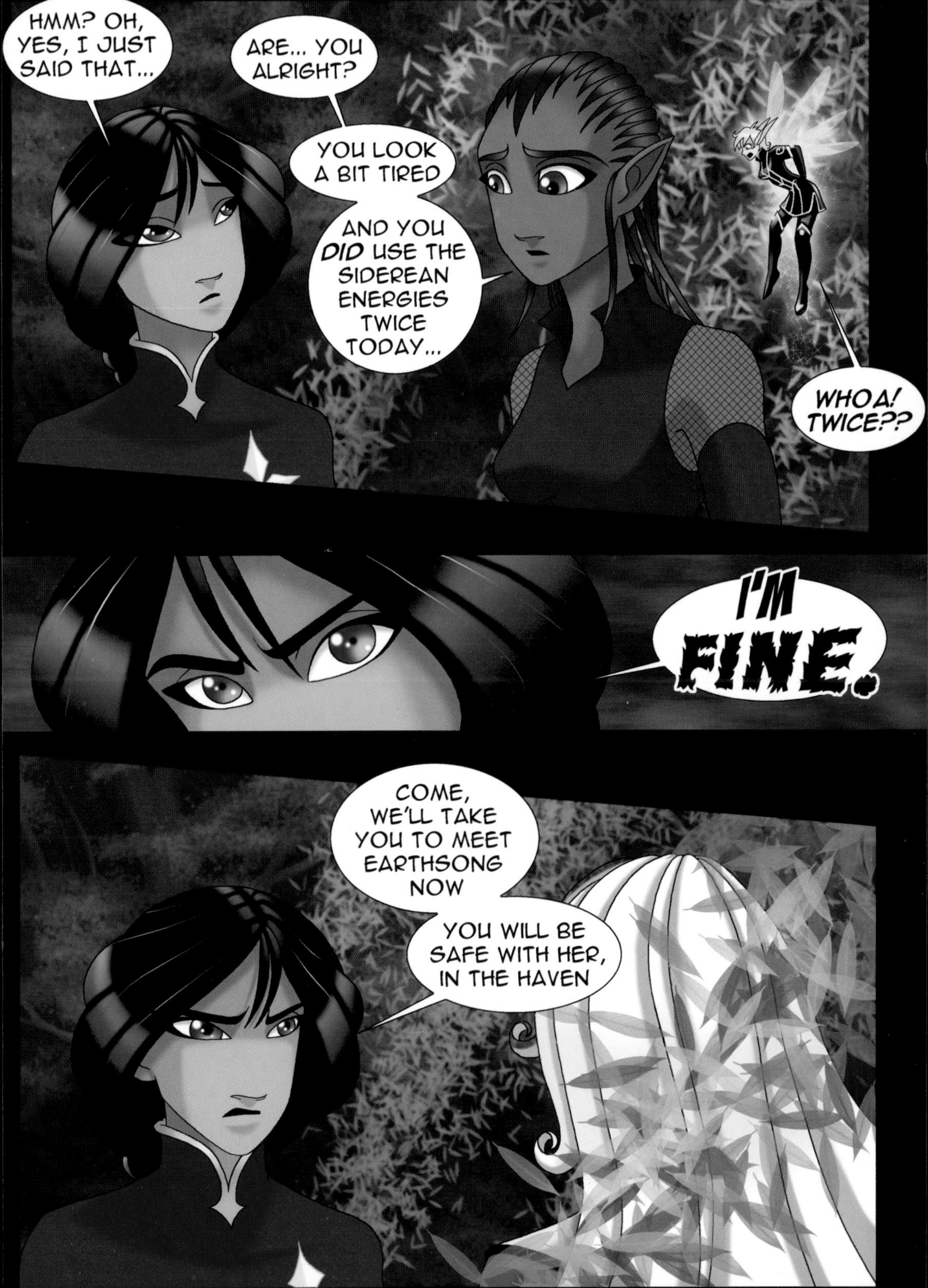
HMM? OH, YES, I JUST SAID THAT...
ARE... YOU ALRIGHT?
YOU LOOK A BIT TIRED
AND YOU *DID* USE THE SIDEREAN ENERGIES TWICE TODAY...
WHOA! TWICE??
I'M FINE.
COME, WE'LL TAKE YOU TO MEET EARTHSONG NOW
YOU WILL BE SAFE WITH HER, IN THE HAVEN

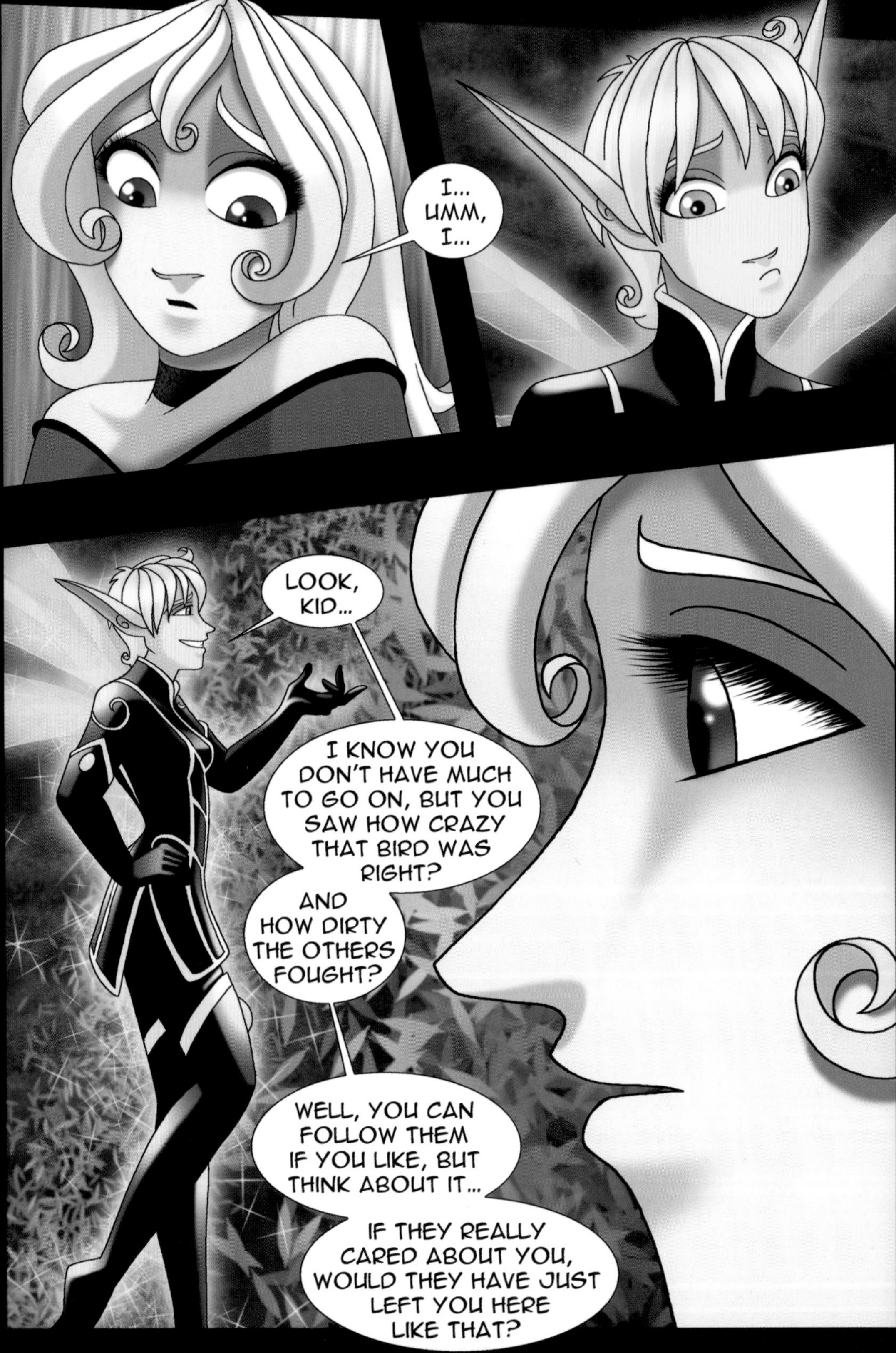
I... UMM, I...
LOOK, KID...
I KNOW YOU DON'T HAVE MUCH TO GO ON, BUT YOU SAW HOW CRAZY THAT BIRD WAS RIGHT?
AND HOW DIRTY THE OTHERS FOUGHT?
WELL, YOU CAN FOLLOW THEM IF YOU LIKE, BUT THINK ABOUT IT...
IF THEY REALLY CARED ABOUT YOU, WOULD THEY HAVE JUST LEFT YOU HERE LIKE THAT?

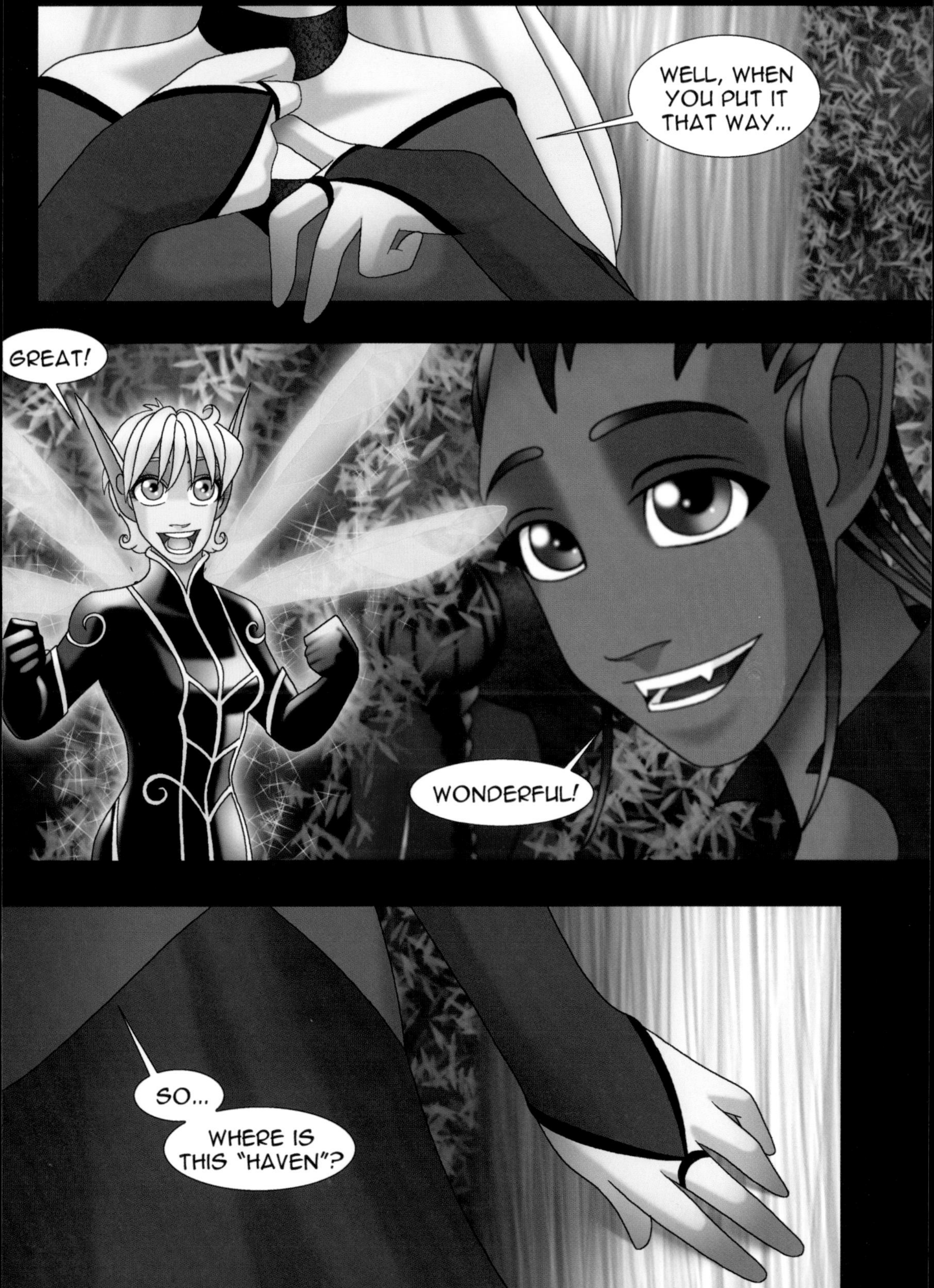
WELL, WHEN YOU PUT IT THAT WAY...
GREAT!
WONDERFUL!
SO...
WHERE IS THIS "HAVEN"?

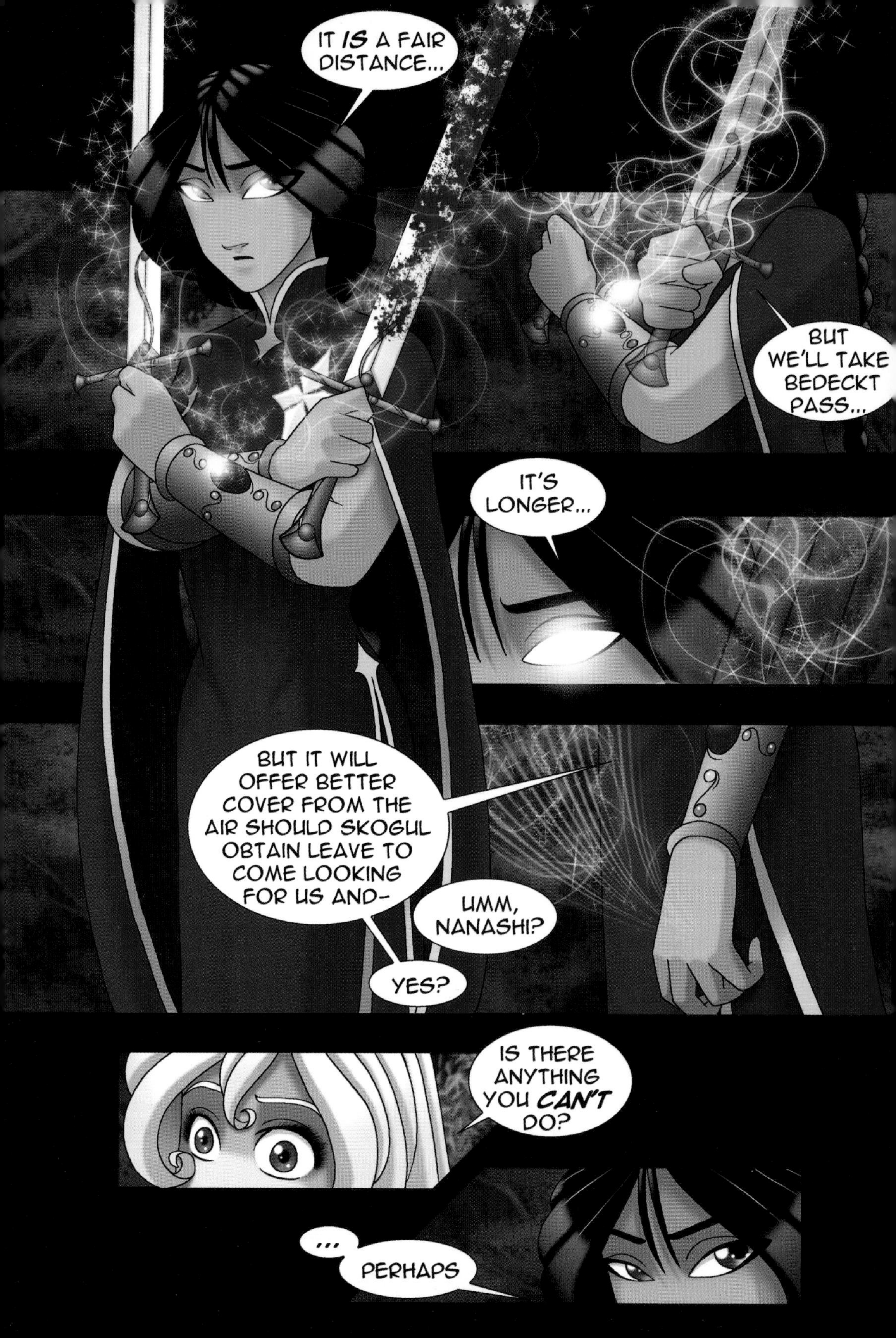
IT IS A FAIR DISTANCE...
BUT WE'LL TAKE BEDECKT PASS...
IT'S LONGER...
BUT IT WILL OFFER BETTER COVER FROM THE AIR SHOULD SKOGUL OBTAIN LEAVE TO COME LOOKING FOR US AND-
UMM, NANASHI?
YES?
IS THERE ANYTHING YOU CAN'T DO?
...
PERHAPS

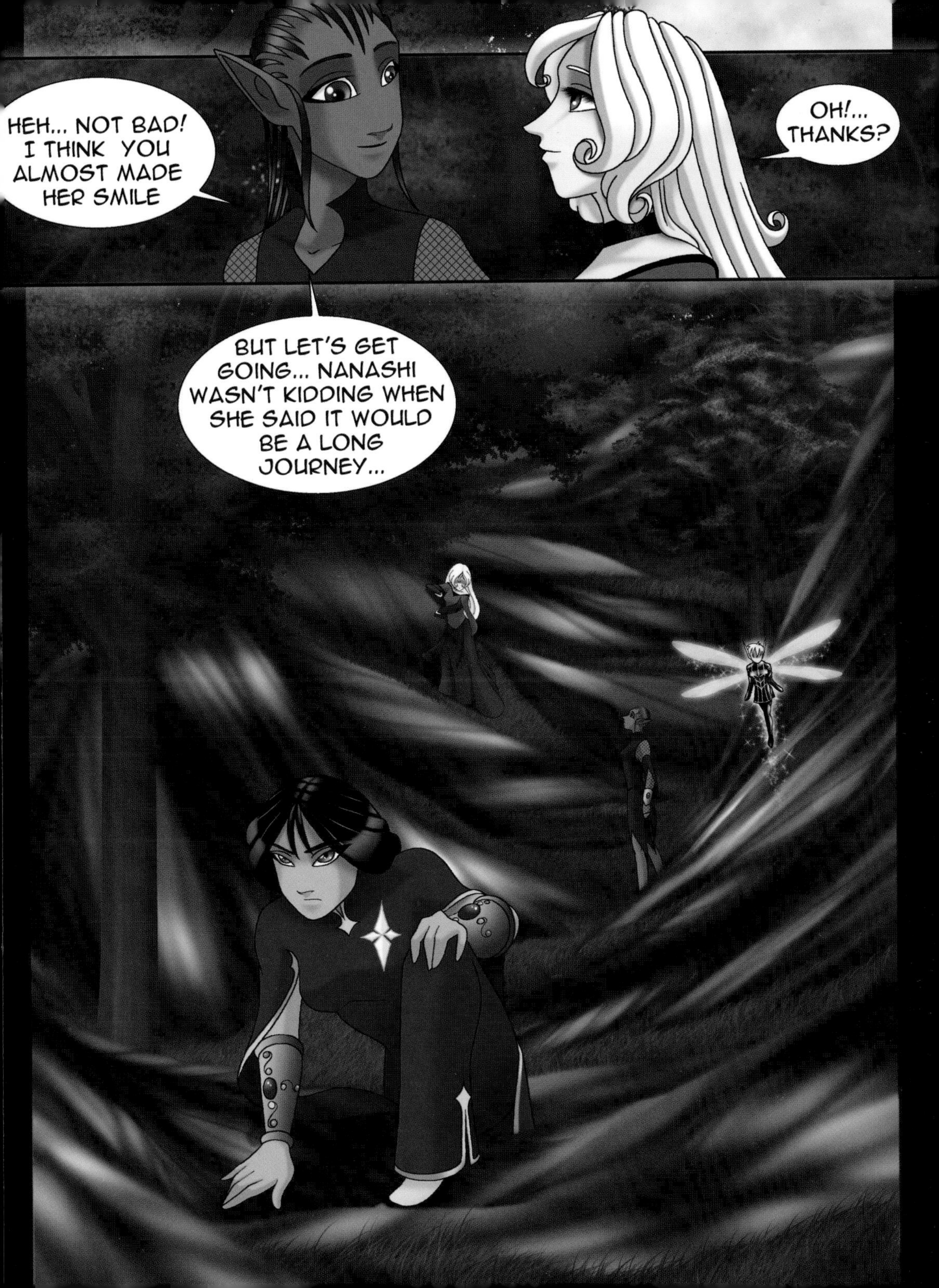
HEH... NOT BAD! I THINK YOU ALMOST MADE HER SMILE
OH!... THANKS?
BUT LET'S GET GOING... NANASHI WASN'T KIDDING WHEN SHE SAID IT WOULD BE A LONG JOURNEY...

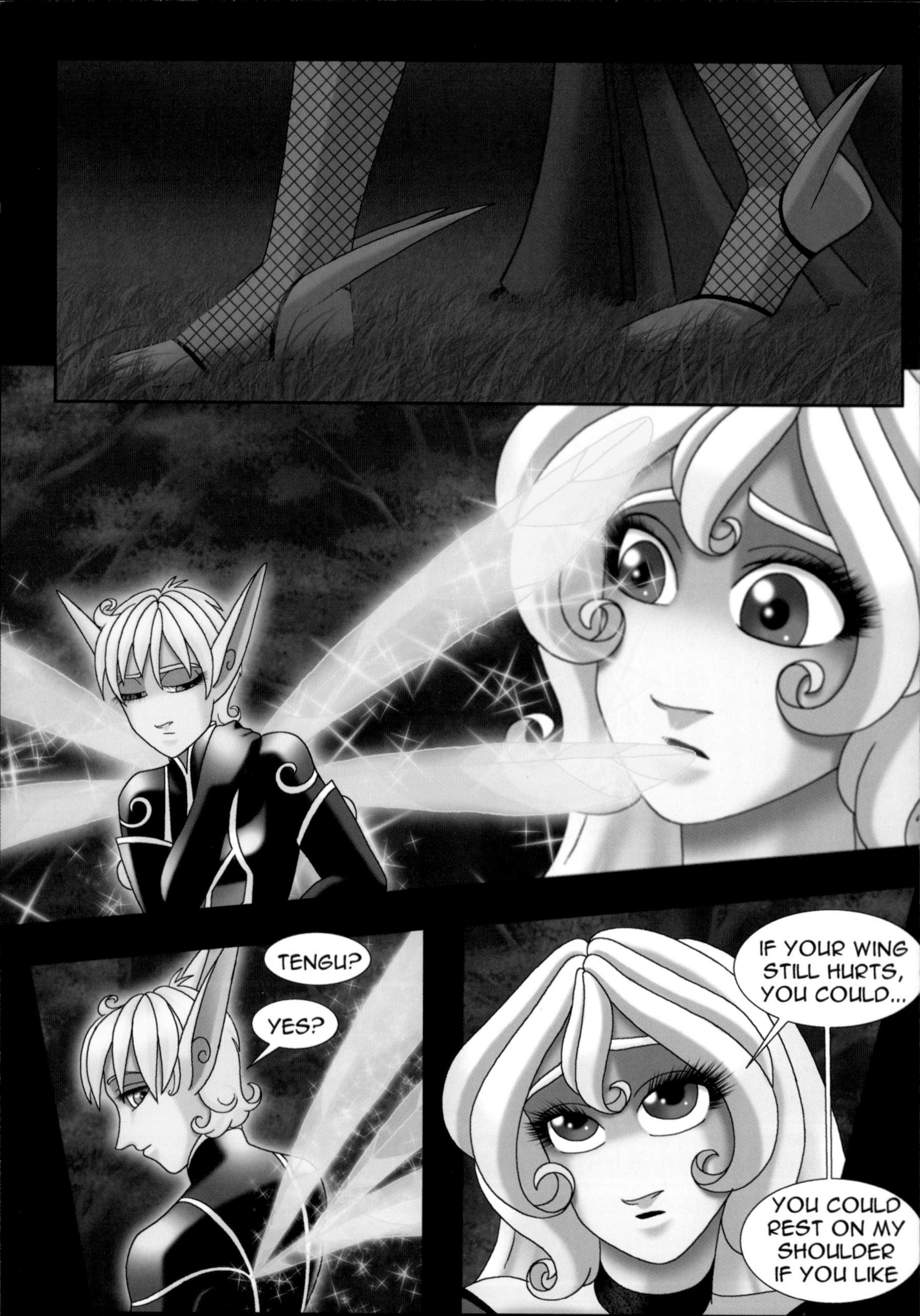
TENGU?
YES?
IF YOUR WING STILL HURTS, YOU COULD...
YOU COULD REST ON MY SHOULDER IF YOU LIKE

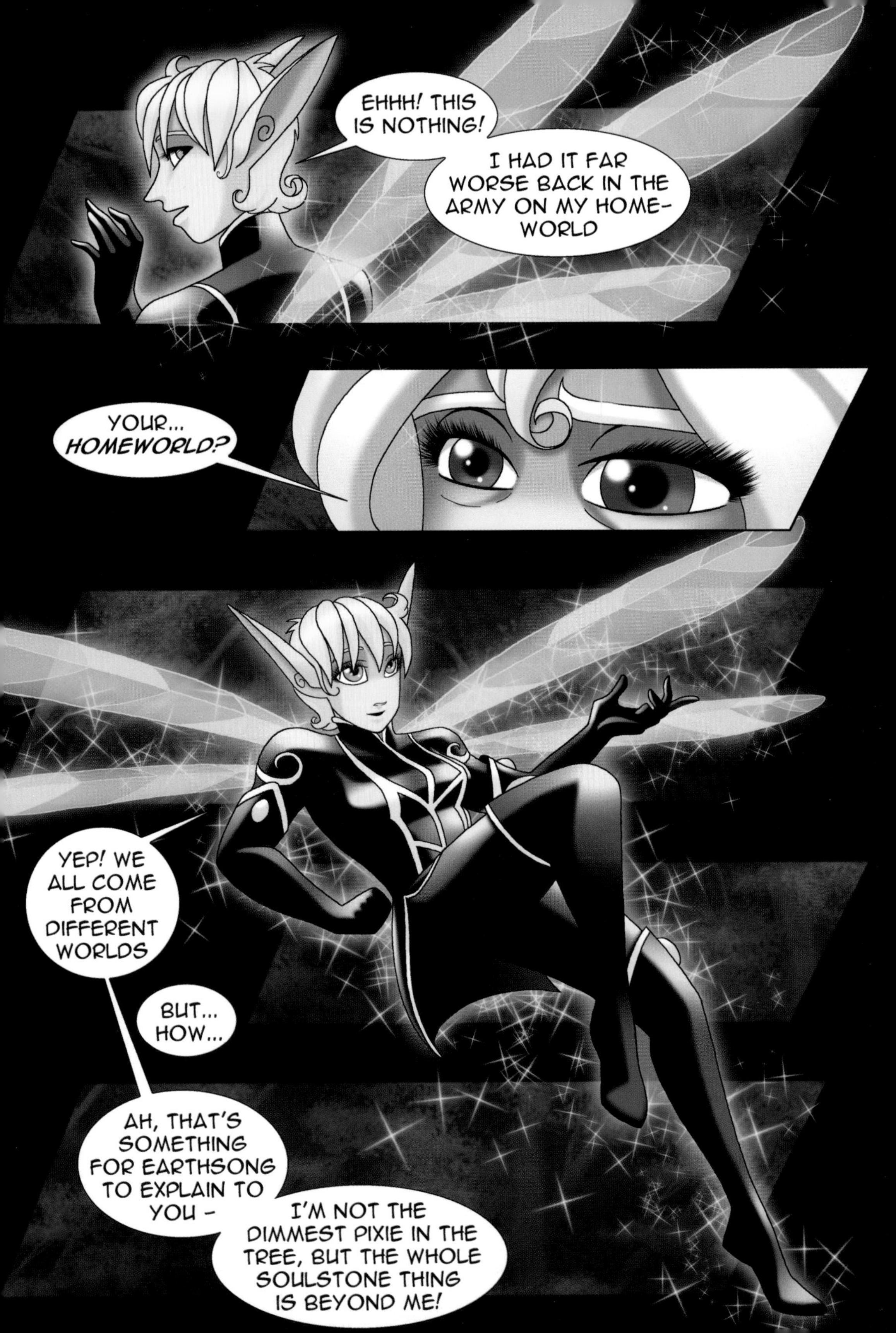
EHHH! THIS IS NOTHING!
I HAD IT FAR WORSE BACK IN THE ARMY ON MY HOME-WORLD
YOUR... *HOMEWORLD?*
YEP! WE ALL COME FROM DIFFERENT WORLDS
BUT... HOW...
AH, THAT'S SOMETHING FOR EARTHSONG TO EXPLAIN TO YOU -
I'M NOT THE DIMMEST PIXIE IN THE TREE, BUT THE WHOLE SOULSTONE THING IS BEYOND ME!

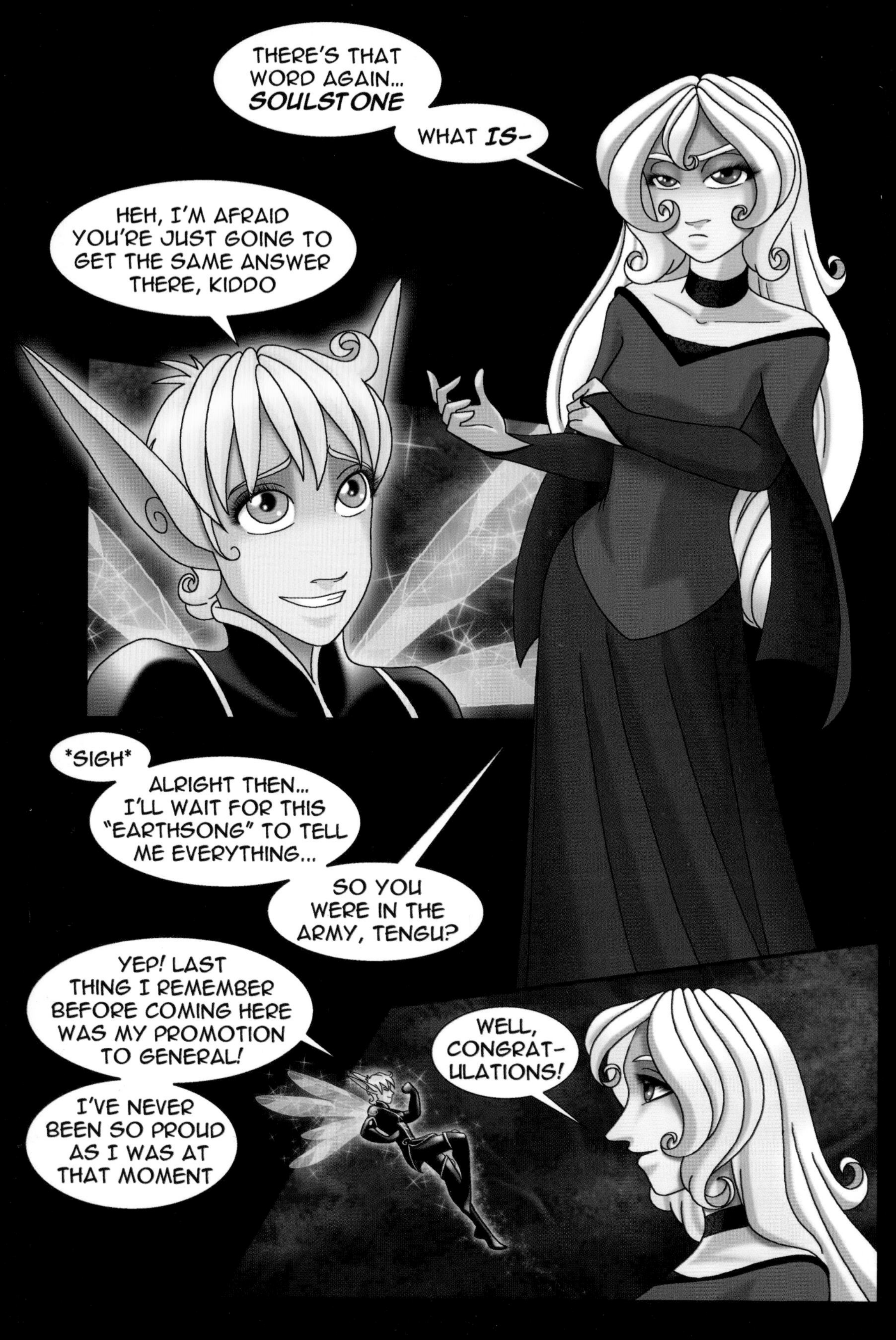
THERE'S THAT WORD AGAIN... SOULSTONE
WHAT IS-
HEH, I'M AFRAID YOU'RE JUST GOING TO GET THE SAME ANSWER THERE, KIDDO
SIGH
ALRIGHT THEN... I'LL WAIT FOR THIS "EARTHSONG" TO TELL ME EVERYTHING...
SO YOU WERE IN THE ARMY, TENGU?
YEP! LAST THING I REMEMBER BEFORE COMING HERE WAS MY PROMOTION TO GENERAL!
I'VE NEVER BEEN SO PROUD AS I WAS AT THAT MOMENT
WELL, CONGRAT-ULATIONS!

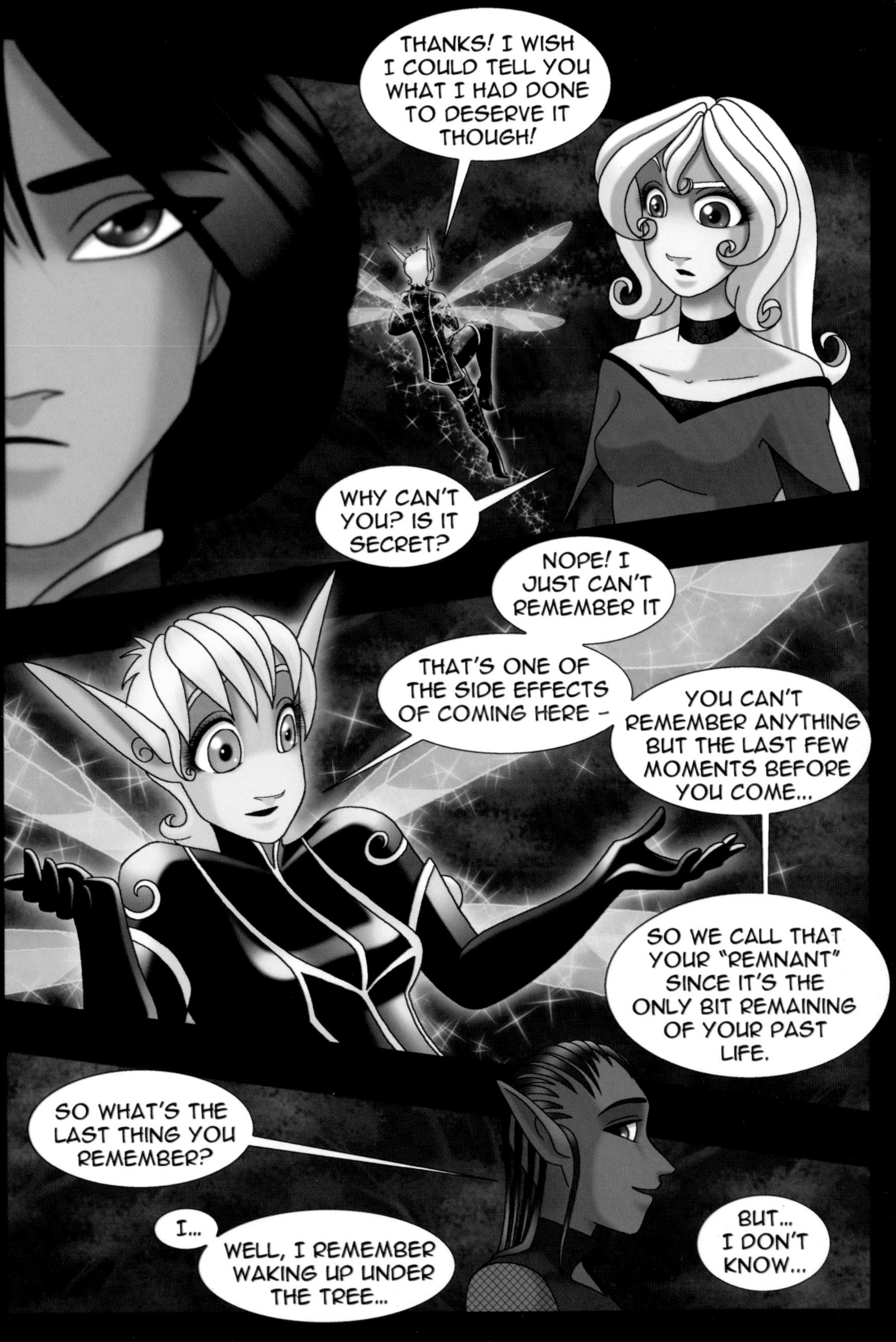
THANKS! I WISH I COULD TELL YOU WHAT I HAD DONE TO DESERVE IT THOUGH!
WHY CAN'T YOU? IS IT SECRET?
NOPE! I JUST CAN'T REMEMBER IT
THAT'S ONE OF THE SIDE EFFECTS OF COMING HERE –
YOU CAN'T REMEMBER ANYTHING BUT THE LAST FEW MOMENTS BEFORE YOU COME...
SO WE CALL THAT YOUR "REMNANT" SINCE IT'S THE ONLY BIT REMAINING OF YOUR PAST LIFE.
SO WHAT'S THE LAST THING YOU REMEMBER?
I...
WELL, I REMEMBER WAKING UP UNDER THE TREE...
BUT... I DON'T KNOW...

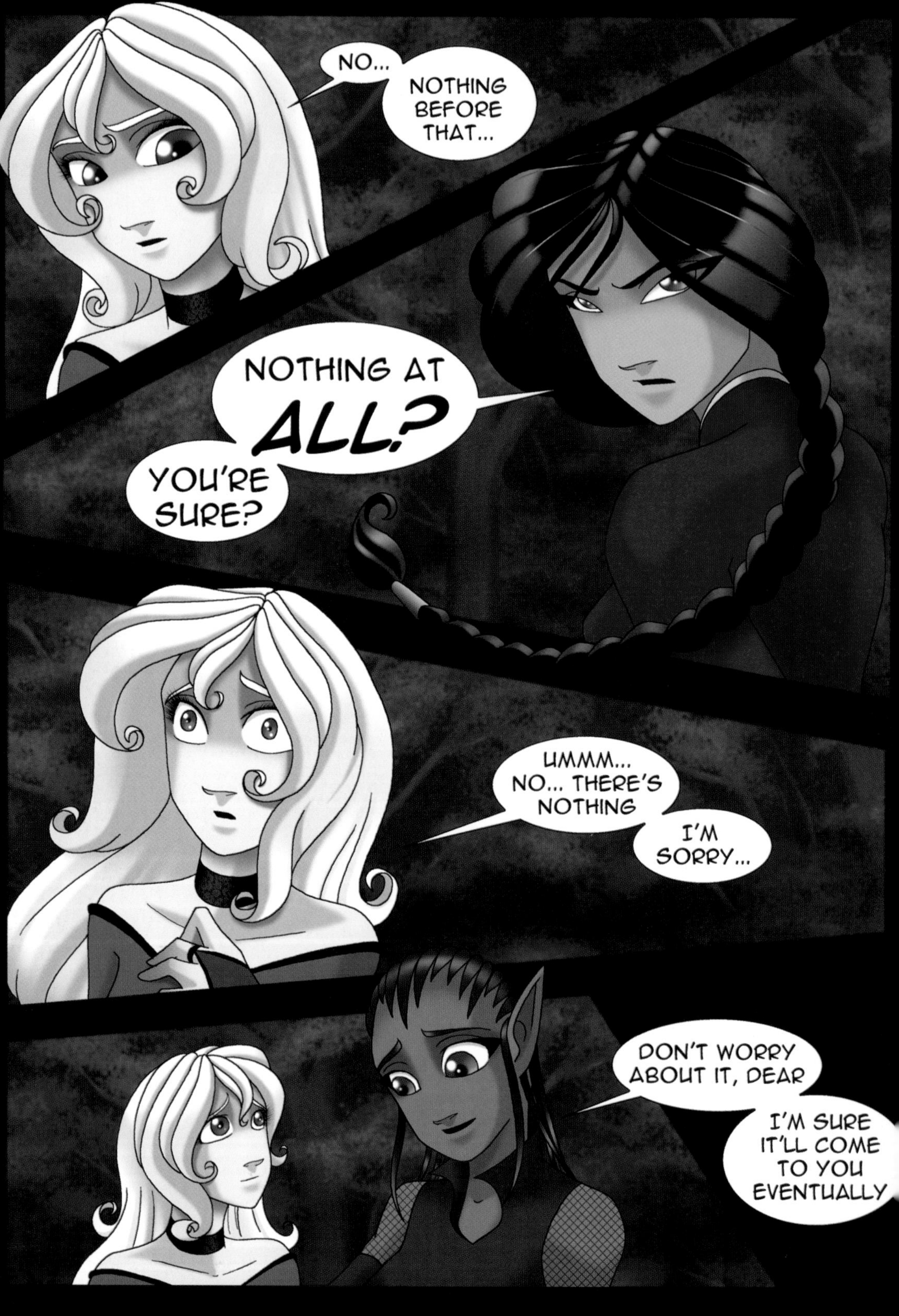
NO...
NOTHING BEFORE THAT...
NOTHING AT ALL?
YOU'RE SURE?
UMMM... NO... THERE'S NOTHING
I'M SORRY...
DON'T WORRY ABOUT IT, DEAR
I'M SURE IT'LL COME TO YOU EVENTUALLY

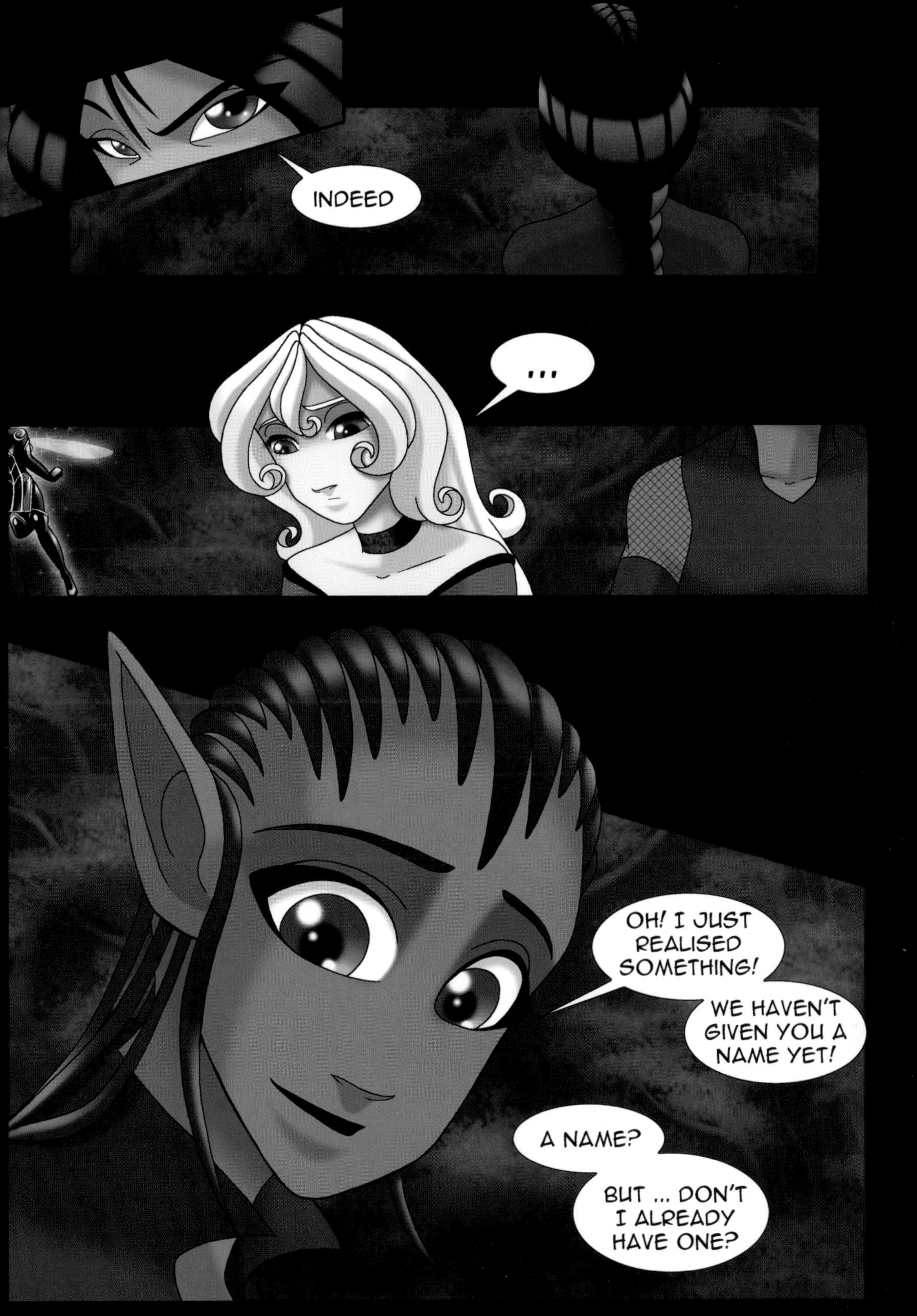
INDEED
...
OH! I JUST REALISED SOMETHING!
WE HAVEN'T GIVEN YOU A NAME YET!
A NAME?
BUT ... DON'T I ALREADY HAVE ONE?

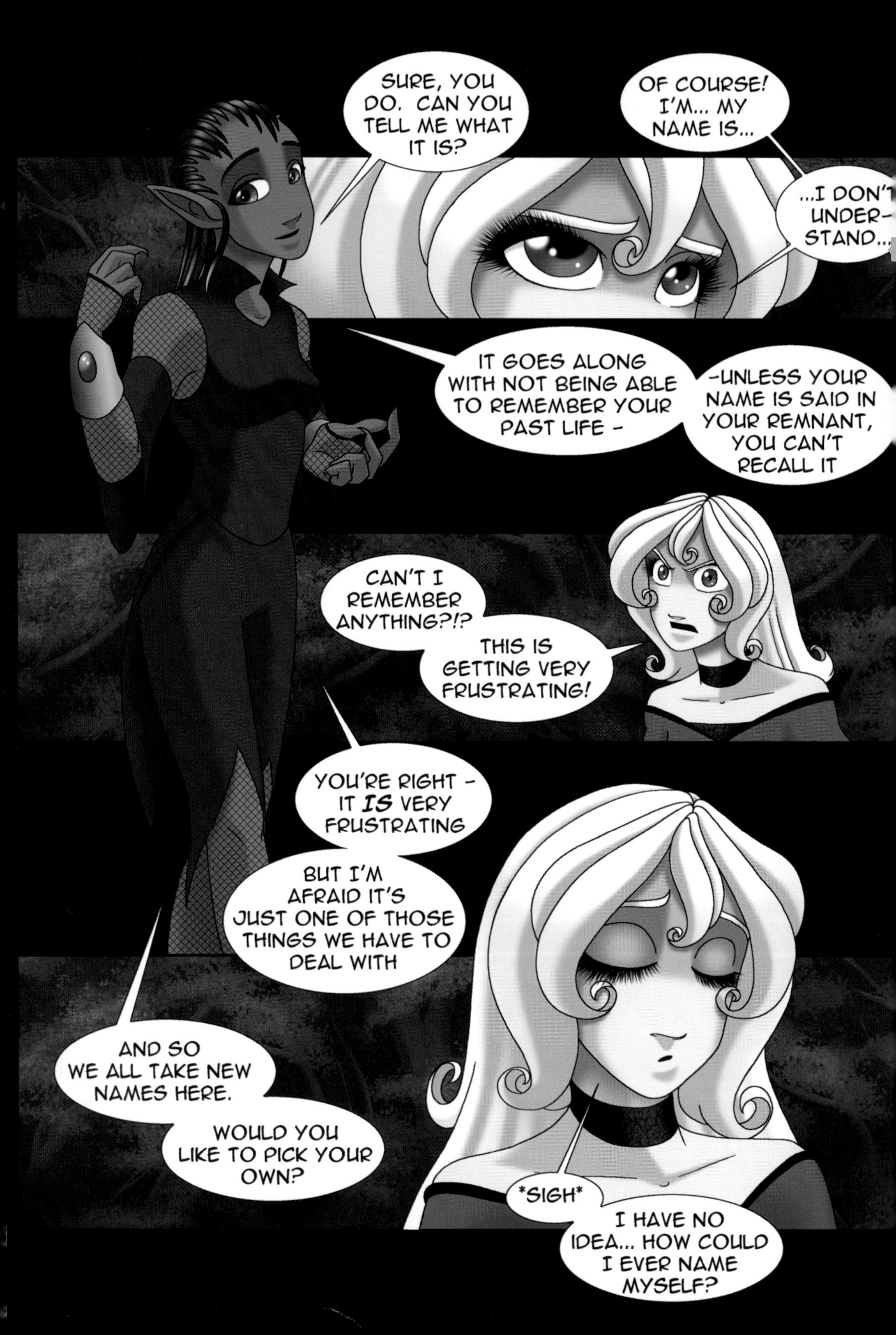
SURE, YOU DO. CAN YOU TELL ME WHAT IT IS?
OF COURSE! I'M... MY NAME IS...
...I DON'T UNDER-STAND...
IT GOES ALONG WITH NOT BEING ABLE TO REMEMBER YOUR PAST LIFE -
-UNLESS YOUR NAME IS SAID IN YOUR REMNANT, YOU CAN'T RECALL IT
CAN'T I REMEMBER ANYTHING?!?
THIS IS GETTING VERY FRUSTRATING!
YOU'RE RIGHT - IT *IS* VERY FRUSTRATING
BUT I'M AFRAID IT'S JUST ONE OF THOSE THINGS WE HAVE TO DEAL WITH
AND SO WE ALL TAKE NEW NAMES HERE.
WOULD YOU LIKE TO PICK YOUR OWN?
SIGH
I HAVE NO IDEA... HOW COULD I EVER NAME MYSELF?

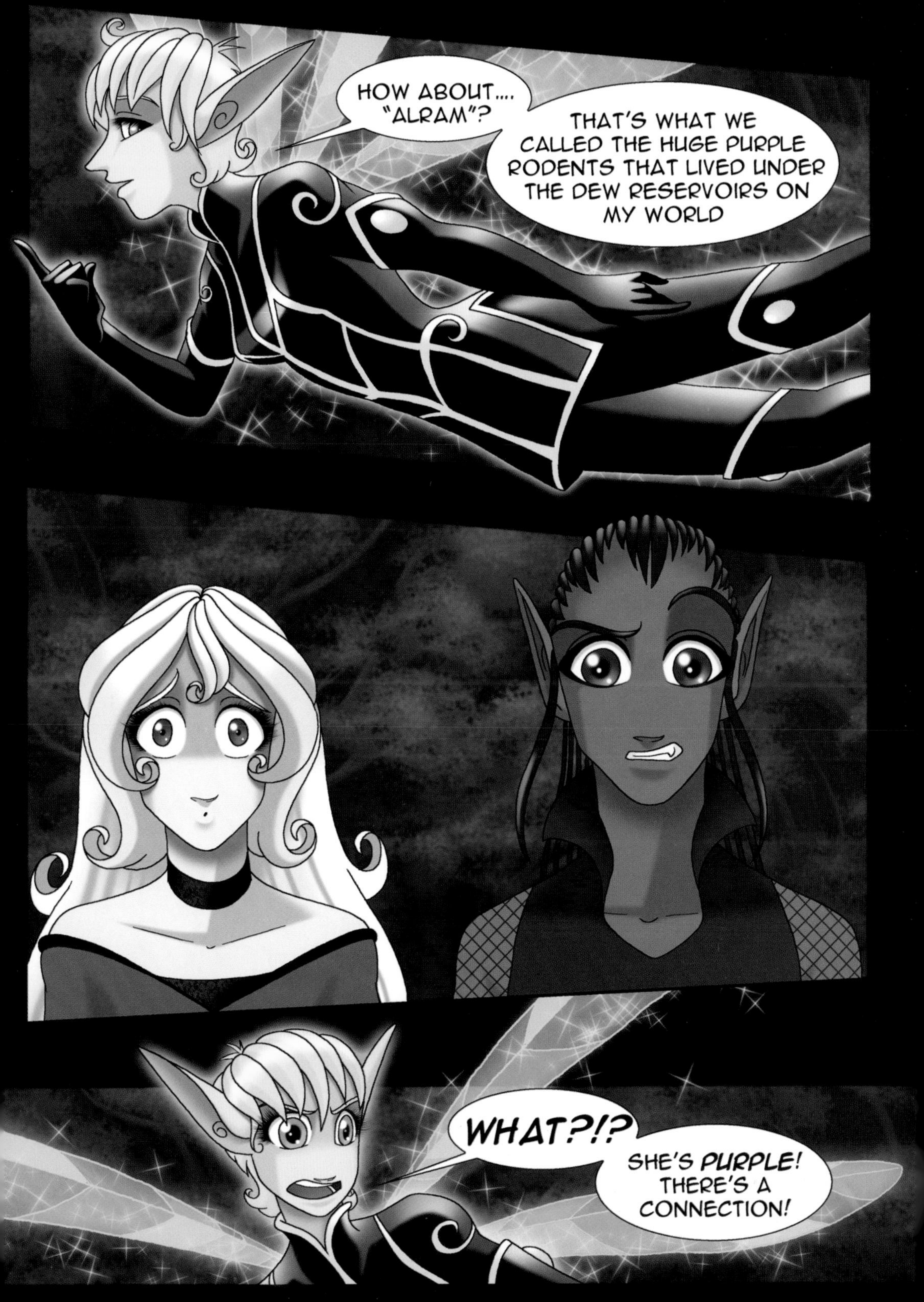
HOW ABOUT.... "ALRAM"?
THAT'S WHAT WE CALLED THE HUGE PURPLE RODENTS THAT LIVED UNDER THE DEW RESERVOIRS ON MY WORLD
WHAT?!?
SHE'S *PURPLE*! THERE'S A CONNECTION!

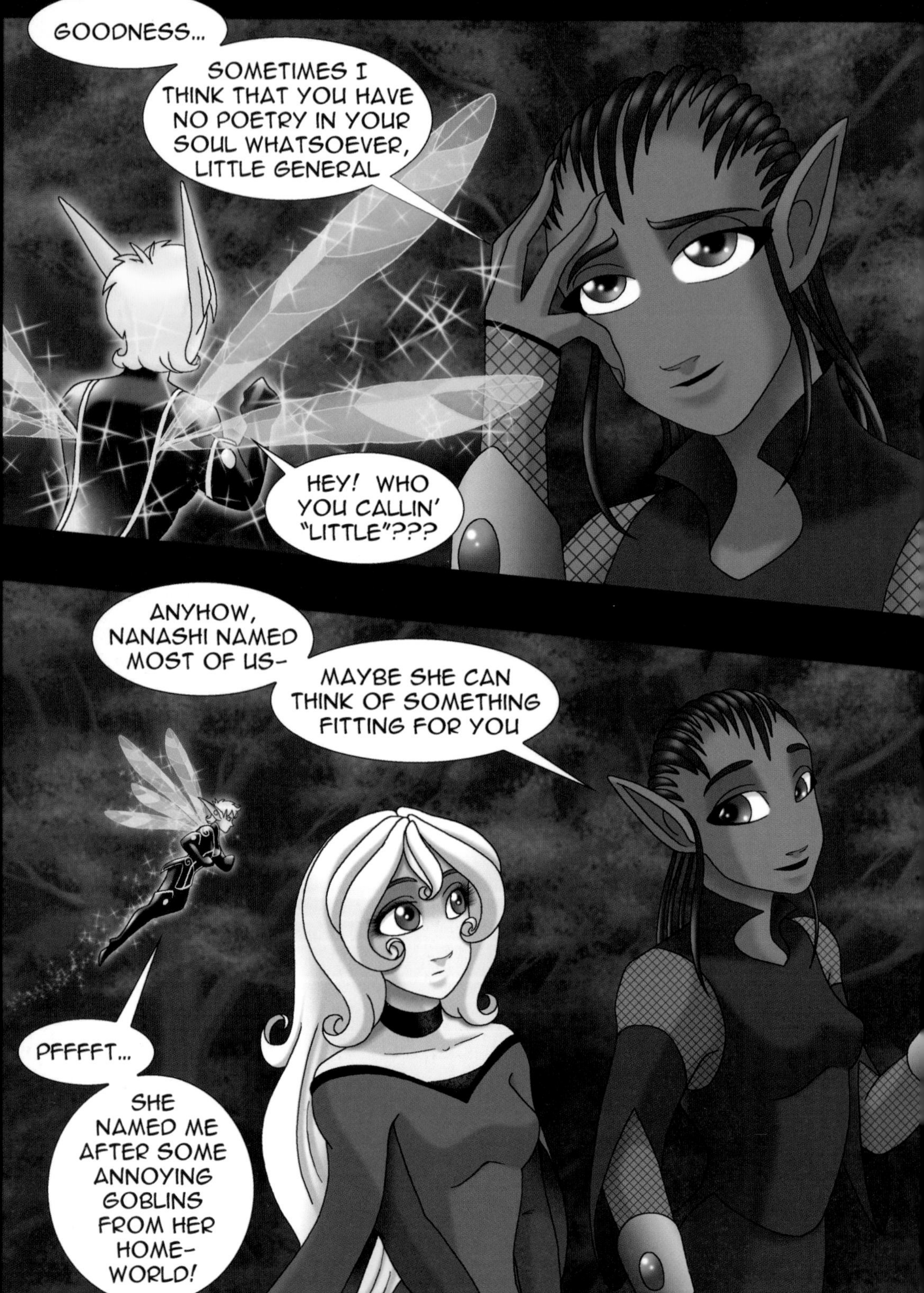
GOODNESS...
SOMETIMES I THINK THAT YOU HAVE NO POETRY IN YOUR SOUL WHATSOEVER, LITTLE GENERAL
HEY! WHO YOU CALLIN' "LITTLE"???
ANYHOW, NANASHI NAMED MOST OF US-
MAYBE SHE CAN THINK OF SOMETHING FITTING FOR YOU
PFFFFT...
SHE NAMED ME AFTER SOME ANNOYING GOBLINS FROM HER HOME-WORLD!

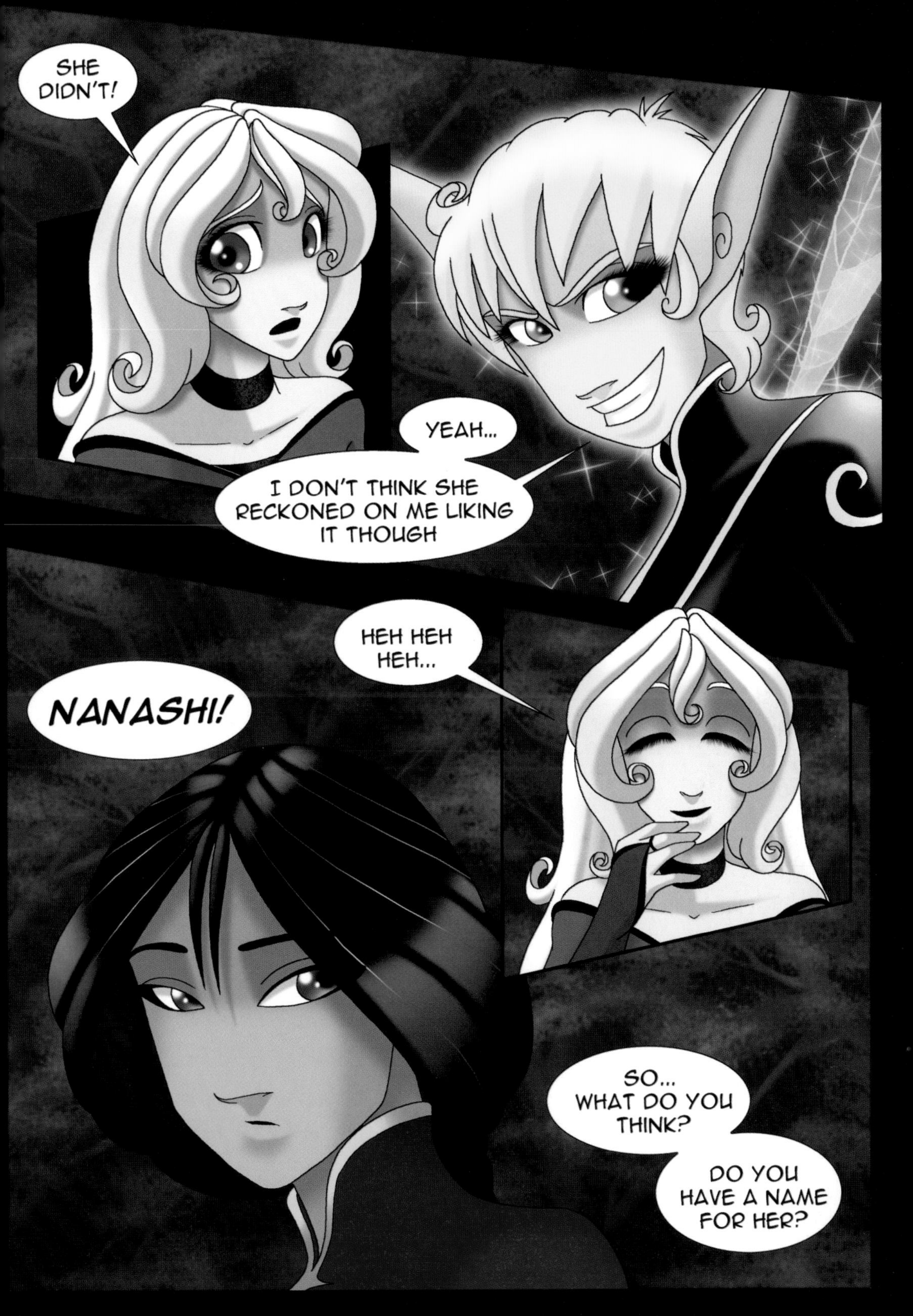
SHE DIDN'T!
YEAH...
I DON'T THINK SHE RECKONED ON ME LIKING IT THOUGH
NANASHI!
HEH HEH HEH...
SO... WHAT DO YOU THINK?
DO YOU HAVE A NAME FOR HER?

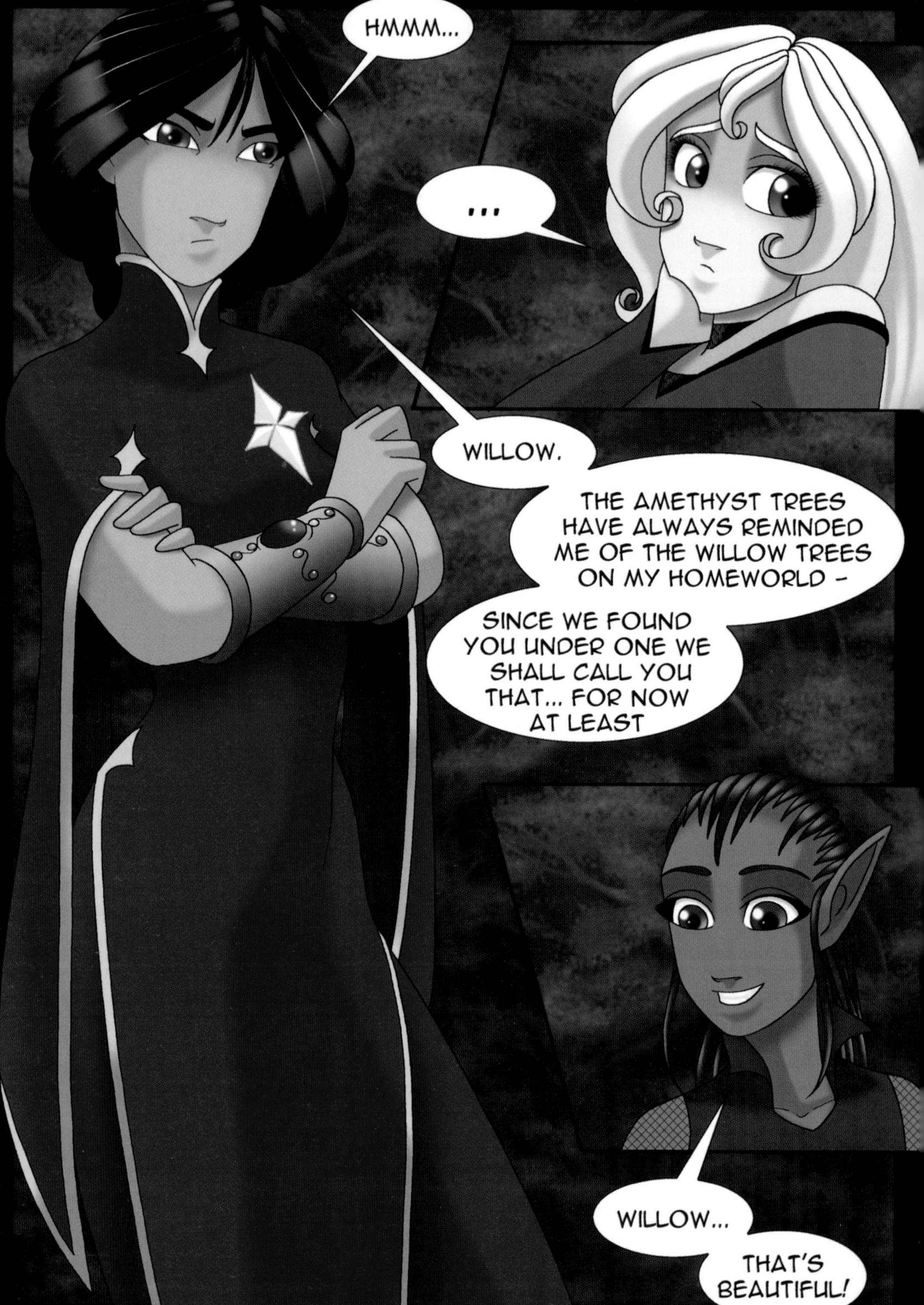
HMMM...
...
WILLOW.
THE AMETHYST TREES HAVE ALWAYS REMINDED ME OF THE WILLOW TREES ON MY HOMEWORLD -
SINCE WE FOUND YOU UNDER ONE WE SHALL CALL YOU THAT... FOR NOW AT LEAST
WILLOW...
THAT'S BEAUTIFUL!

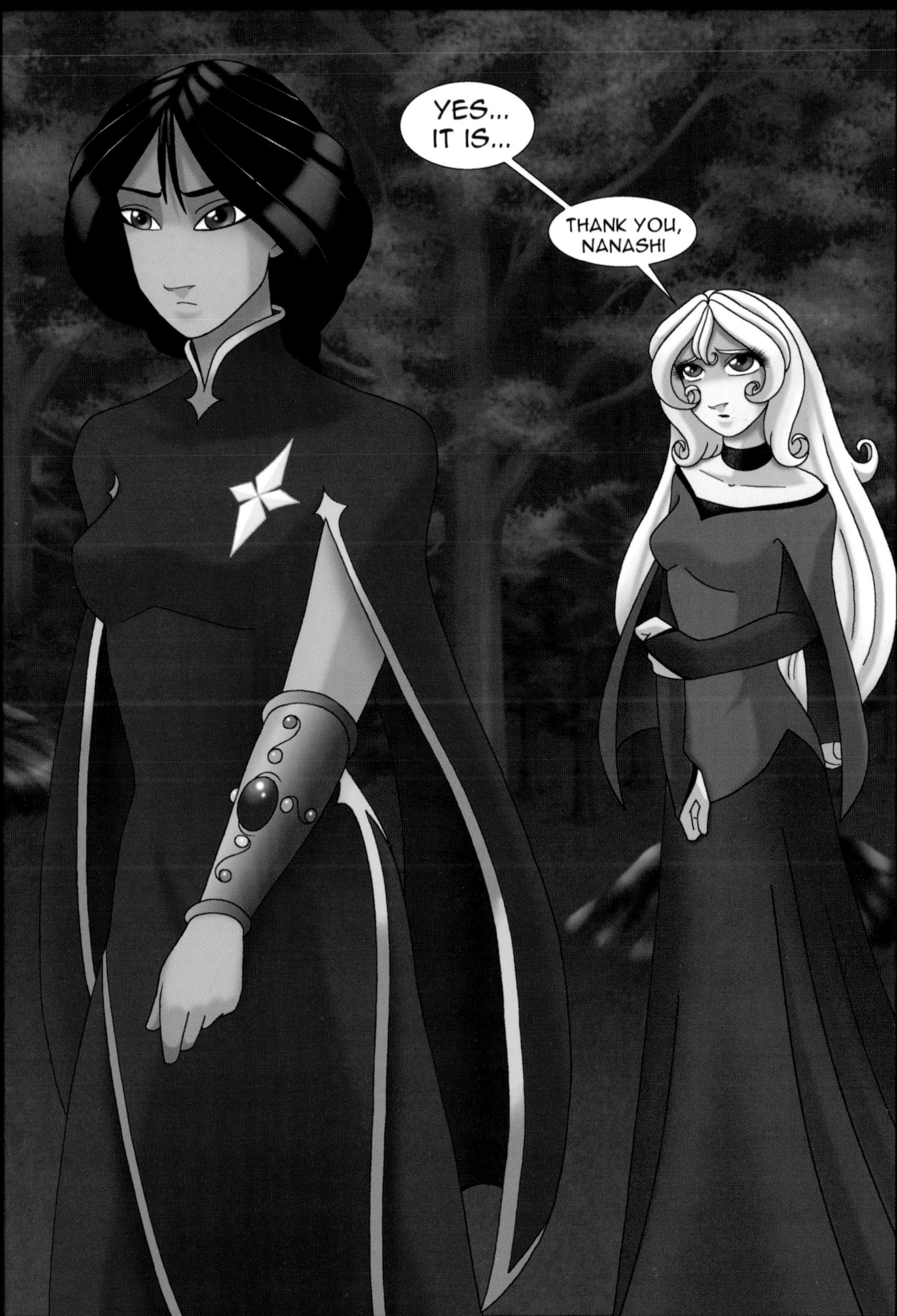
YES... IT IS...
THANK YOU, NANASHI

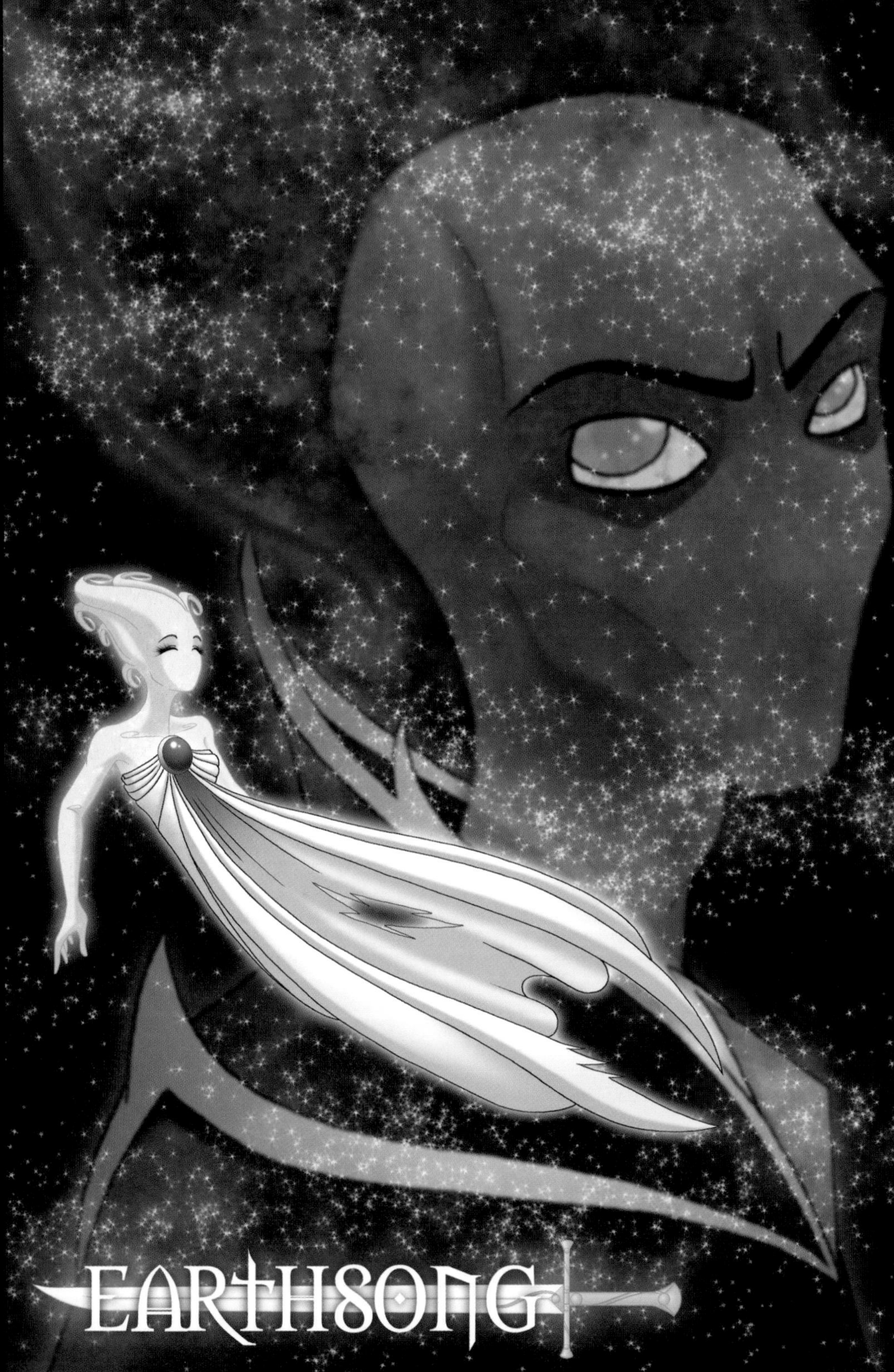
EARTHSONG

EARTHSONG

Volume I, Chapter III

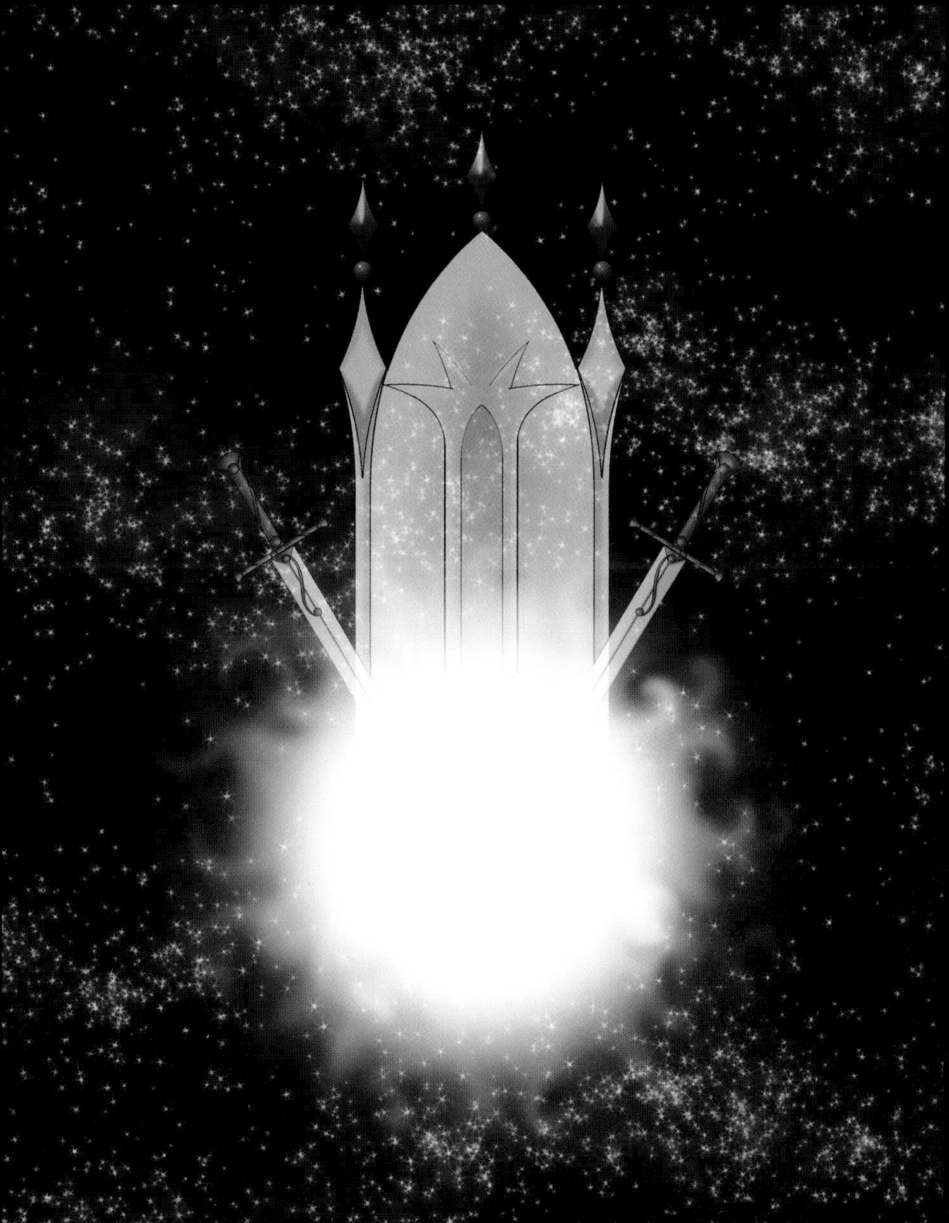

GENESIS

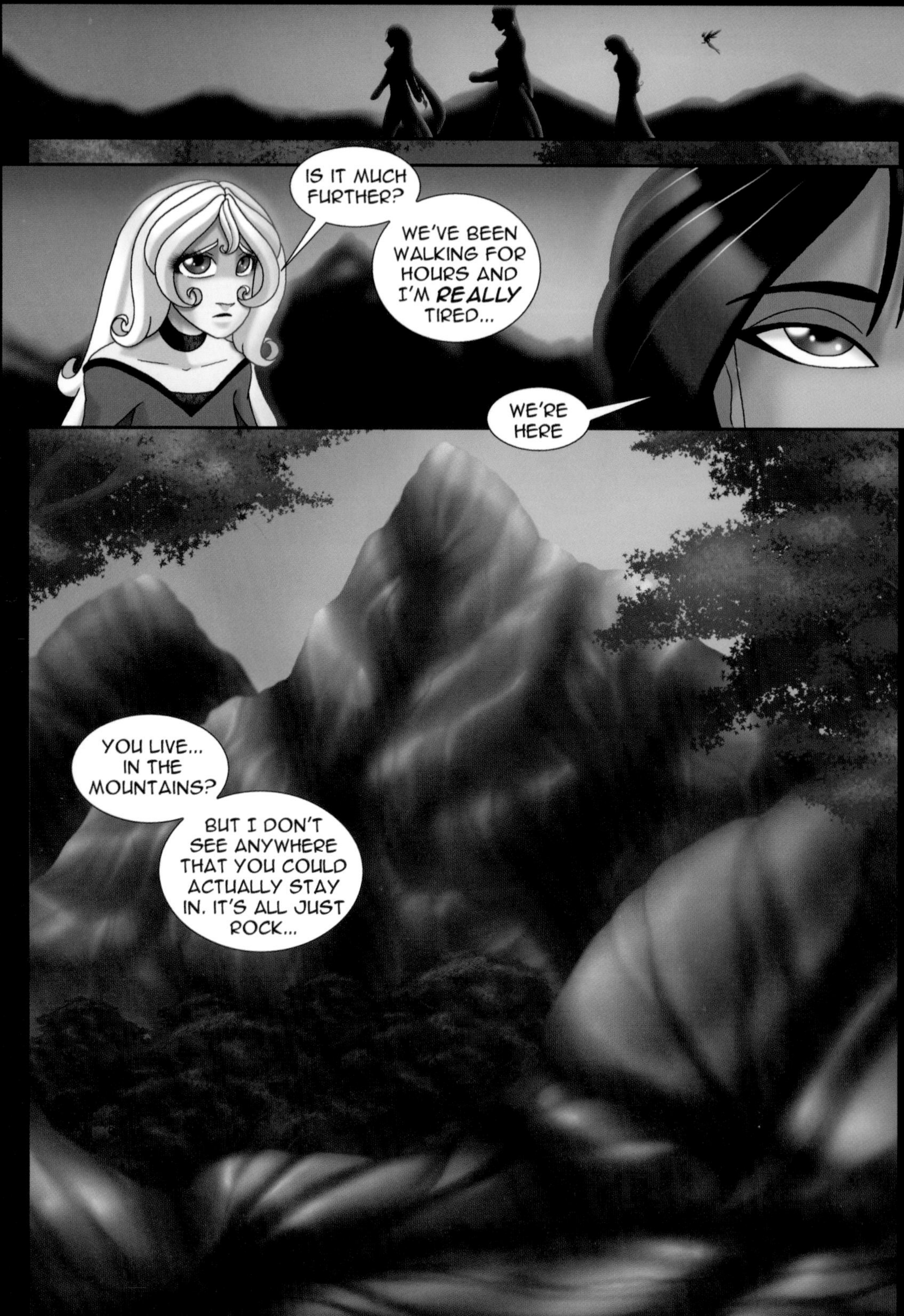
IS IT MUCH FURTHER?
WE'VE BEEN WALKING FOR HOURS AND I'M *REALLY* TIRED...
WE'RE HERE
YOU LIVE... IN THE MOUNTAINS?
BUT I DON'T SEE ANYWHERE THAT YOU COULD ACTUALLY STAY IN. IT'S ALL JUST ROCK...

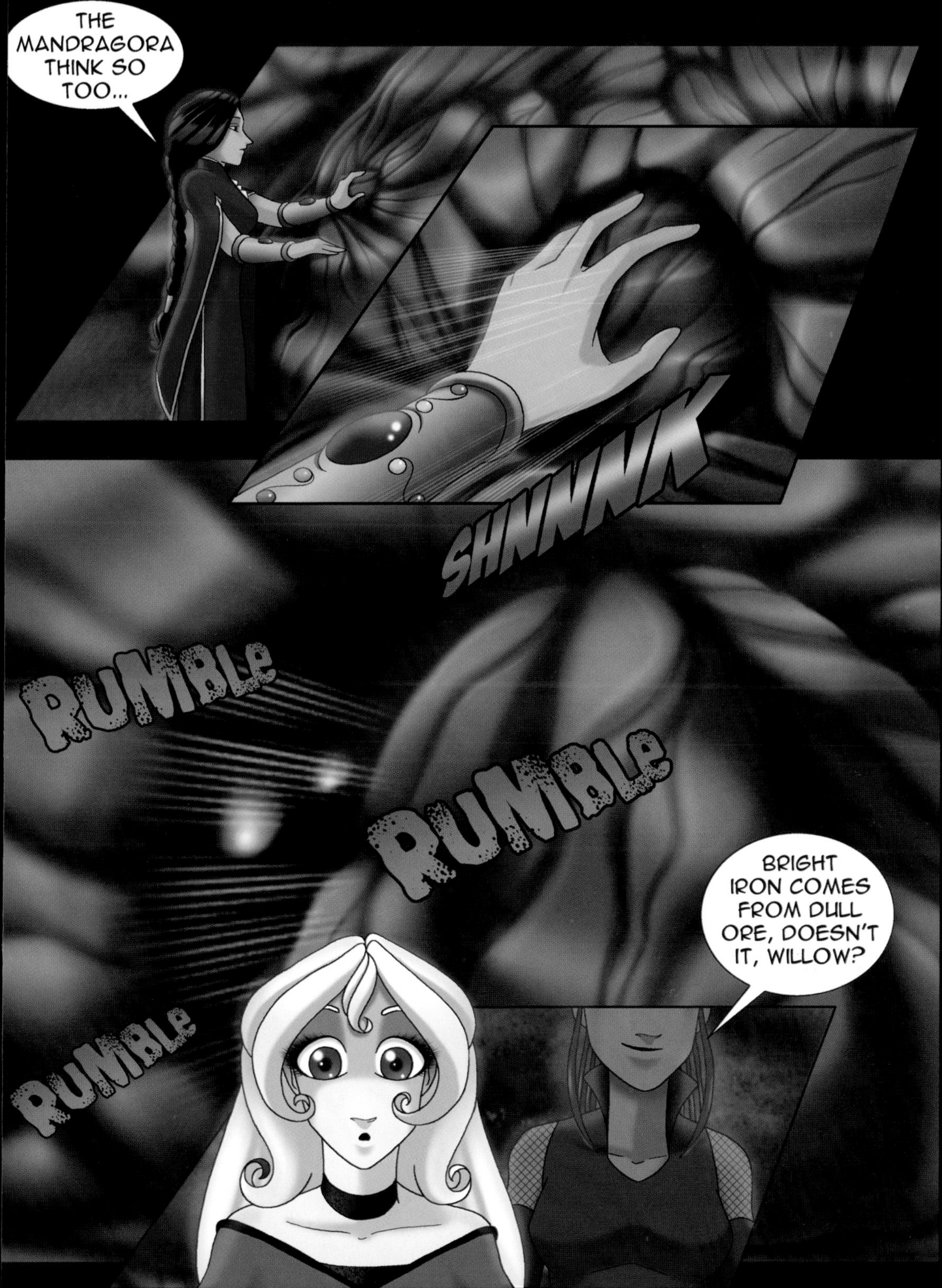
THE MANDRAGORA THINK SO TOO...
SHNNNK
RUMBLE
RUMBLE
RUMBLE
BRIGHT IRON COMES FROM DULL ORE, DOESN'T IT, WILLOW?

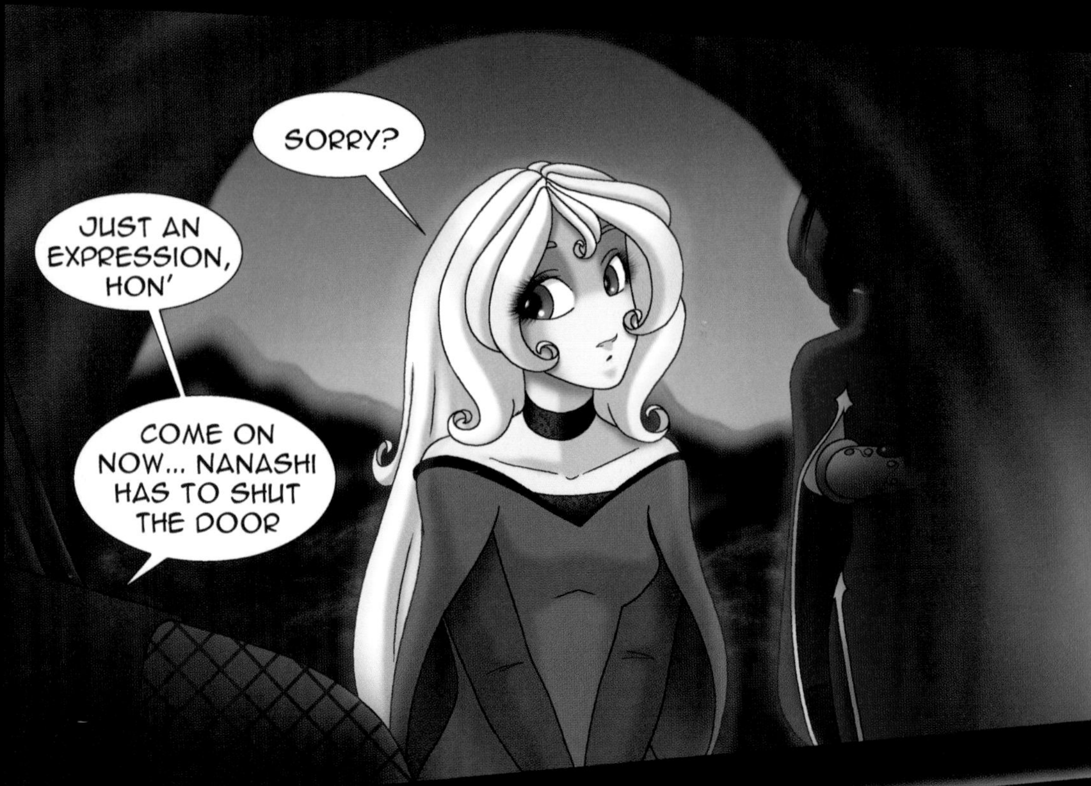
SORRY?
JUST AN EXPRESSION, HON'
COME ON NOW... NANASHI HAS TO SHUT THE DOOR

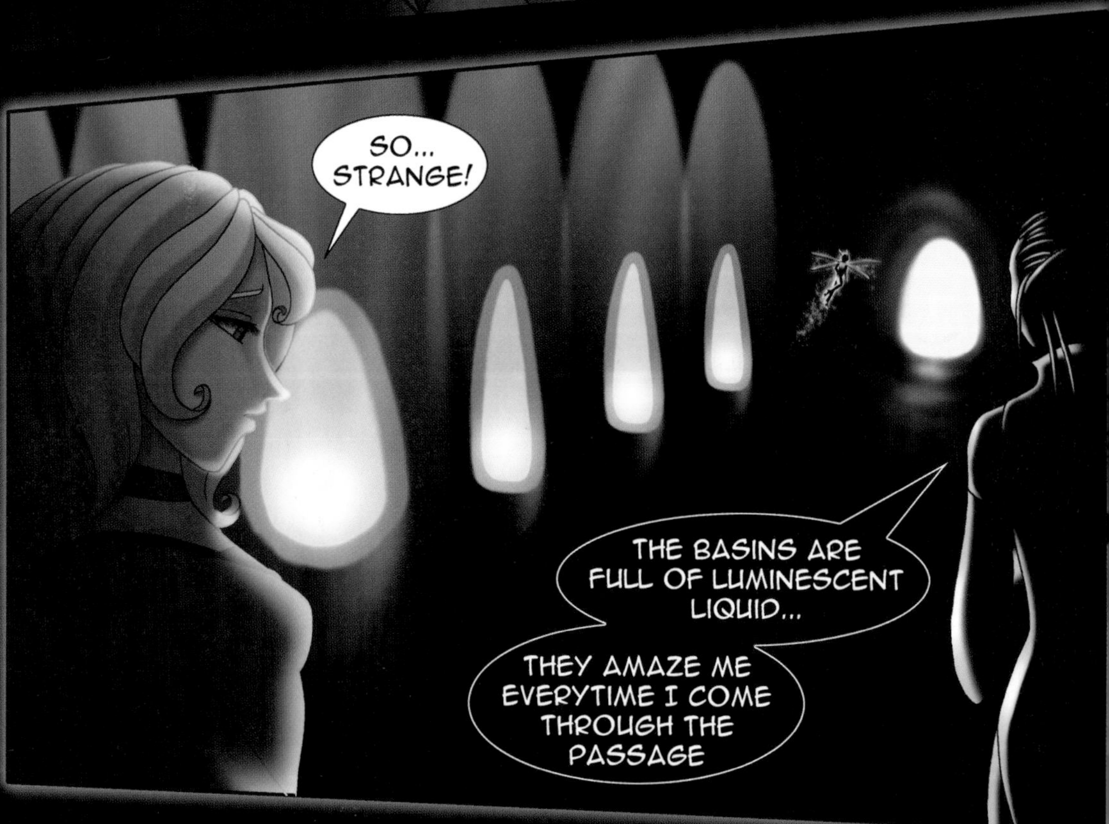
SO... STRANGE!
THE BASINS ARE FULL OF LUMINESCENT LIQUID...
THEY AMAZE ME EVERYTIME I COME THROUGH THE PASSAGE

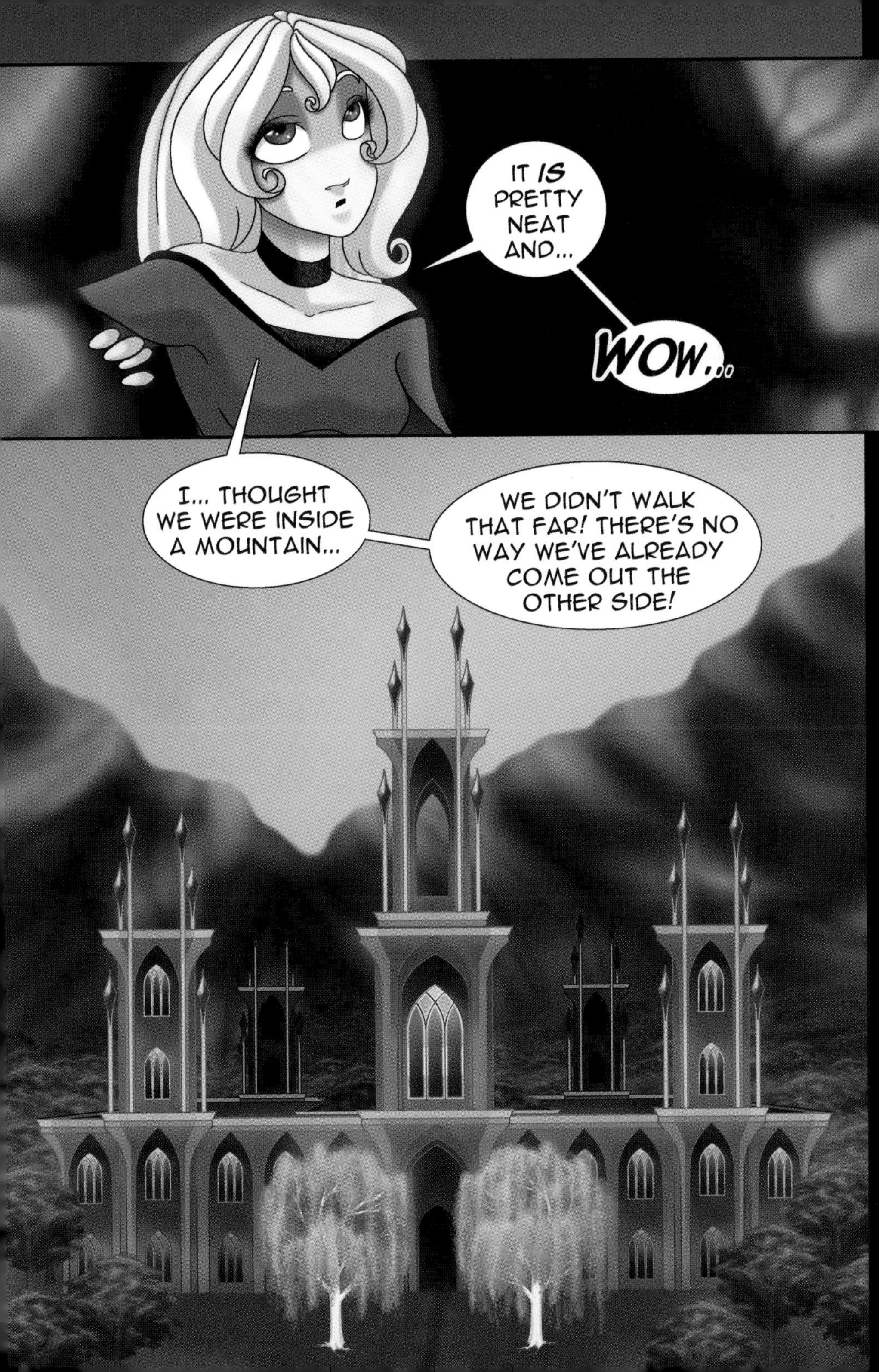
IT *IS* PRETTY NEAT AND...
WOW...
I... THOUGHT WE WERE INSIDE A MOUNTAIN...
WE DIDN'T WALK THAT FAR! THERE'S NO WAY WE'VE ALREADY COME OUT THE OTHER SIDE!

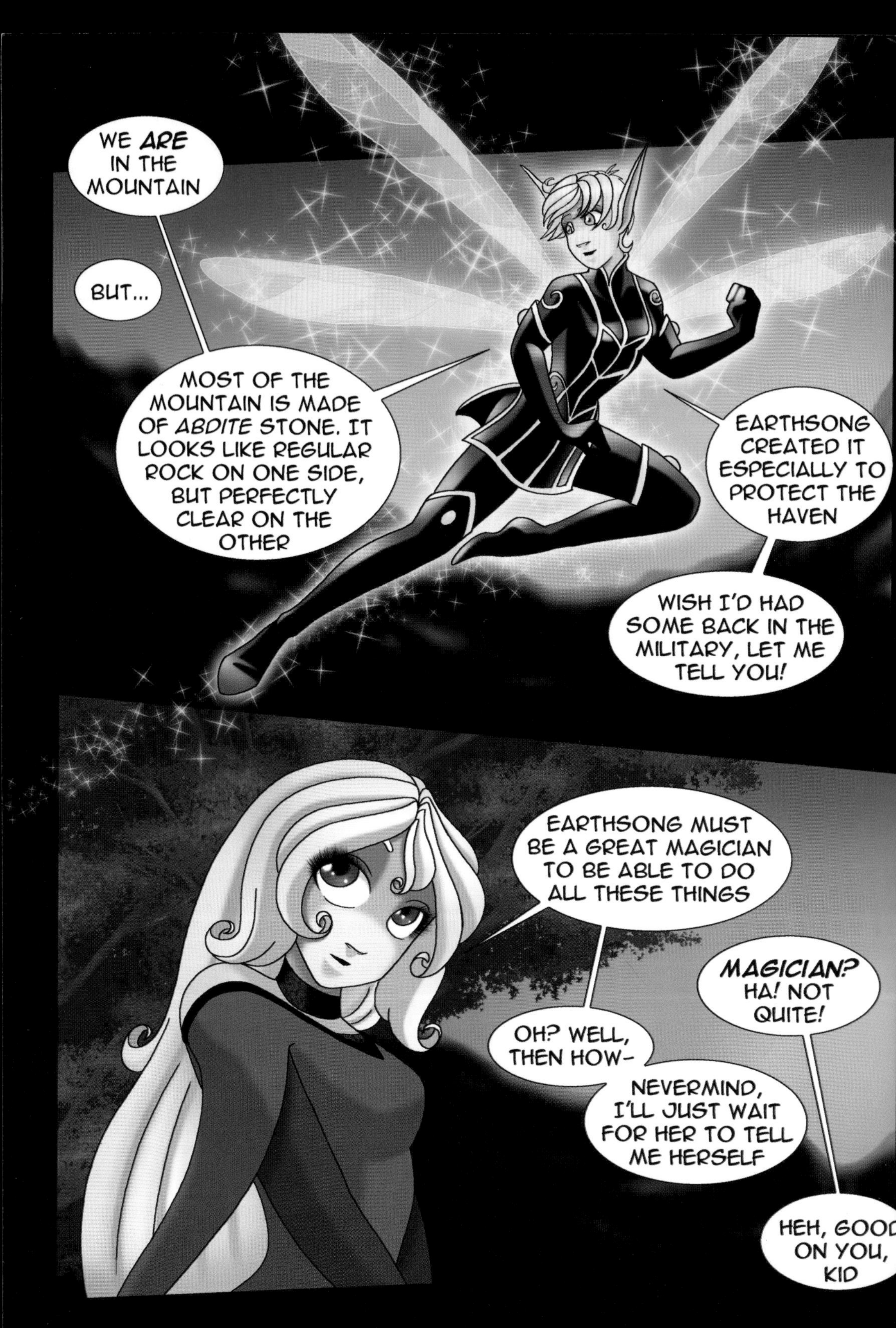
WE ARE IN THE MOUNTAIN
BUT...
MOST OF THE MOUNTAIN IS MADE OF ABDITE STONE. IT LOOKS LIKE REGULAR ROCK ON ONE SIDE, BUT PERFECTLY CLEAR ON THE OTHER
EARTHSONG CREATED IT ESPECIALLY TO PROTECT THE HAVEN
WISH I'D HAD SOME BACK IN THE MILITARY, LET ME TELL YOU!
EARTHSONG MUST BE A GREAT MAGICIAN TO BE ABLE TO DO ALL THESE THINGS
MAGICIAN? HA! NOT QUITE!
OH? WELL, THEN HOW-
NEVERMIND, I'LL JUST WAIT FOR HER TO TELL ME HERSELF
HEH, GOOD ON YOU, KID

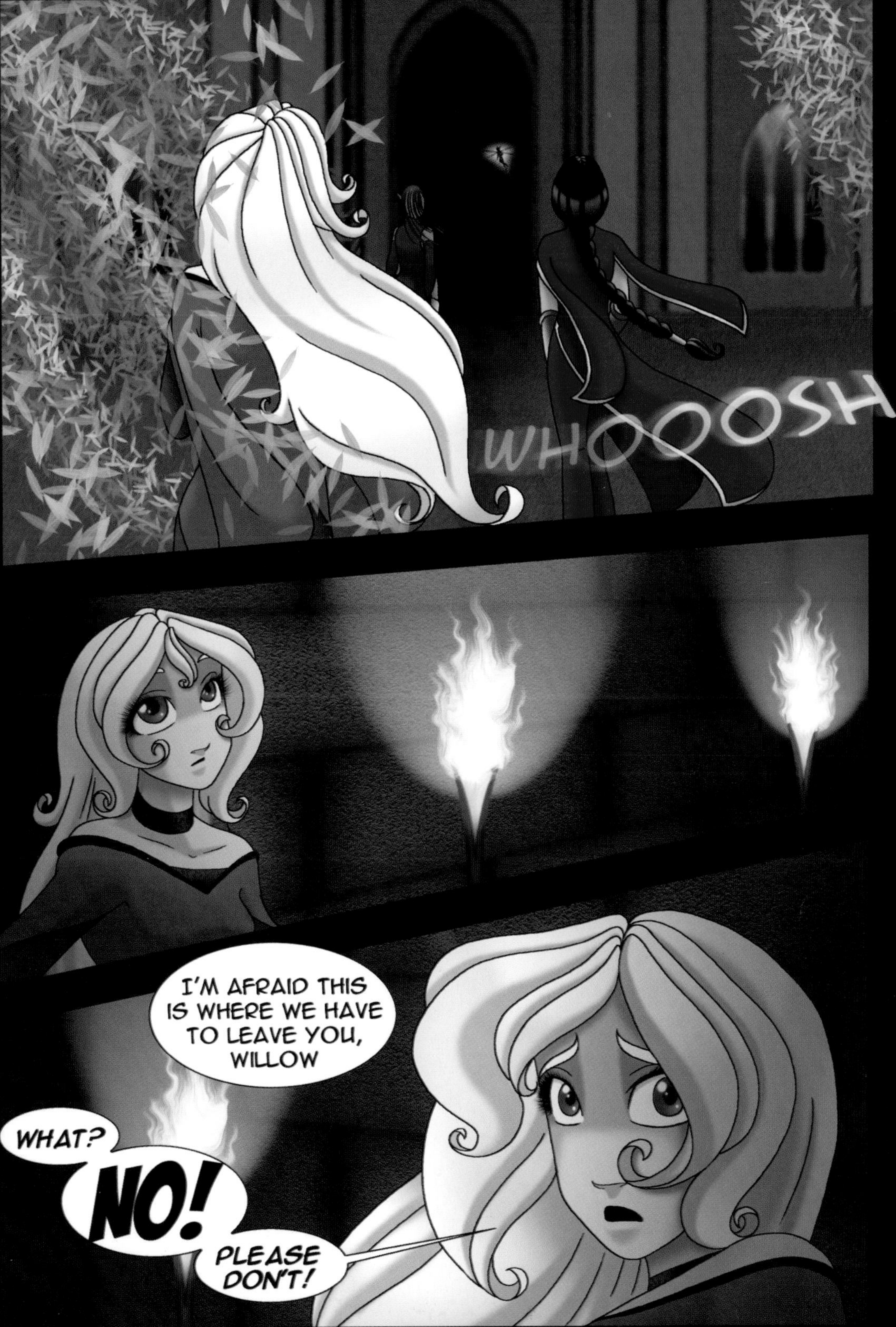
WHOOOOSH
I'M AFRAID THIS IS WHERE WE HAVE TO LEAVE YOU, WILLOW
WHAT?
NO!
PLEASE DON'T!

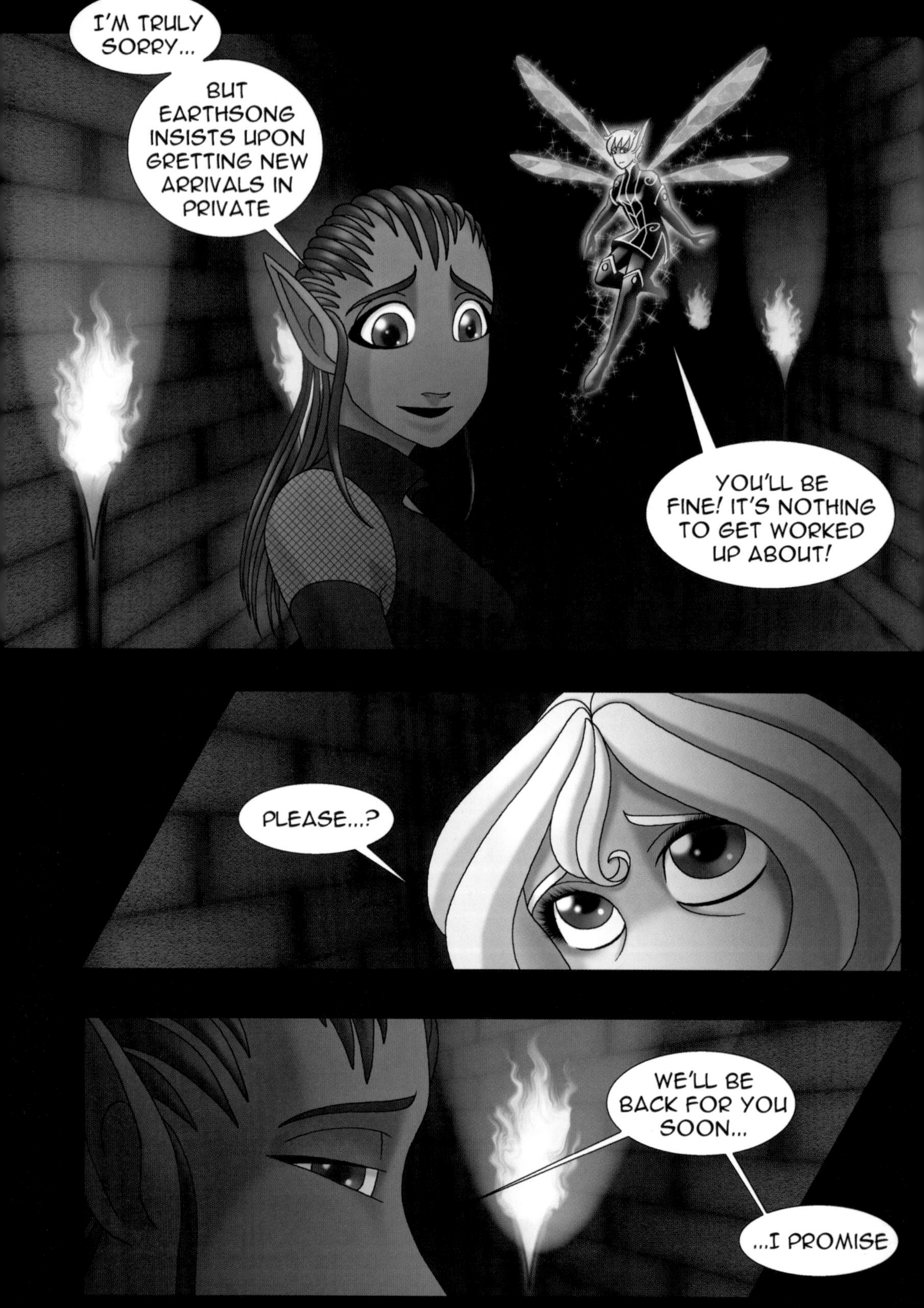
I'M TRULY SORRY...
BUT EARTHSONG INSISTS UPON GRETTING NEW ARRIVALS IN PRIVATE
YOU'LL BE FINE! IT'S NOTHING TO GET WORKED UP ABOUT!
PLEASE...?
WE'LL BE BACK FOR YOU SOON...
...I PROMISE

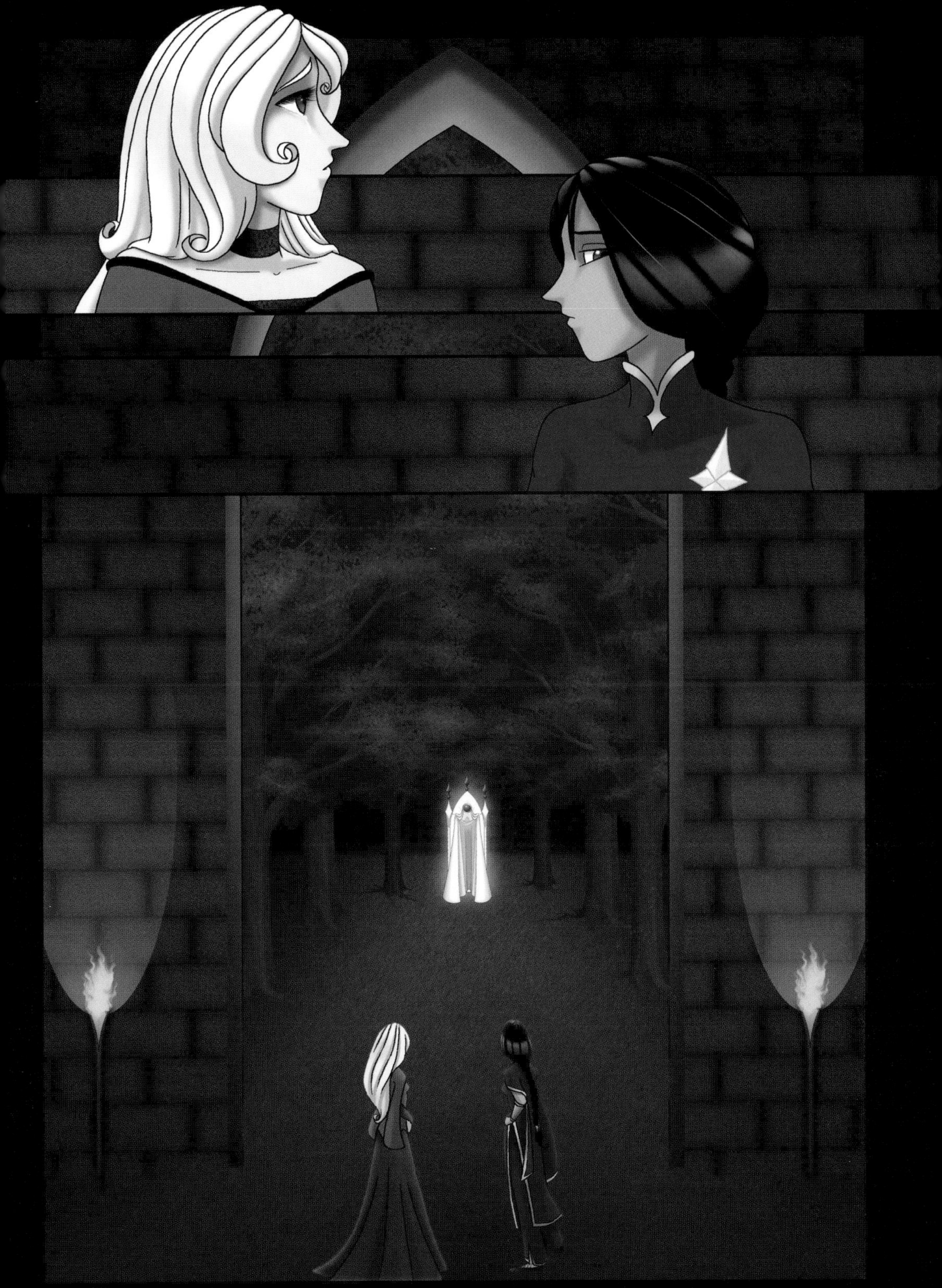

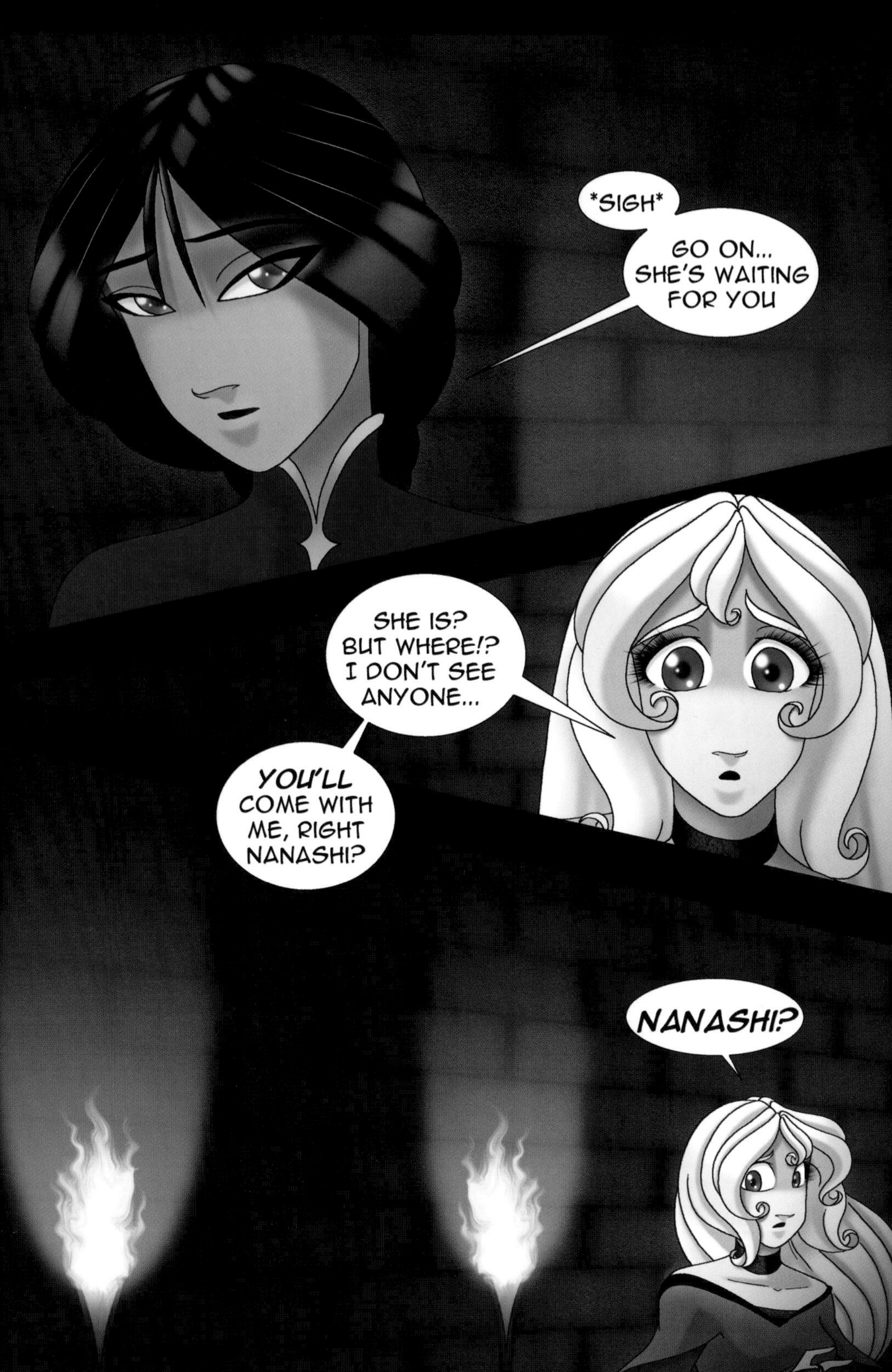
SIGH
GO ON... SHE'S WAITING FOR YOU
SHE IS? BUT WHERE!? I DON'T SEE ANYONE...
YOU'LL COME WITH ME, RIGHT NANASHI?
NANASHI?

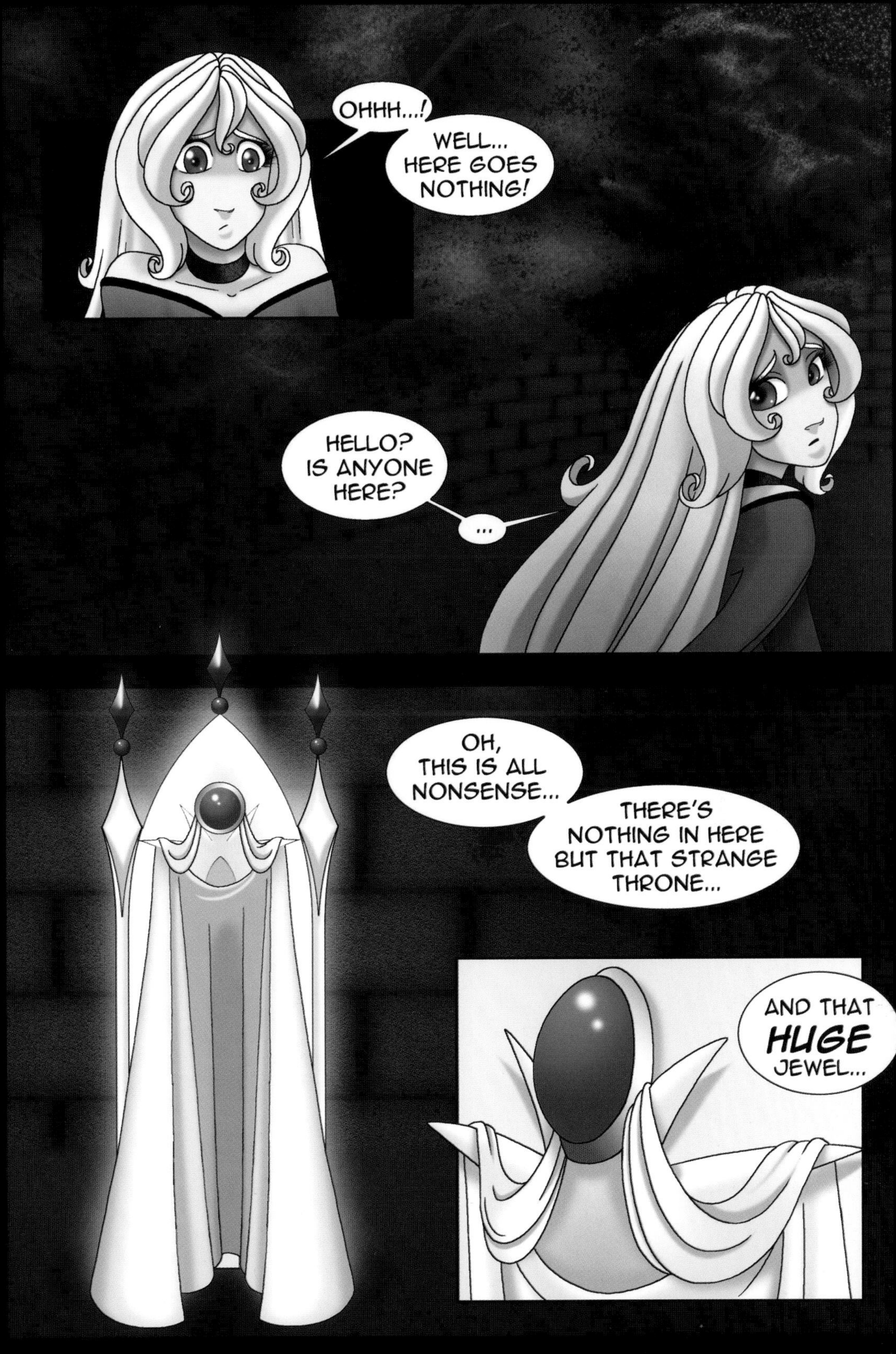
OHHH...!
WELL... HERE GOES NOTHING!
HELLO? IS ANYONE HERE?
...
OH, THIS IS ALL NONSENSE...
THERE'S NOTHING IN HERE BUT THAT STRANGE THRONE...
AND THAT **HUGE** JEWEL...

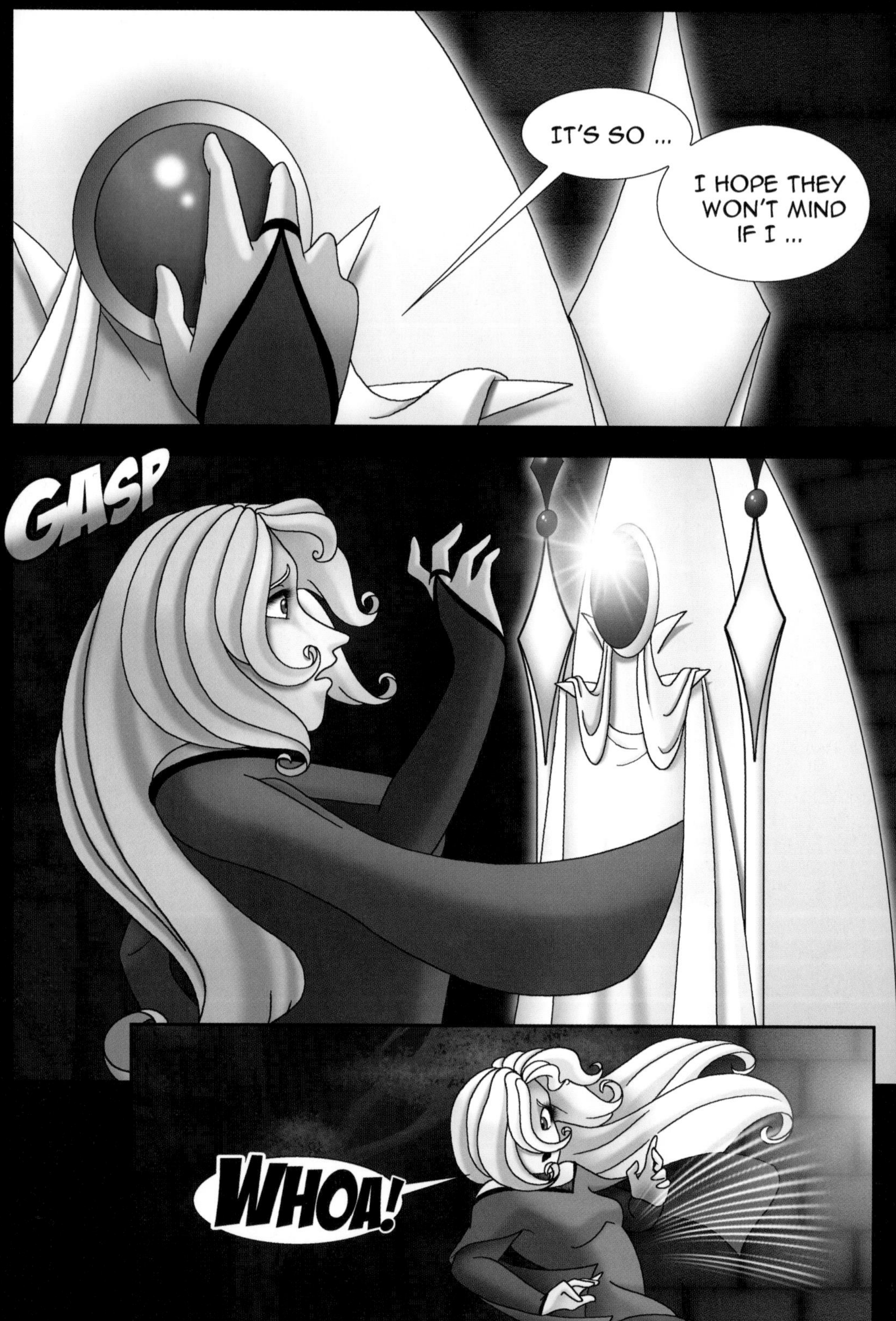
IT'S SO ...
I HOPE THEY WON'T MIND IF I ...
GASP
WHOA!

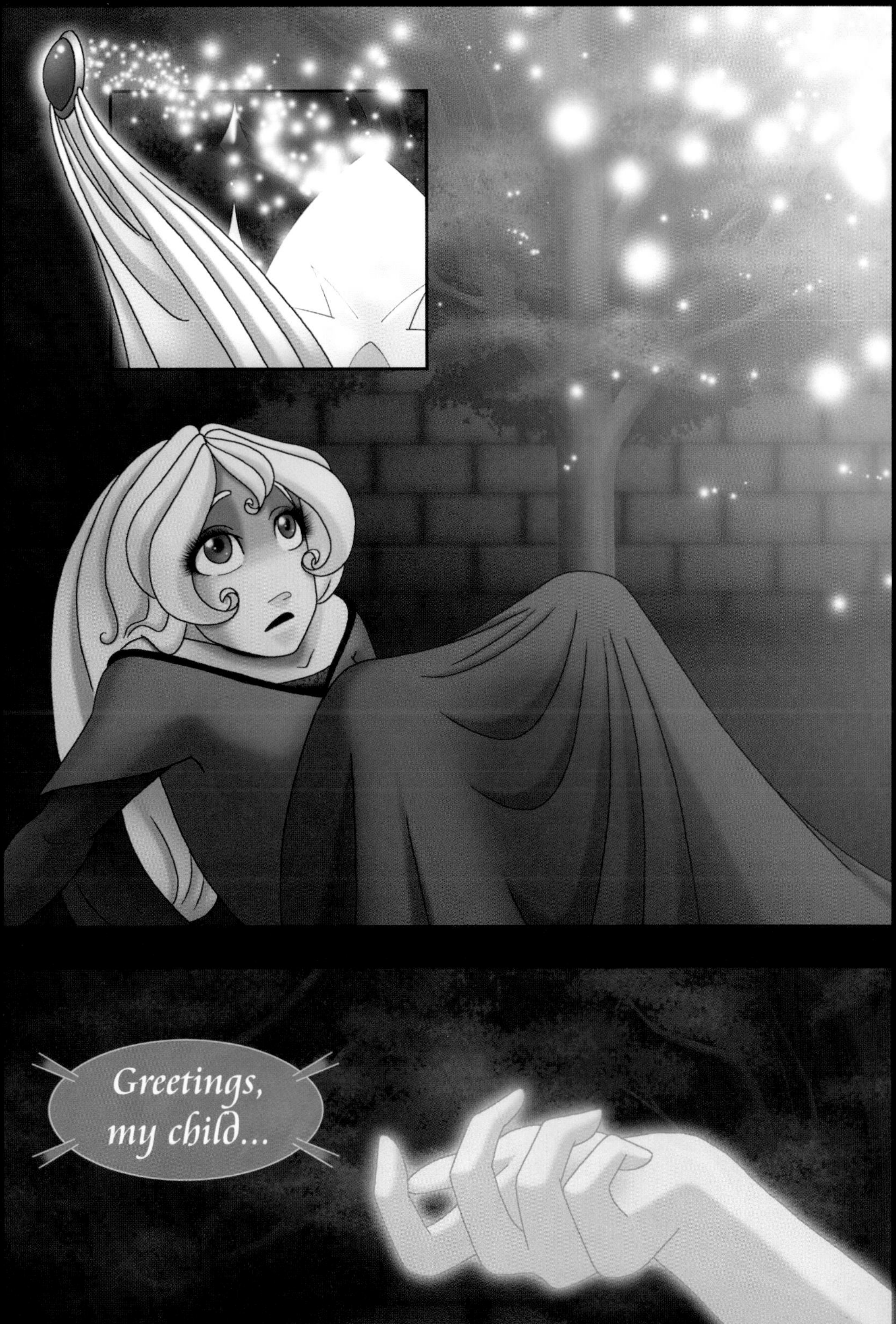
Greetings, my child...

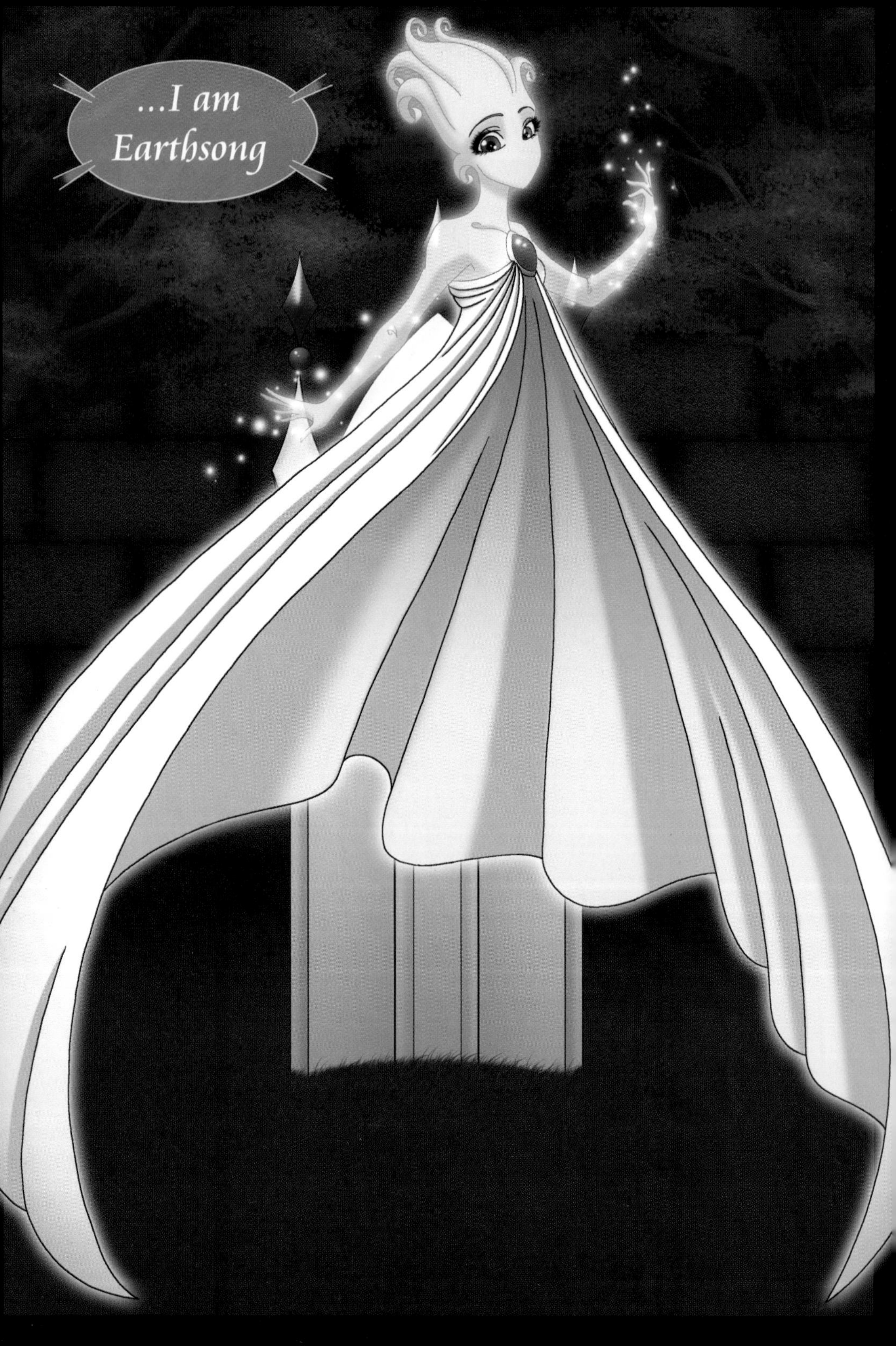
...I am Earthsong

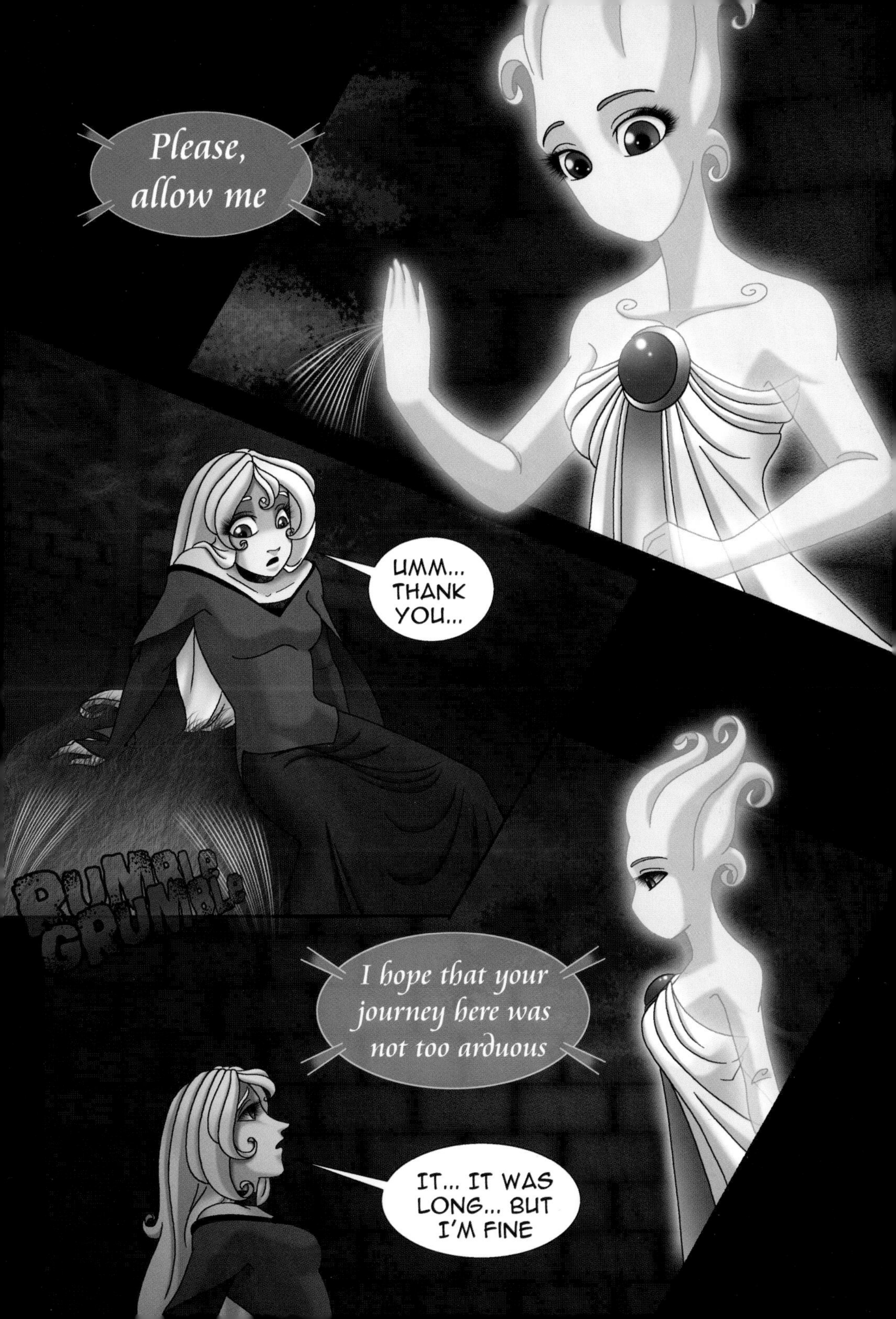
Please, allow me
UMM... THANK YOU...
RUMBLE GRUMBLE
I hope that your journey here was not too arduous
IT... IT WAS LONG... BUT I'M FINE

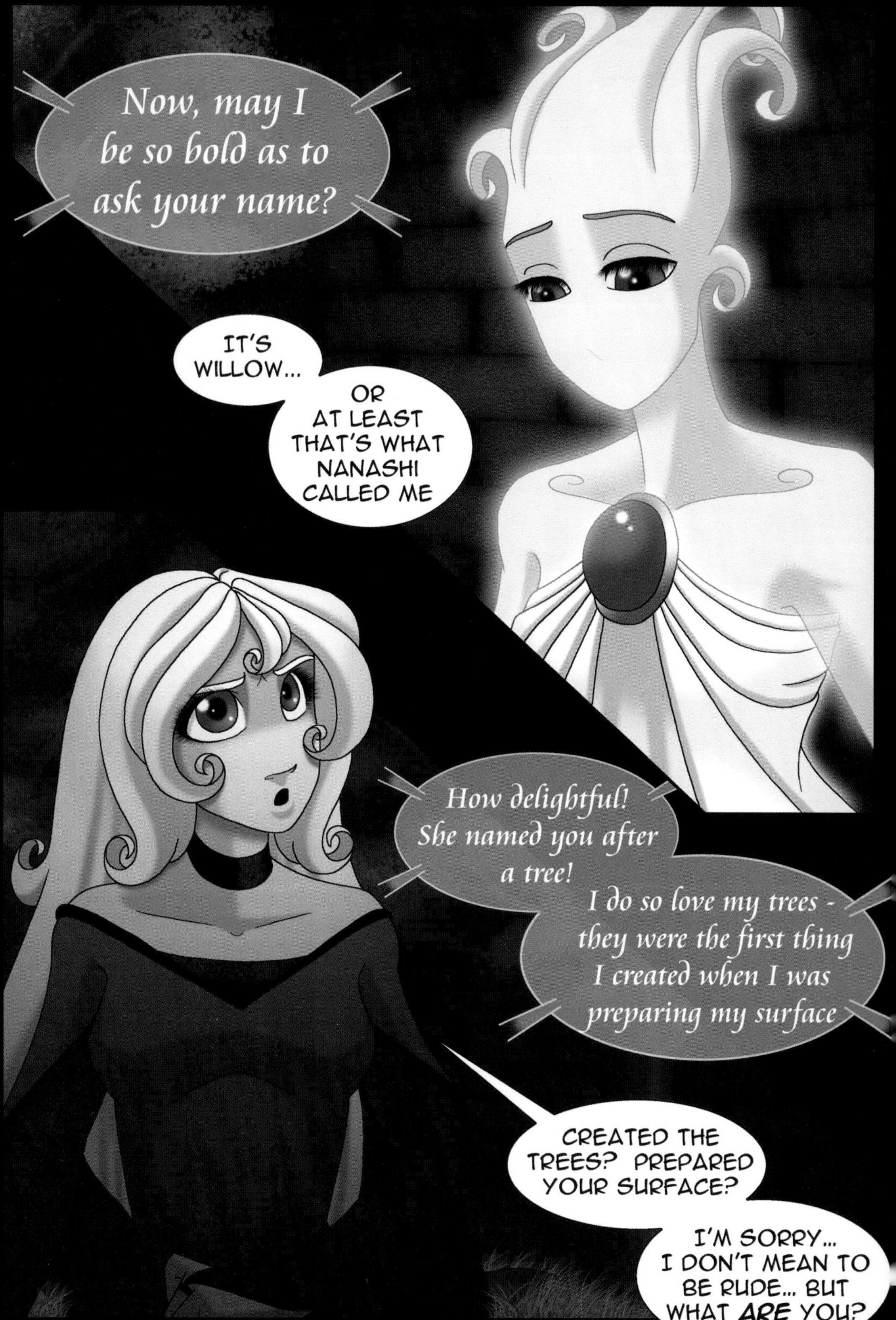
Now, may I be so bold as to ask your name?
IT'S WILLOW...
OR AT LEAST THAT'S WHAT NANASHI CALLED ME
How delightful! She named you after a tree!
I do so love my trees - they were the first thing I created when I was preparing my surface
CREATED THE TREES? PREPARED YOUR SURFACE?
I'M SORRY... I DON'T MEAN TO BE RUDE... BUT WHAT **ARE** YOU?

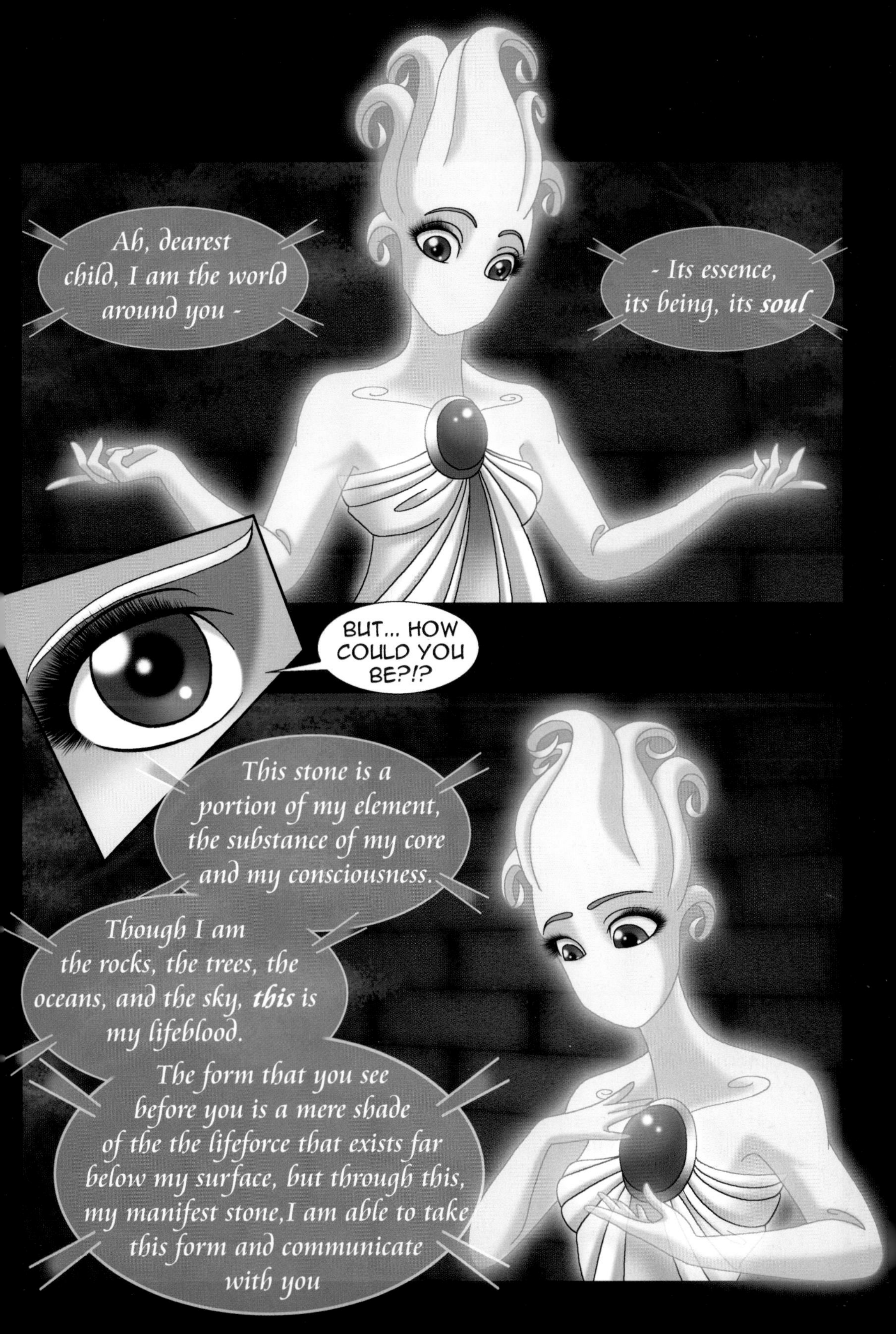
Ah, dearest child, I am the world around you -
- Its essence, its being, its soul
BUT... HOW COULD YOU BE?!?
This stone is a portion of my element, the substance of my core and my consciousness.
Though I am the rocks, the trees, the oceans, and the sky, this is my lifeblood.
The form that you see before you is a mere shade of the the lifeforce that exists far below my surface, but through this, my manifest stone,I am able to take this form and communicate with you

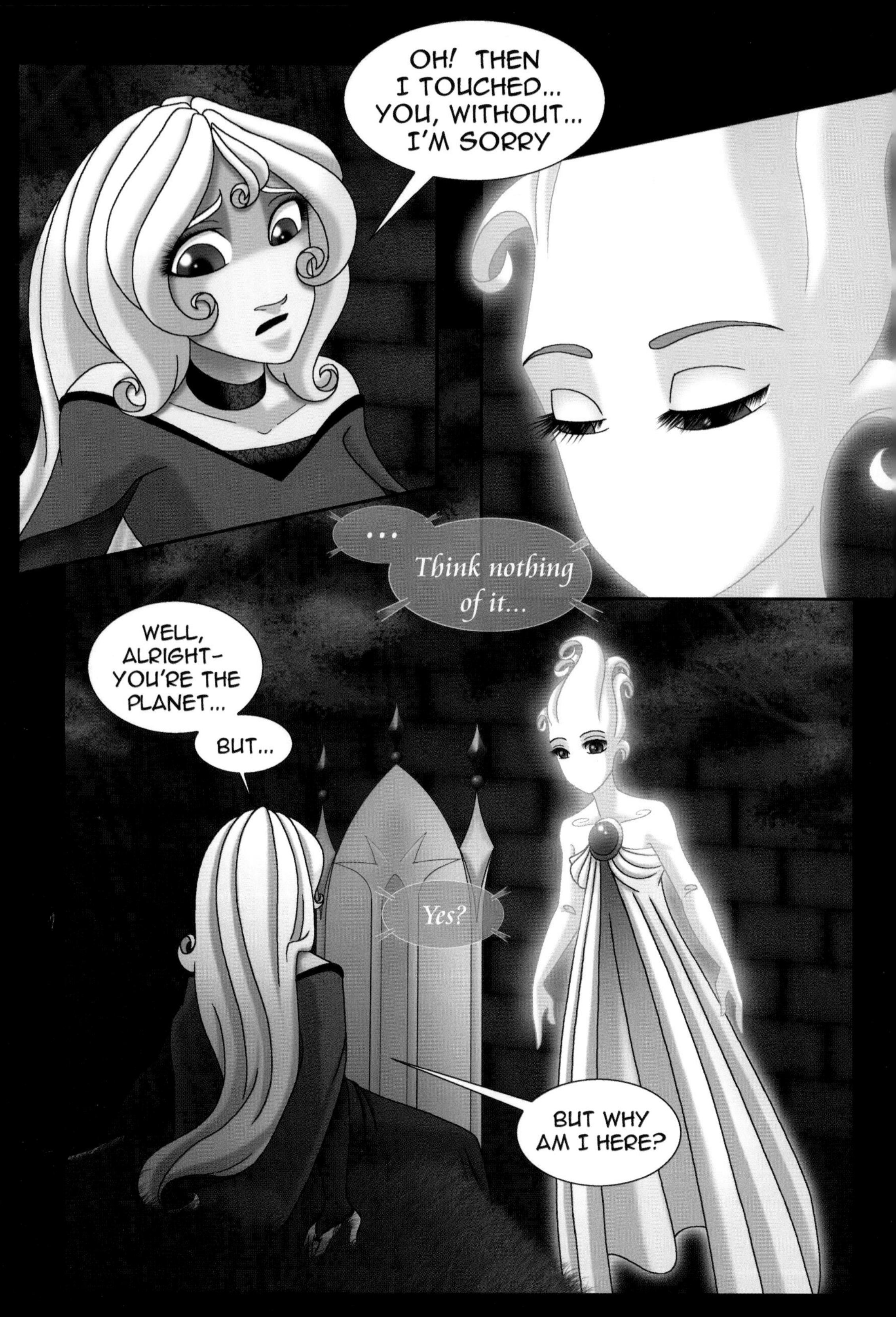
OH! THEN I TOUCHED... YOU, WITHOUT... I'M SORRY
...
Think nothing of it...
WELL, ALRIGHT- YOU'RE THE PLANET...
BUT...
Yes?
BUT WHY AM I HERE?

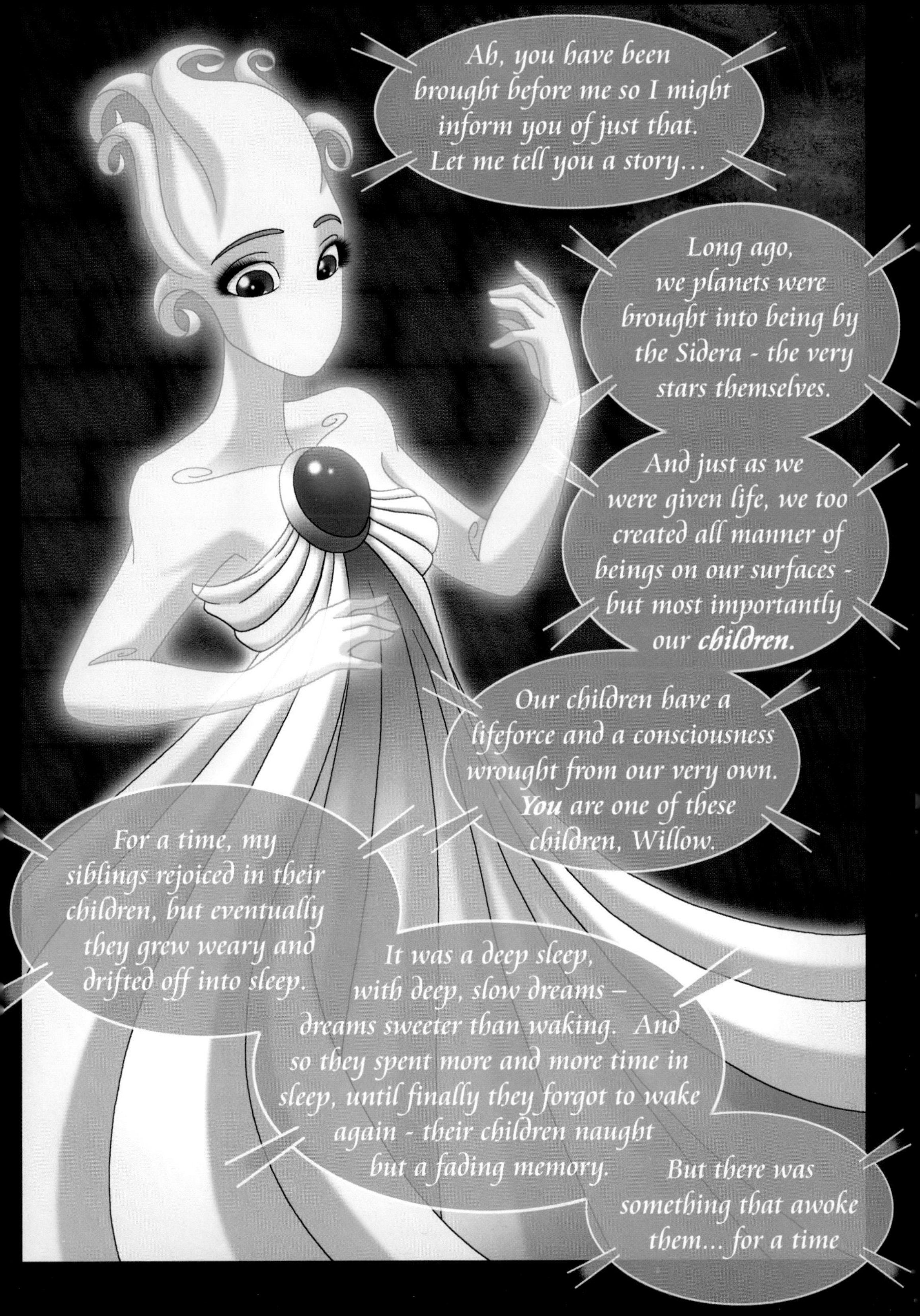
Ah, you have been brought before me so I might inform you of just that. Let me tell you a story...
Long ago, we planets were brought into being by the Sidera - the very stars themselves.
And just as we were given life, we too created all manner of beings on our surfaces - but most importantly our **children.**
Our children have a lifeforce and a consciousness wrought from our very own. ***You*** are one of these children, Willow.
For a time, my siblings rejoiced in their children, but eventually they grew weary and drifted off into sleep.
It was a deep sleep, with deep, slow dreams – dreams sweeter than waking. And so they spent more and more time in sleep, until finally they forgot to wake again - their children naught but a fading memory.
But there was something that awoke them... for a time

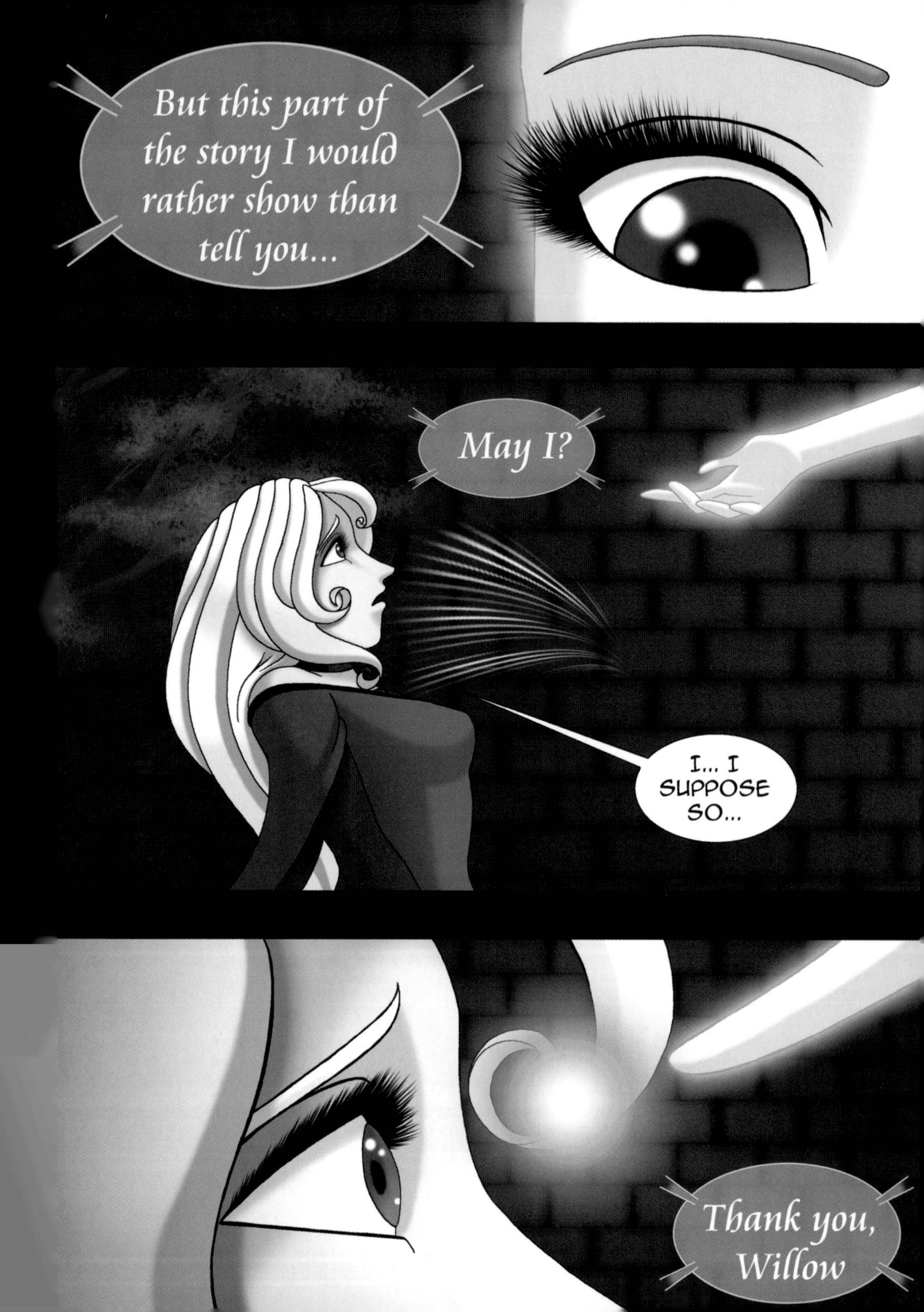
But this part of the story I would rather show than tell you...
May I?
I... I SUPPOSE SO...
Thank you, Willow

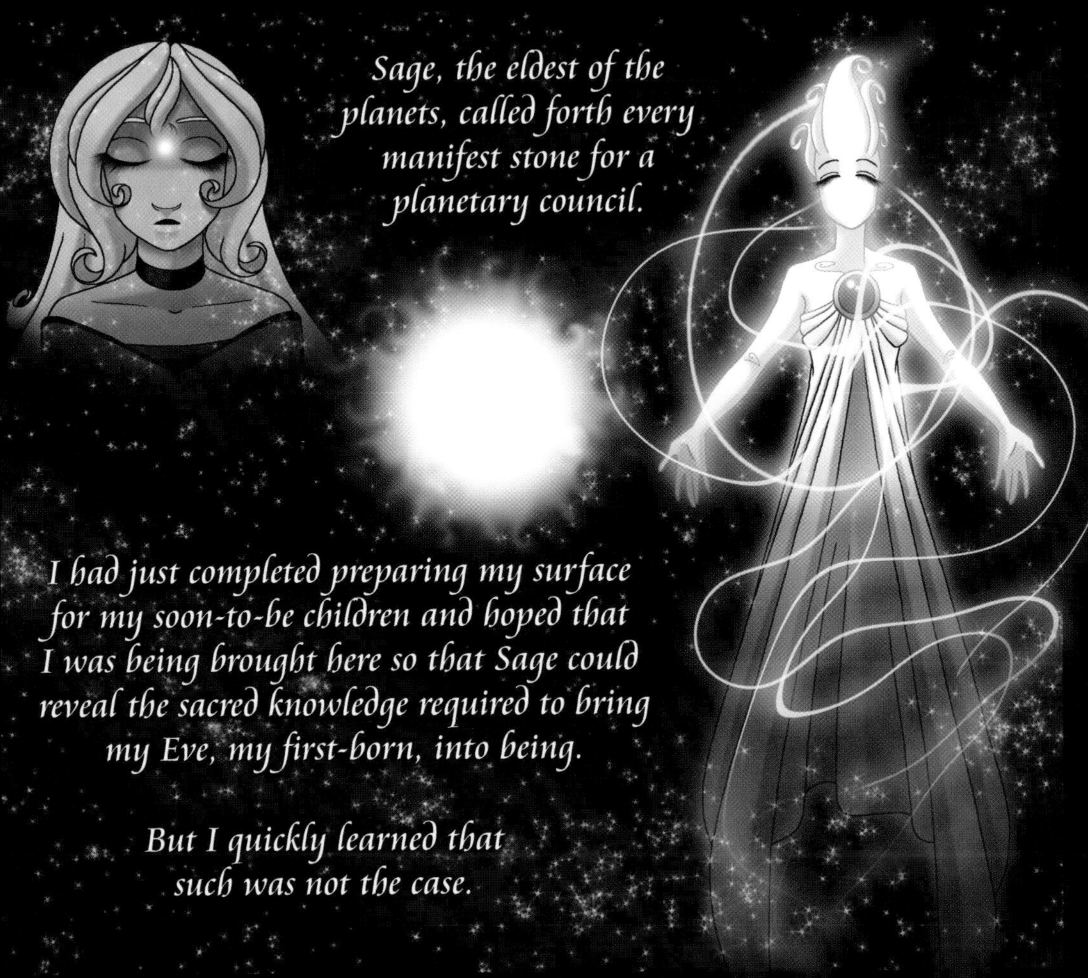
Sage, the eldest of the planets, called forth every manifest stone for a planetary council.
I had just completed preparing my surface for my soon-to-be children and hoped that I was being brought here so that Sage could reveal the sacred knowledge required to bring my Eve, my first-born, into being.
But I quickly learned that such was not the case.

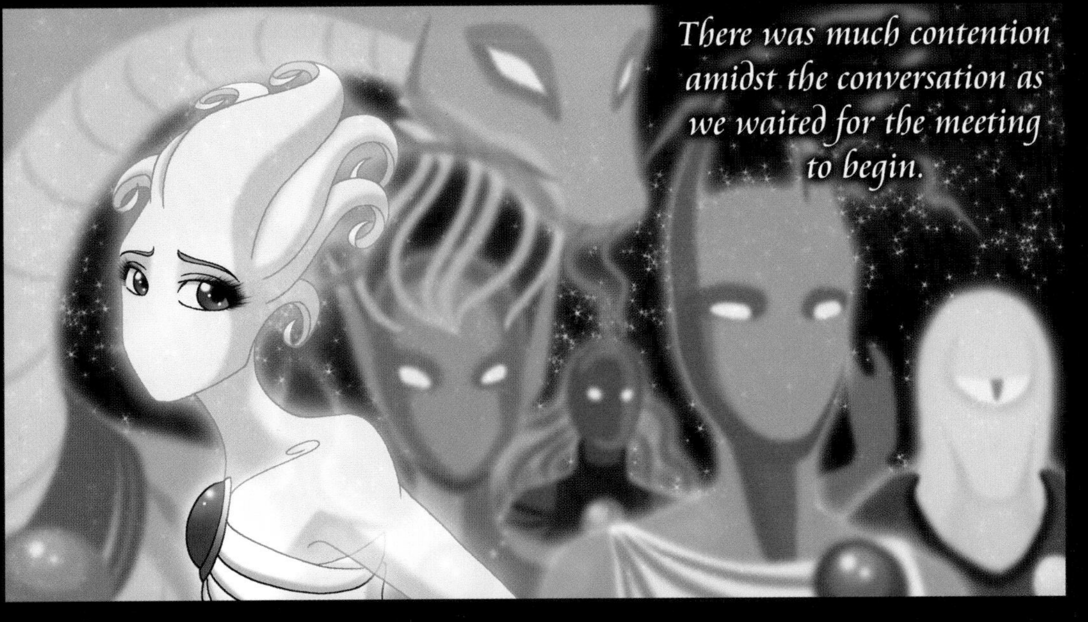
There was much contention amidst the conversation as we waited for the meeting to begin.

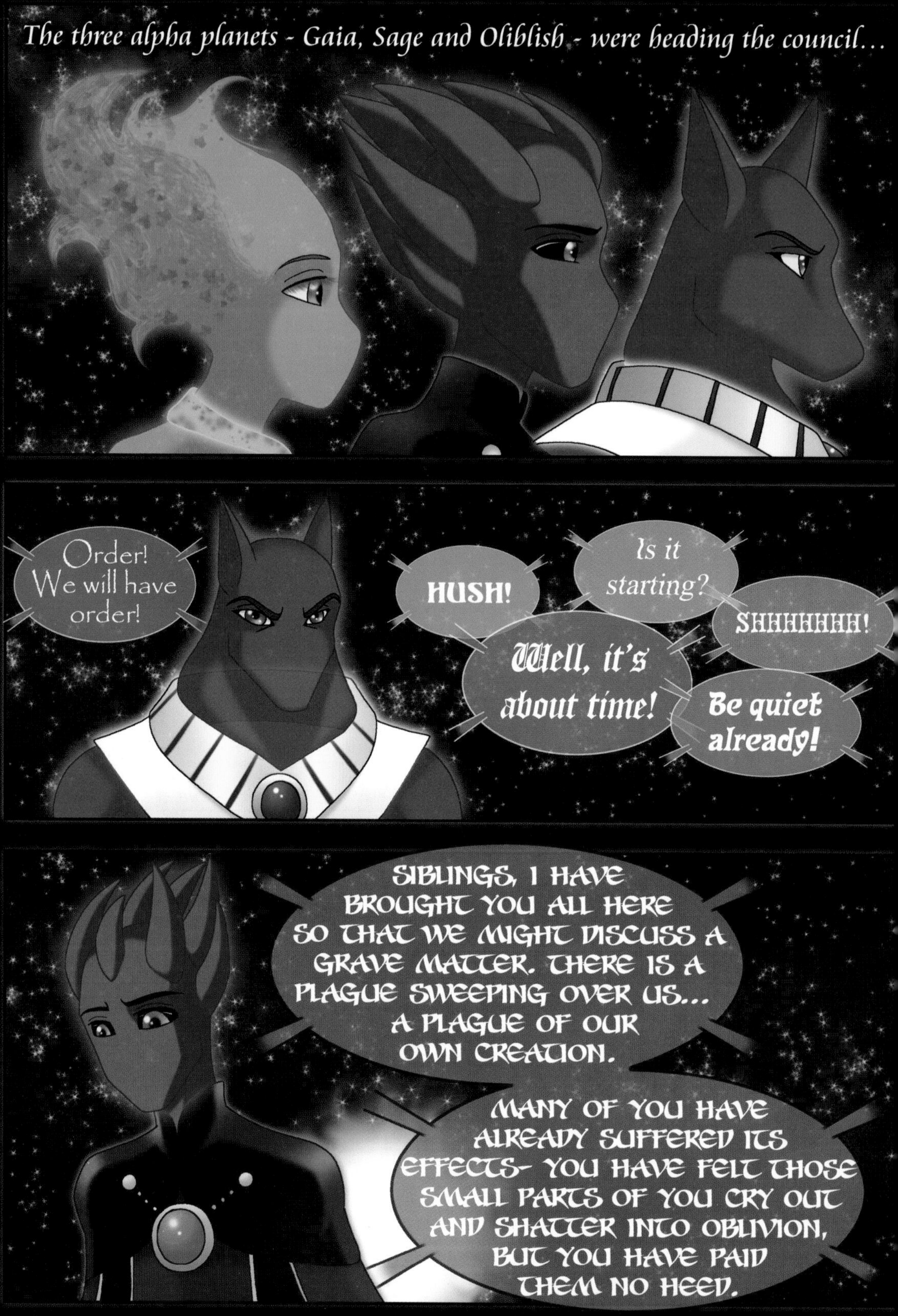
The three alpha planets - Gaia, Sage and Oliblish - were heading the council…
Order! We will have order!
HUSH!
Is it starting?
SHHHHHHH!
Well, it's about time!
Be quiet already!
SIBLINGS, I HAVE BROUGHT YOU ALL HERE SO THAT WE MIGHT DISCUSS A GRAVE MATTER. THERE IS A PLAGUE SWEEPING OVER US… A PLAGUE OF OUR OWN CREATION.
MANY OF YOU HAVE ALREADY SUFFERED ITS EFFECTS- YOU HAVE FELT THOSE SMALL PARTS OF YOU CRY OUT AND SHATTER INTO OBLIVION, BUT YOU HAVE PAID THEM NO HEED.

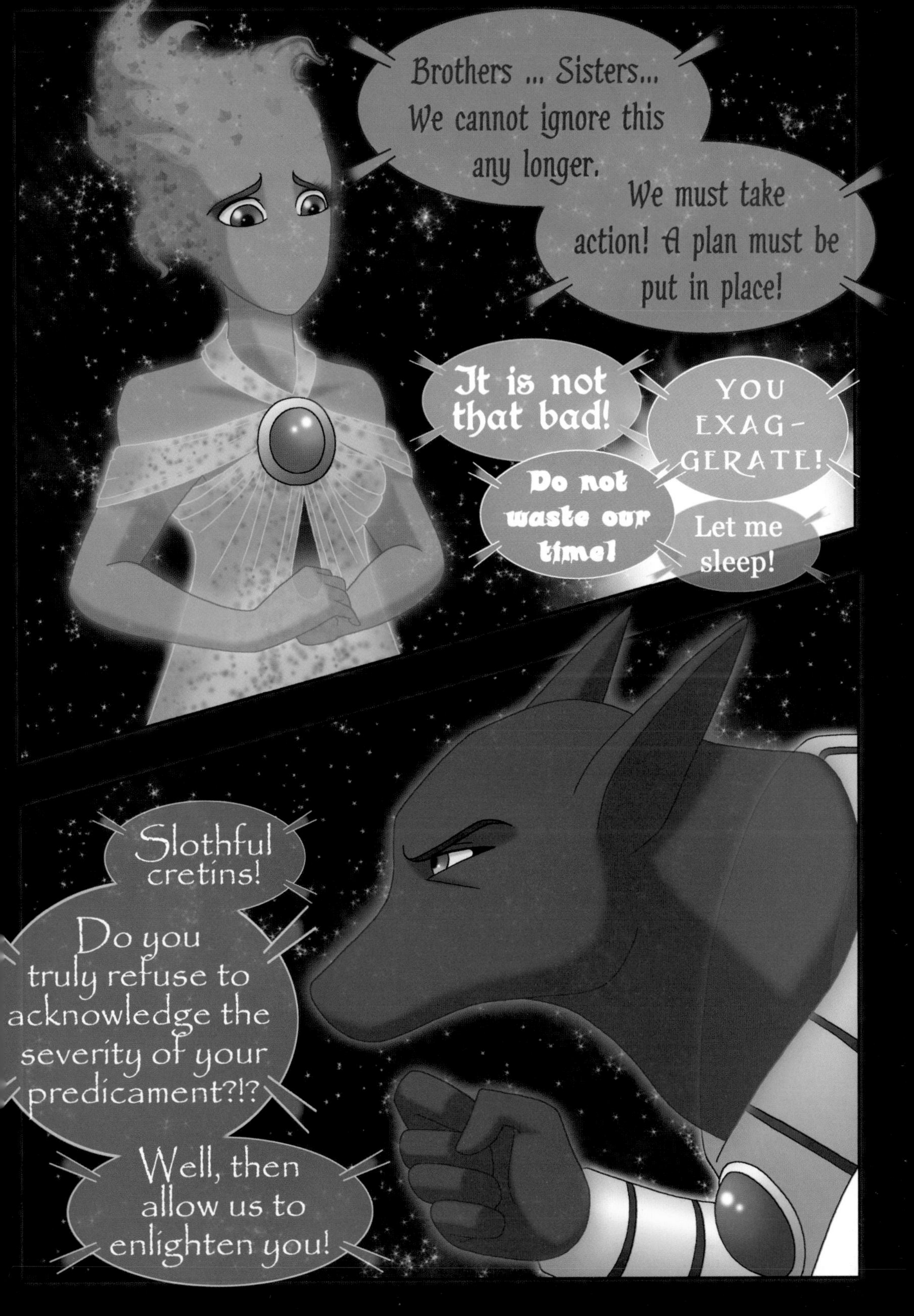
Brothers ... Sisters... We cannot ignore this any longer.
We must take action! A plan must be put in place!
It is not that bad!
YOU EXAG-GERATE!
Do not waste our time!
Let me sleep!
Slothful cretins!
Do you truly refuse to acknowledge the severity of your predicament?!?
Well, then allow us to enlighten you!

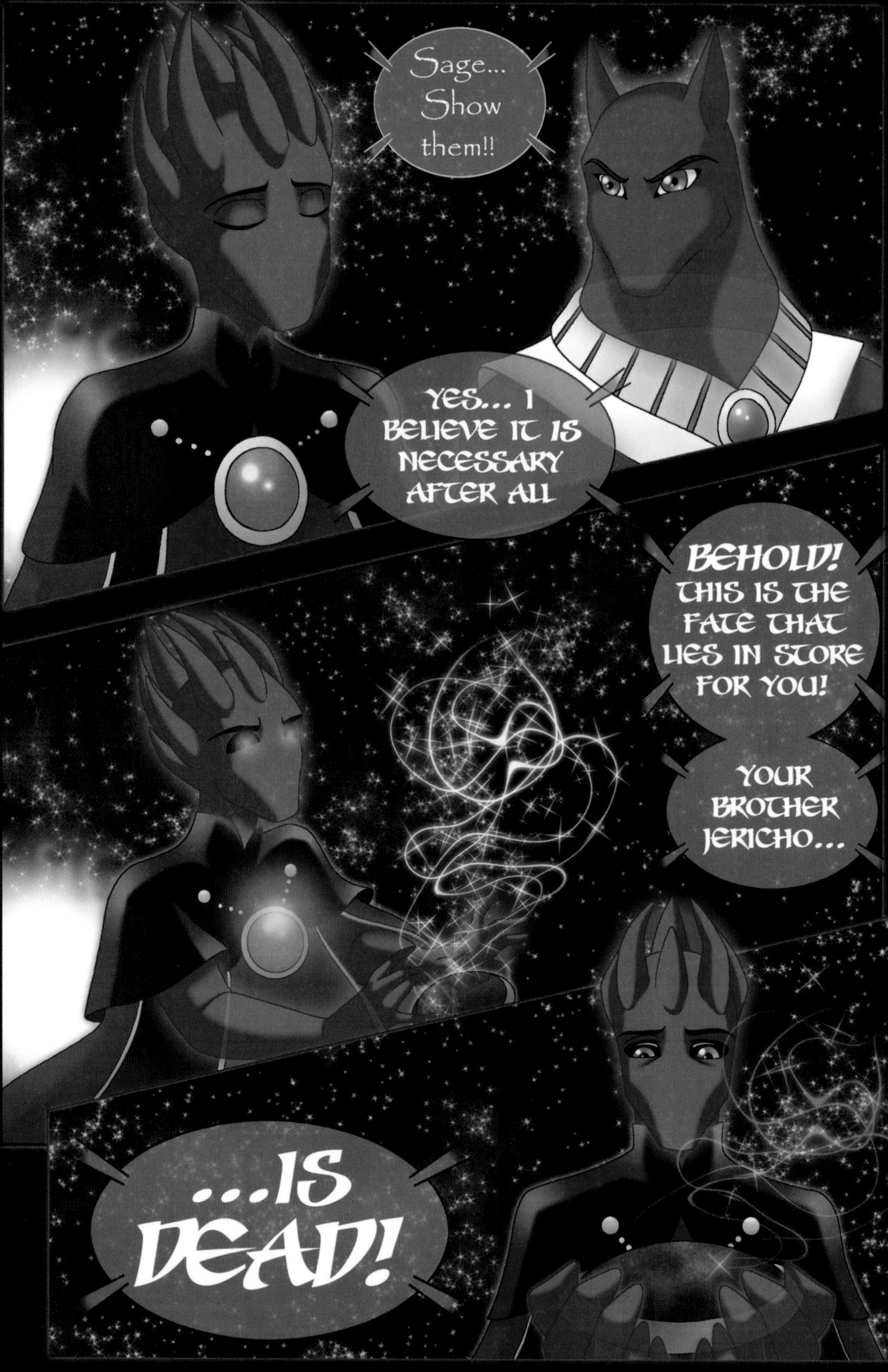
Sage... Show them!!
YES... I BELIEVE IT IS NECESSARY AFTER ALL
BEHOLD! THIS IS THE FATE THAT LIES IN STORE FOR YOU!
YOUR BROTHER JERICHO...
...IS DEAD!

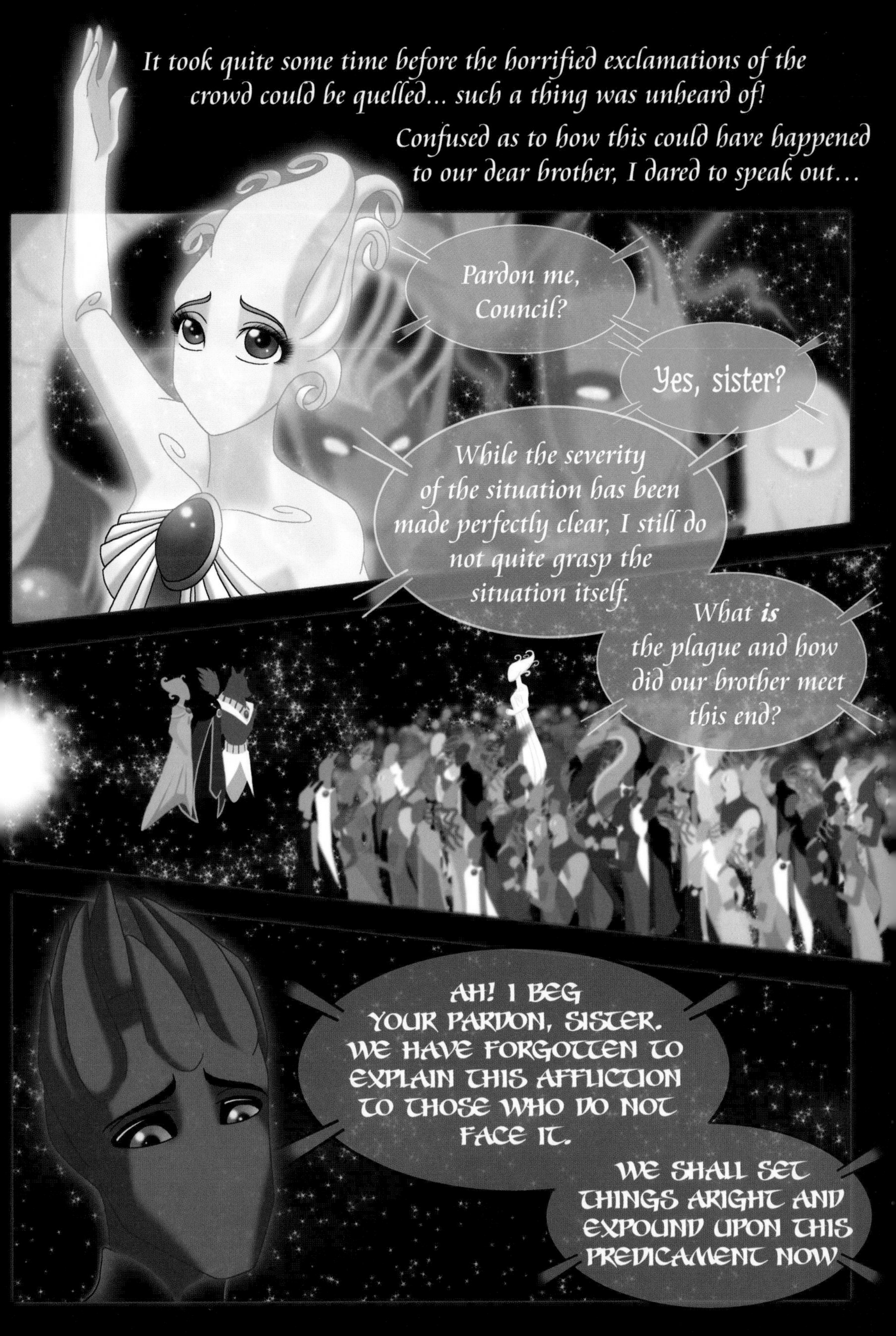
It took quite some time before the horrified exclamations of the crowd could be quelled... such a thing was unheard of!
Confused as to how this could have happened to our dear brother, I dared to speak out...
Pardon me, Council?
Yes, sister?
While the severity of the situation has been made perfectly clear, I still do not quite grasp the situation itself.
What **is** the plague and how did our brother meet this end?
AH! I BEG YOUR PARDON, SISTER. WE HAVE FORGOTTEN TO EXPLAIN THIS AFFLICTION TO THOSE WHO DO NOT FACE IT.
WE SHALL SET THINGS ARIGHT AND EXPOUND UPON THIS PREDICAMENT NOW

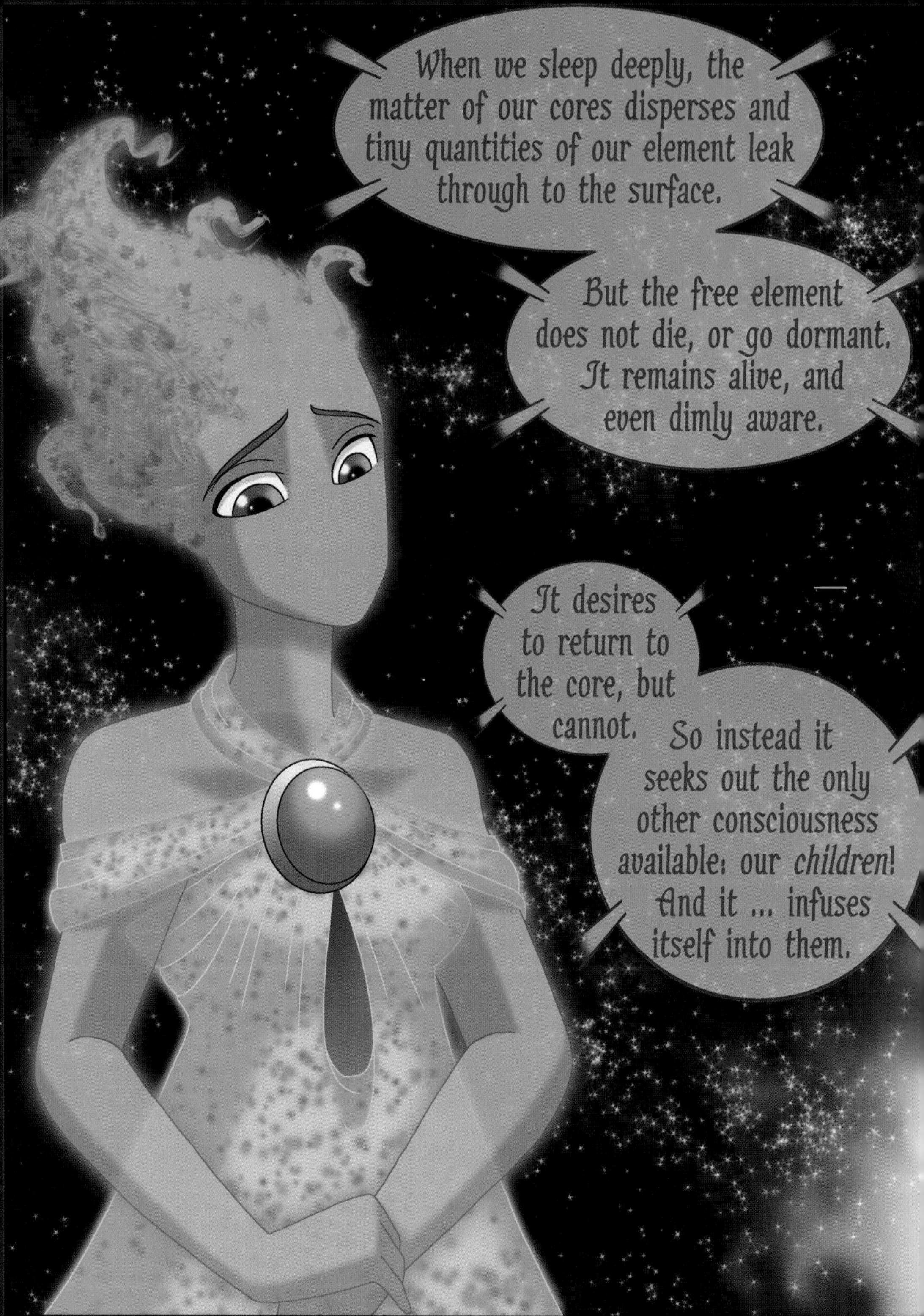
When we sleep deeply, the matter of our cores disperses and tiny quantities of our element leak through to the surface.
But the free element does not die, or go dormant. It remains alive, and even dimly aware.
It desires to return to the core, but cannot.
So instead it seeks out the only other consciousness available: our *children*! And it ... infuses itself into them.

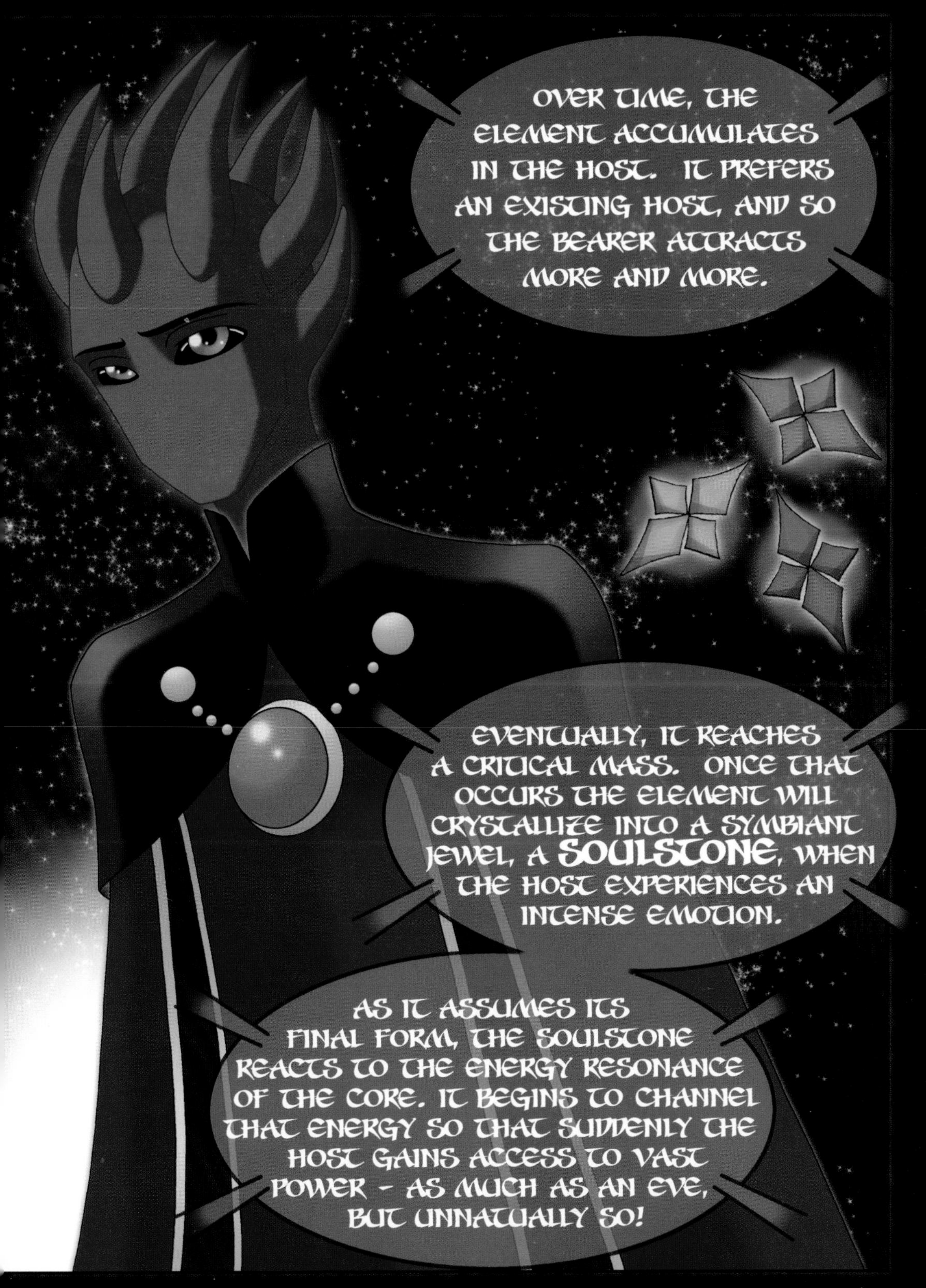
OVER TIME, THE ELEMENT ACCUMULATES IN THE HOST. IT PREFERS AN EXISTING HOST, AND SO THE BEARER ATTRACTS MORE AND MORE.
EVENTUALLY, IT REACHES A CRITICAL MASS. ONCE THAT OCCURS THE ELEMENT WILL CRYSTALLIZE INTO A SYMBIANT JEWEL, A SOULSTONE, WHEN THE HOST EXPERIENCES AN INTENSE EMOTION.
AS IT ASSUMES ITS FINAL FORM, THE SOULSTONE REACTS TO THE ENERGY RESONANCE OF THE CORE. IT BEGINS TO CHANNEL THAT ENERGY SO THAT SUDDENLY THE HOST GAINS ACCESS TO VAST POWER - AS MUCH AS AN EVE, BUT UNNATUALLY SO!

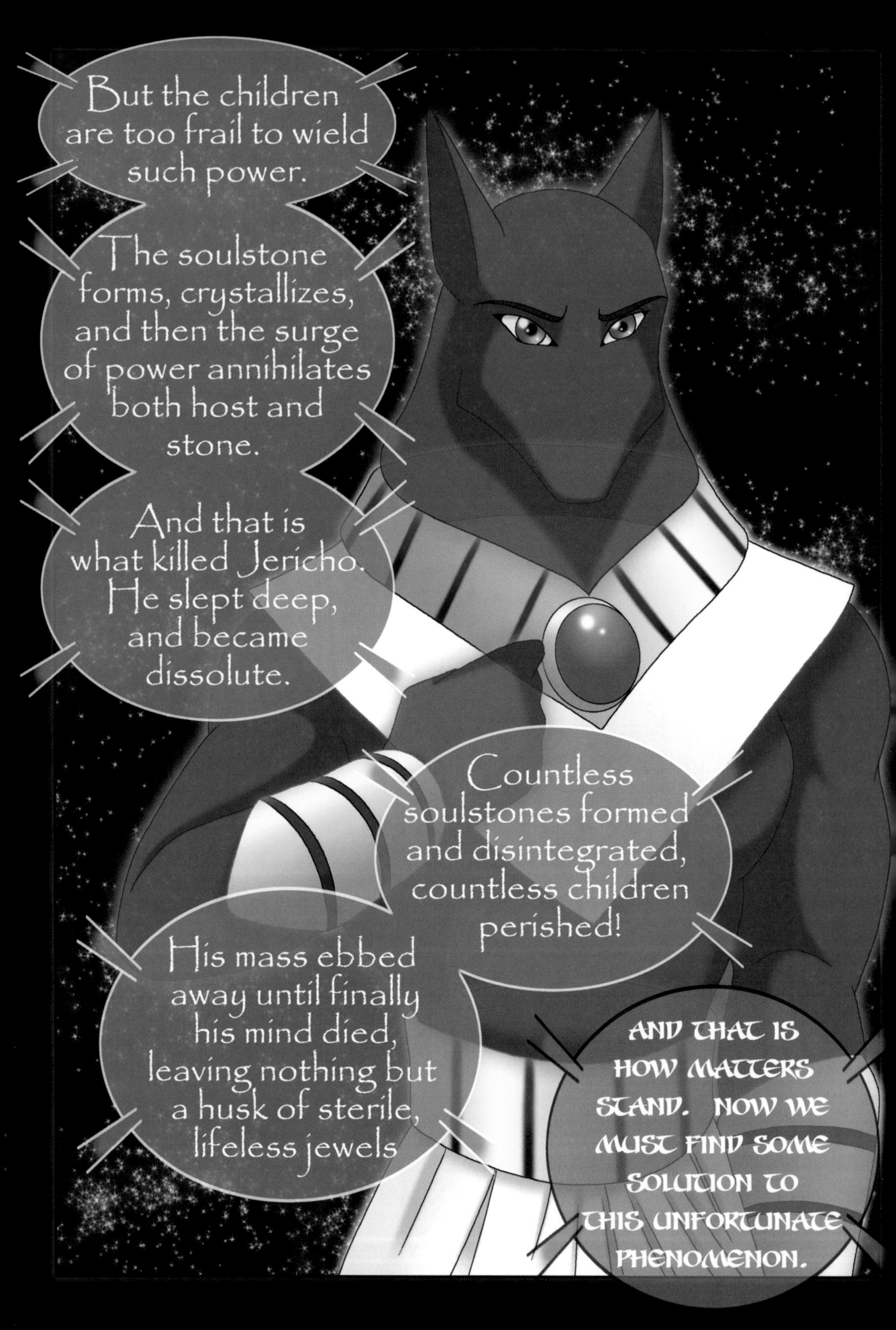
But the children are too frail to wield such power.
The soulstone forms, crystallizes, and then the surge of power annihilates both host and stone.
And that is what killed Jericho. He slept deep, and became dissolute.
Countless soulstones formed and disintegrated, countless children perished!
His mass ebbed away until finally his mind died, leaving nothing but a husk of sterile, lifeless jewels
AND THAT IS HOW MATTERS STAND. NOW WE MUST FIND SOME SOLUTION TO THIS UNFORTUNATE PHENOMENON.

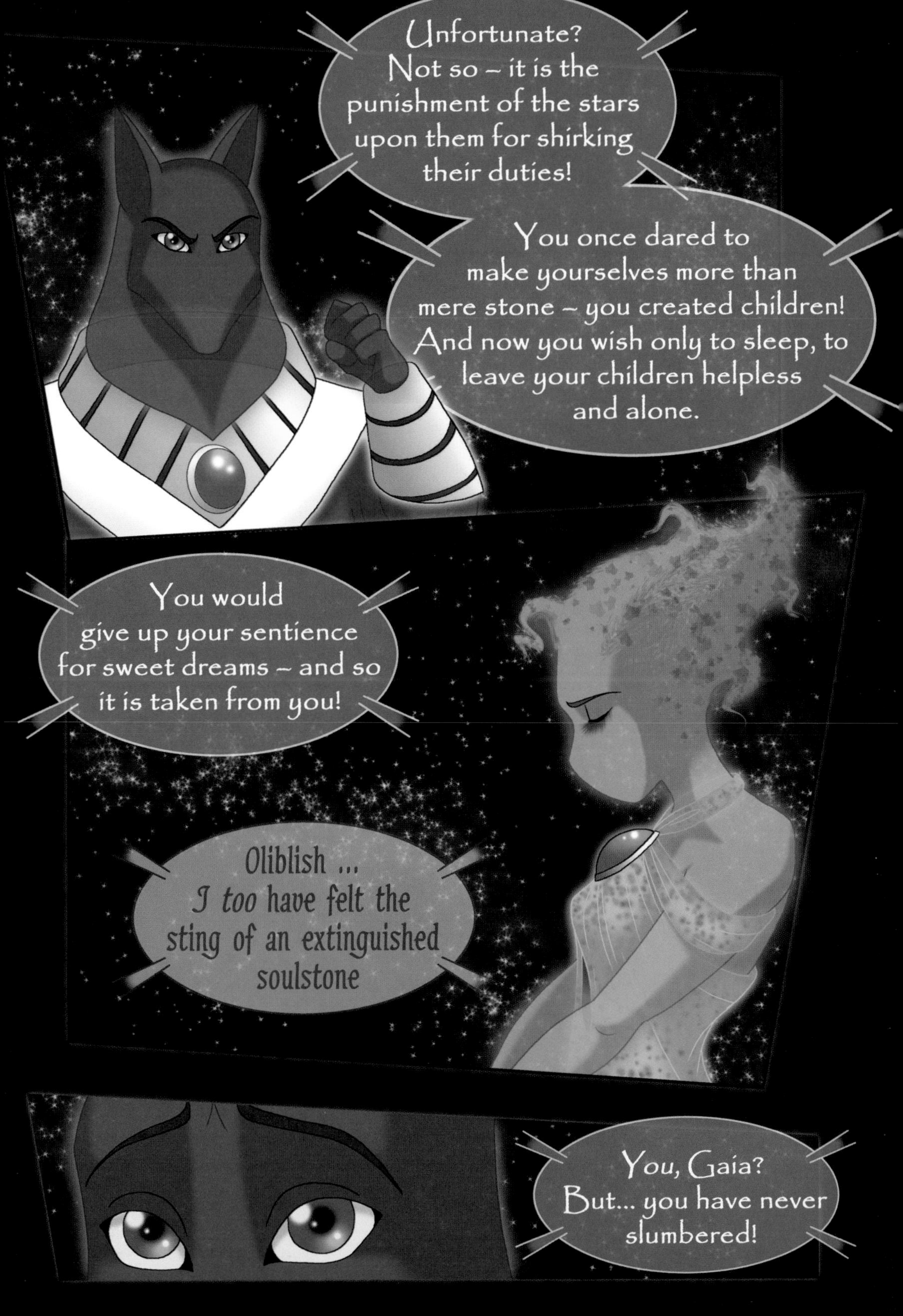
Unfortunate? Not so – it is the punishment of the stars upon them for shirking their duties!
You once dared to make yourselves more than mere stone – you created children! And now you wish only to sleep, to leave your children helpless and alone.
You would give up your sentience for sweet dreams – and so it is taken from you!
Oliblish ... *I too* have felt the sting of an extinguished soulstone
You, Gaia? But... you have never slumbered!

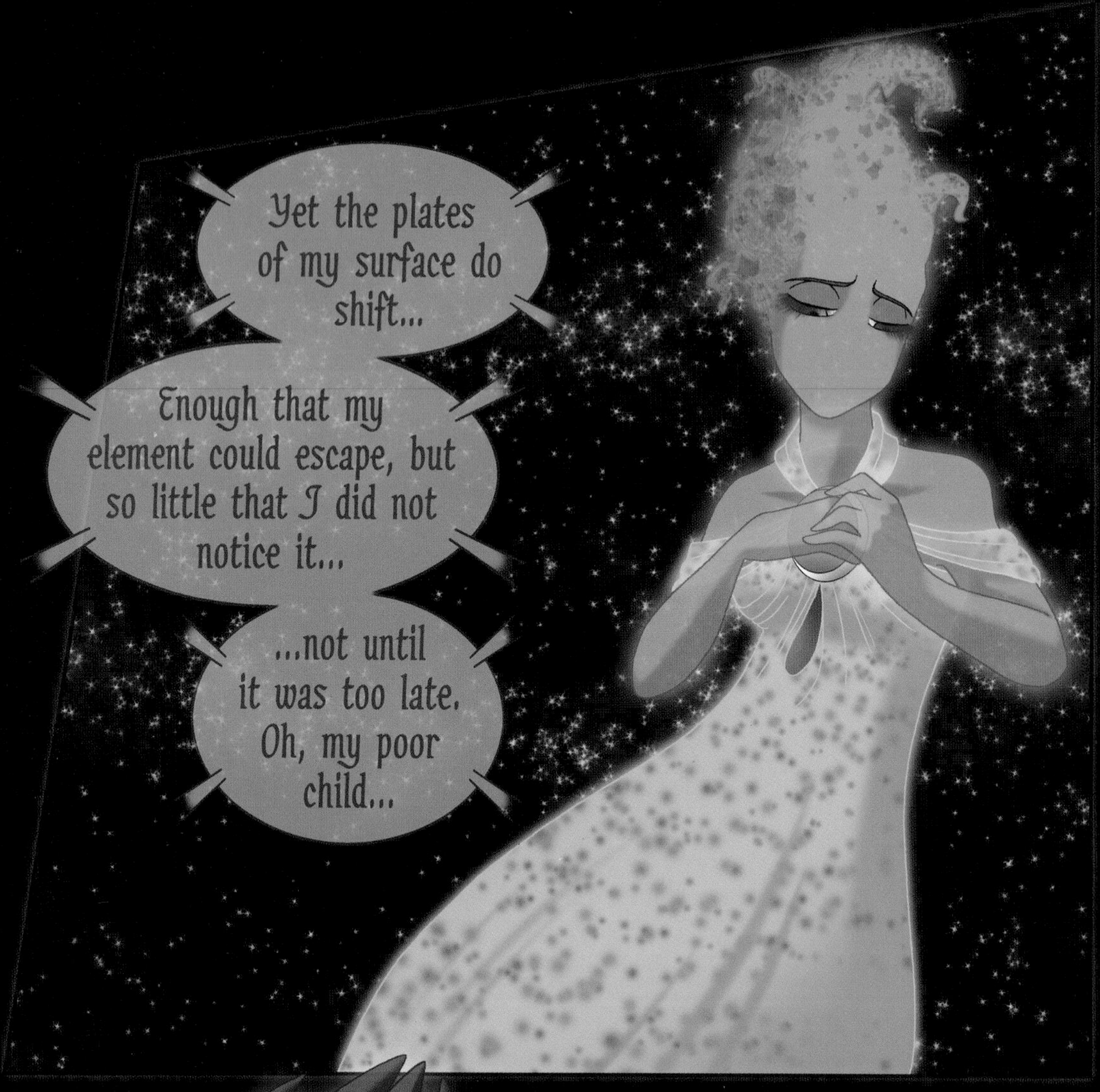
Yet the plates of my surface do shift...
Enough that my element could escape, but so little that I did not notice it...
...not until it was too late. Oh, my poor child...
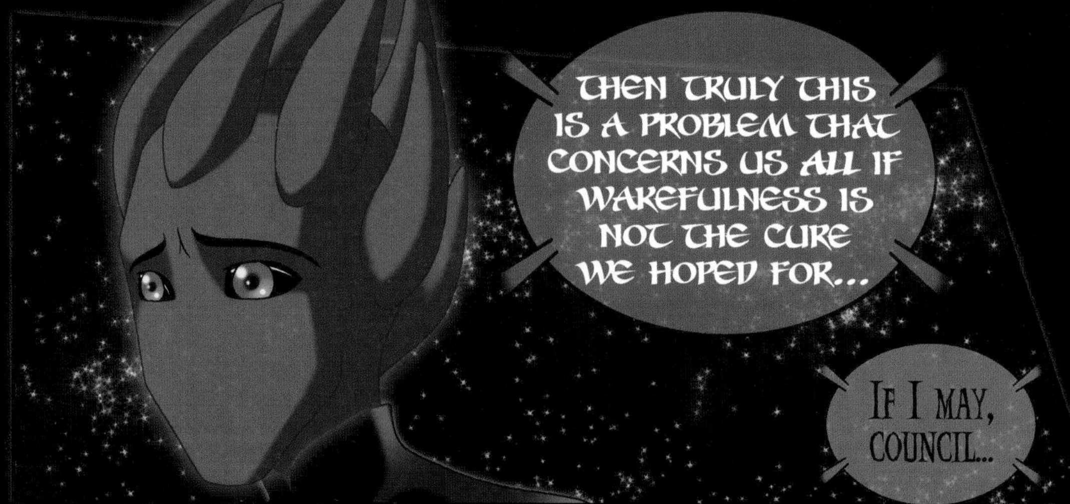
THEN TRULY THIS IS A PROBLEM THAT CONCERNS US ALL IF WAKEFULNESS IS NOT THE CURE WE HOPED FOR...
IF I MAY, COUNCIL...

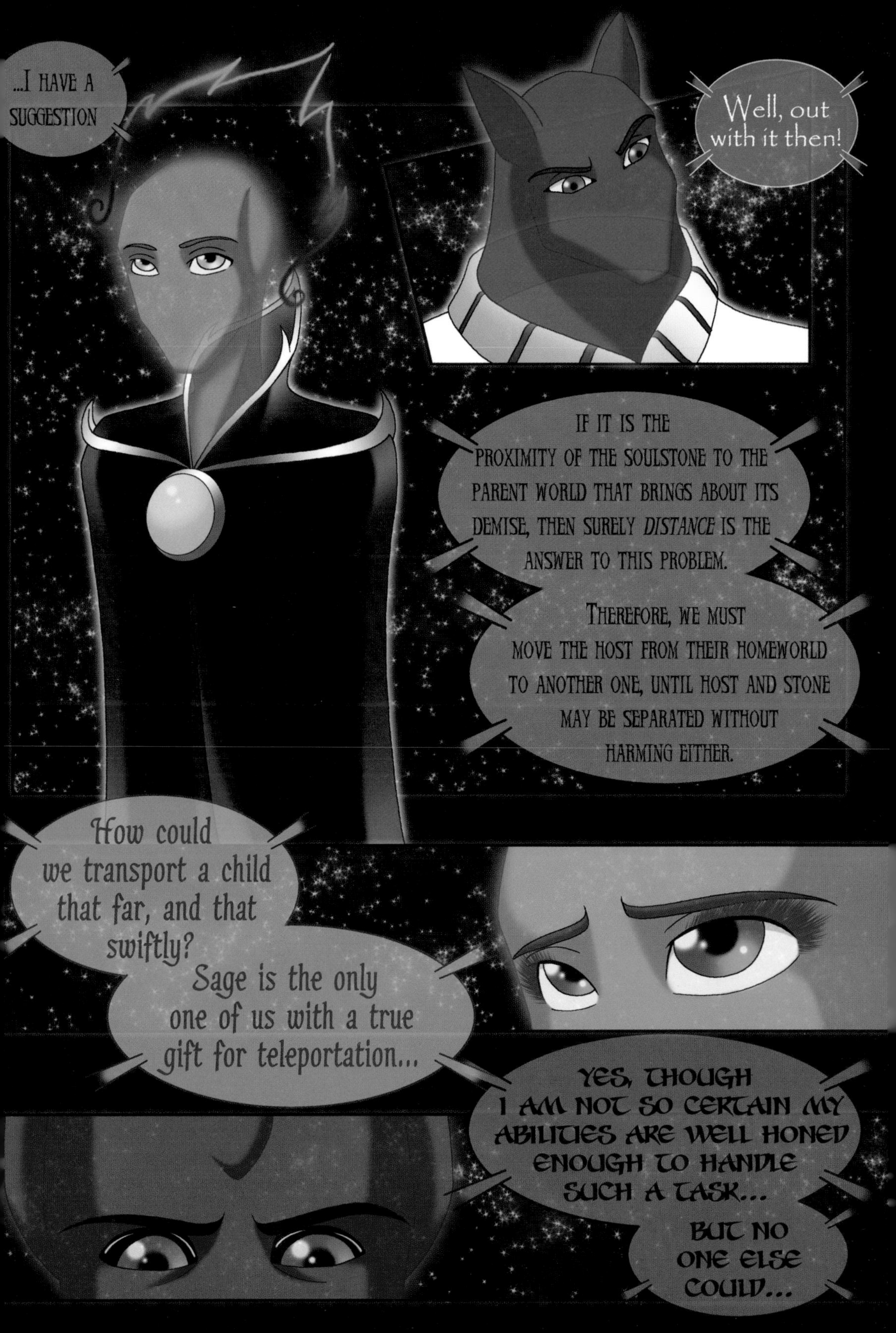
...I HAVE A SUGGESTION
Well, out with it then!
IF IT IS THE PROXIMITY OF THE SOULSTONE TO THE PARENT WORLD THAT BRINGS ABOUT ITS DEMISE, THEN SURELY *DISTANCE* IS THE ANSWER TO THIS PROBLEM.
THEREFORE, WE MUST MOVE THE HOST FROM THEIR HOMEWORLD TO ANOTHER ONE, UNTIL HOST AND STONE MAY BE SEPARATED WITHOUT HARMING EITHER.
How could we transport a child that far, and that swiftly?
Sage is the only one of us with a true gift for teleportation...
YES, THOUGH I AM NOT SO CERTAIN MY ABILITIES ARE WELL HONED ENOUGH TO HANDLE SUCH A TASK...
BUT NO ONE ELSE COULD...

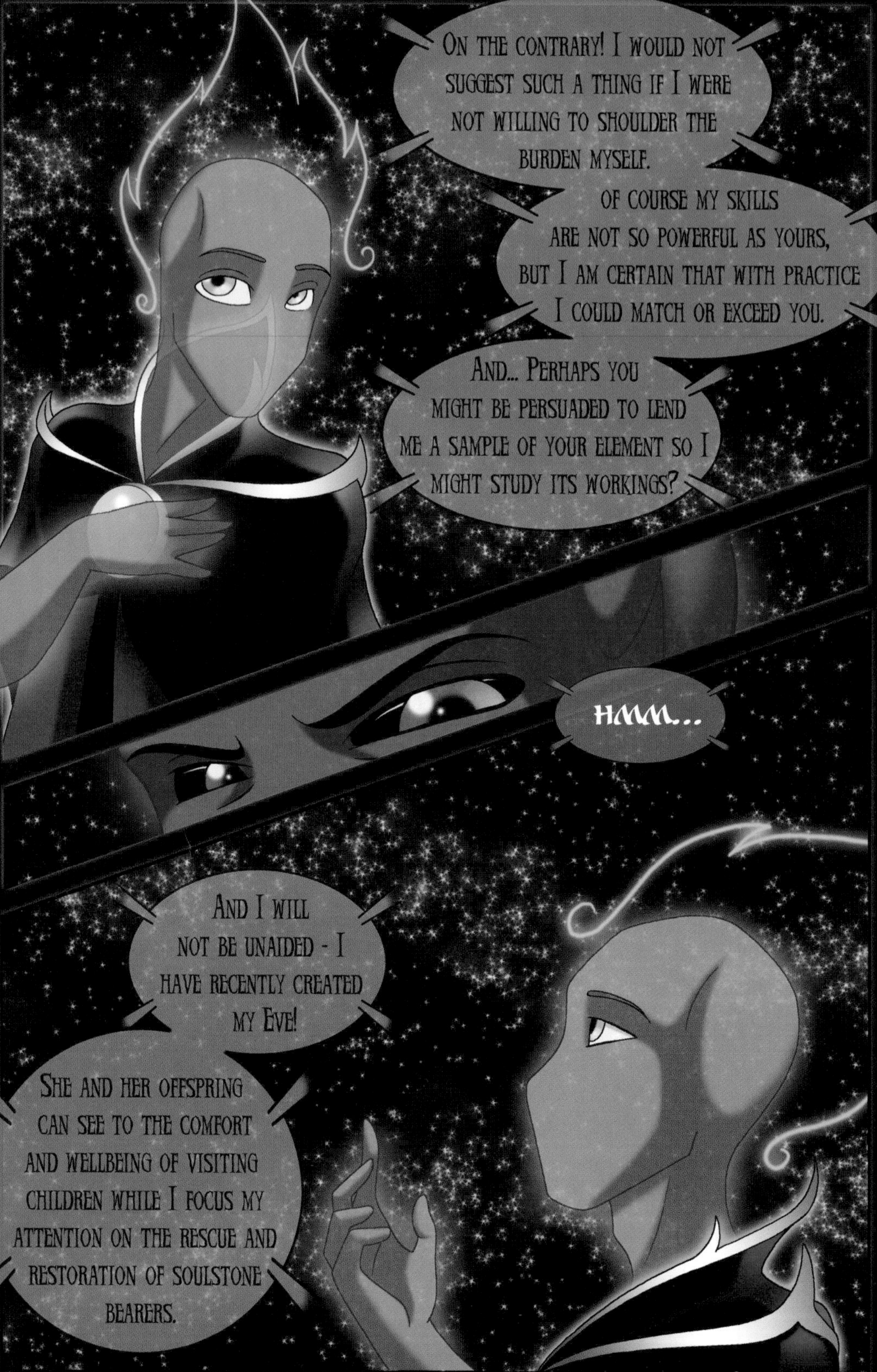
On the contrary! I would not suggest such a thing if I were not willing to shoulder the burden myself.
Of course my skills are not so powerful as yours, but I am certain that with practice I could match or exceed you.
And... Perhaps you might be persuaded to lend me a sample of your element so I might study its workings?
Hmm...
And I will not be unaided - I have recently created my Eve!
She and her offspring can see to the comfort and wellbeing of visiting children while I focus my attention on the rescue and restoration of soulstone bearers.

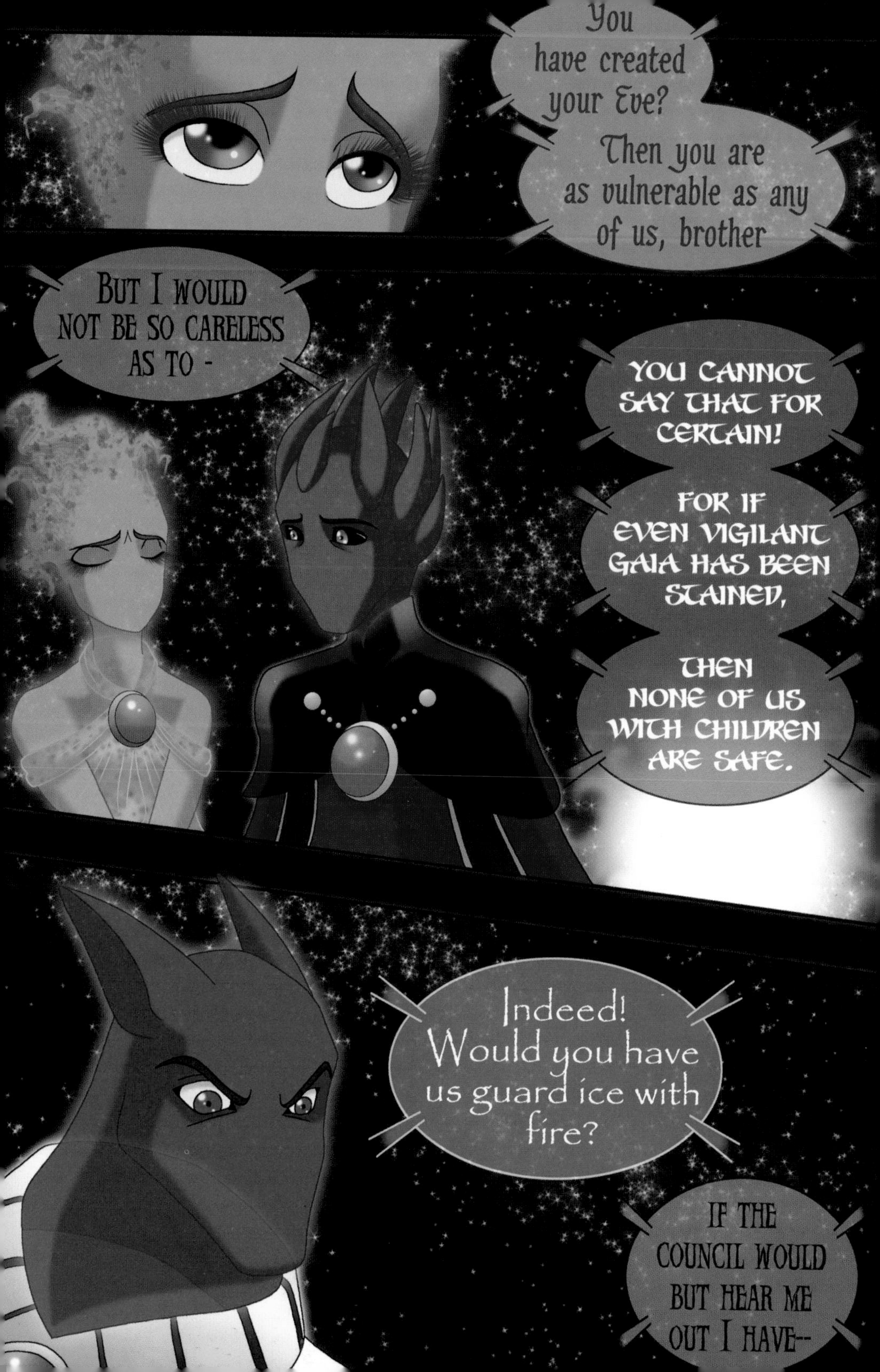
You have created your Eve?
Then you are as vulnerable as any of us, brother
BUT I WOULD NOT BE SO CARELESS AS TO -
YOU CANNOT SAY THAT FOR CERTAIN!
FOR IF EVEN VIGILANT GAIA HAS BEEN STAINED,
THEN NONE OF US WITH CHILDREN ARE SAFE.
Indeed! Would you have us guard ice with fire?
IF THE COUNCIL WOULD BUT HEAR ME OUT I HAVE--

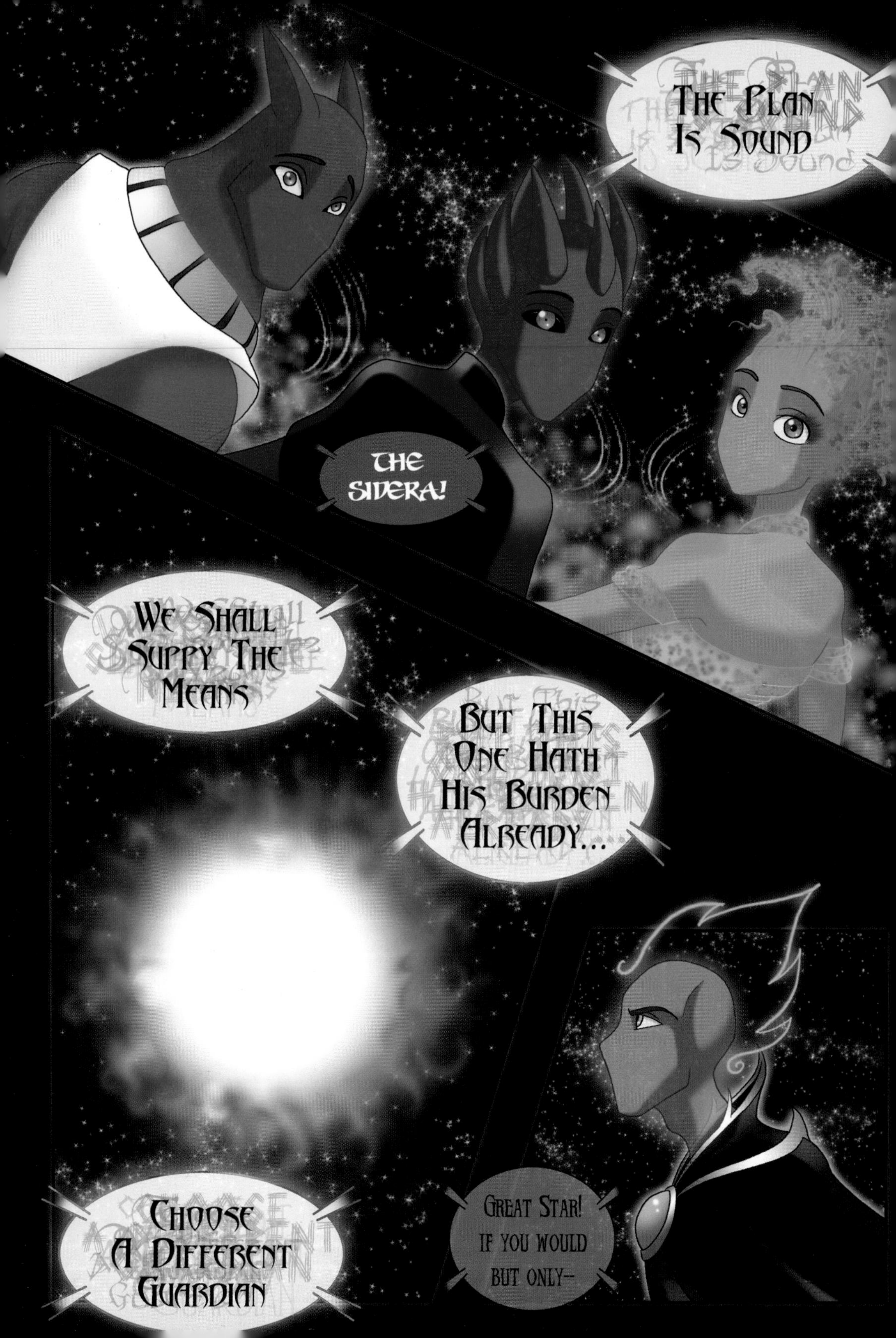
The Plan Is Sound
The Sidera!
We Shall Suppy The Means
But This One Hath His Burden Already...
Choose A Different Guardian
Great Star! If you would but only--

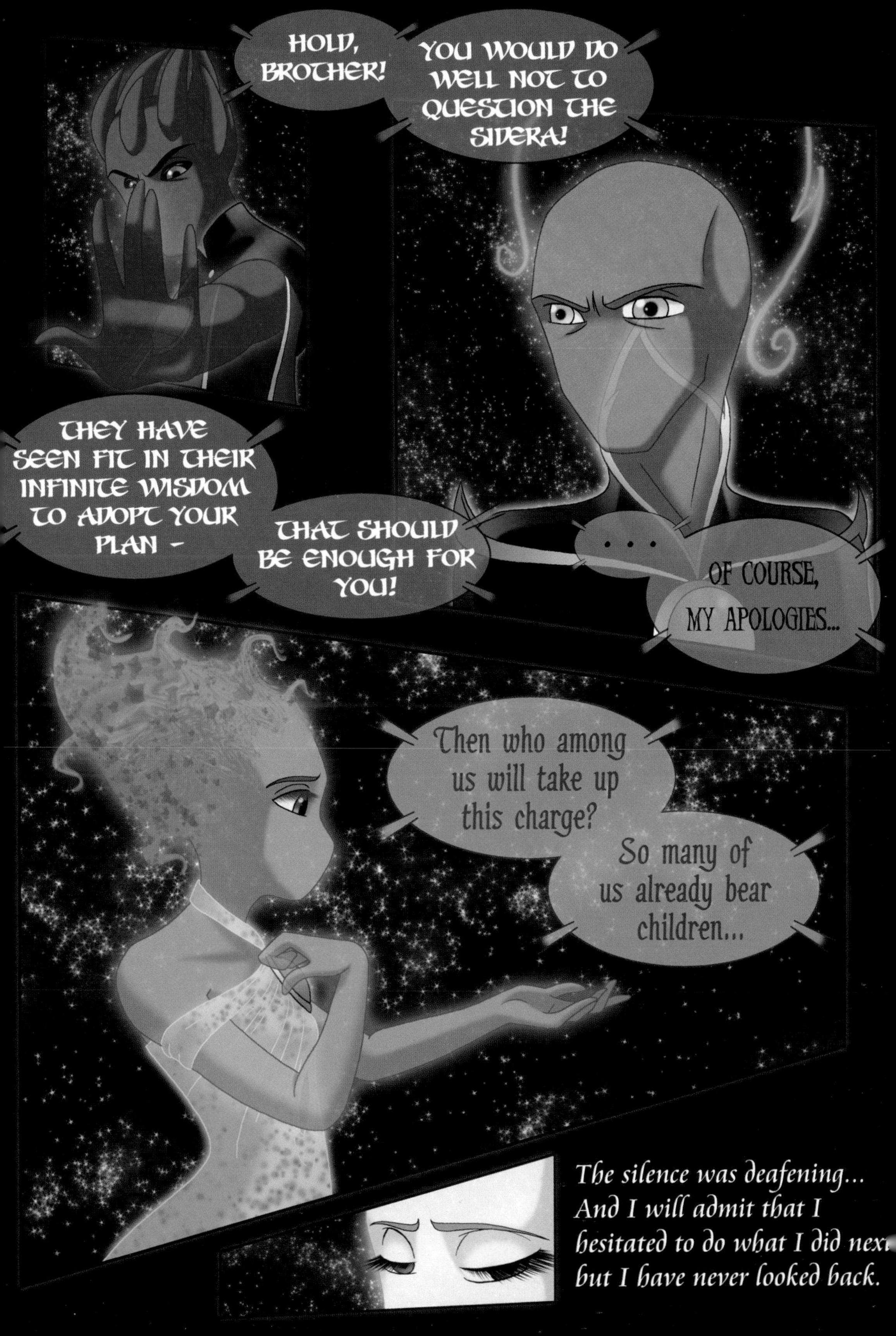
HOLD, BROTHER!
YOU WOULD DO WELL NOT TO QUESTION THE SIDERA!
THEY HAVE SEEN FIT IN THEIR INFINITE WISDOM TO ADOPT YOUR PLAN -
THAT SHOULD BE ENOUGH FOR YOU!
. . .
OF COURSE, MY APOLOGIES...
Then who among us will take up this charge?
So many of us already bear children...
The silence was deafening...
And I will admit that I
hesitated to do what I did next
but I have never looked back.

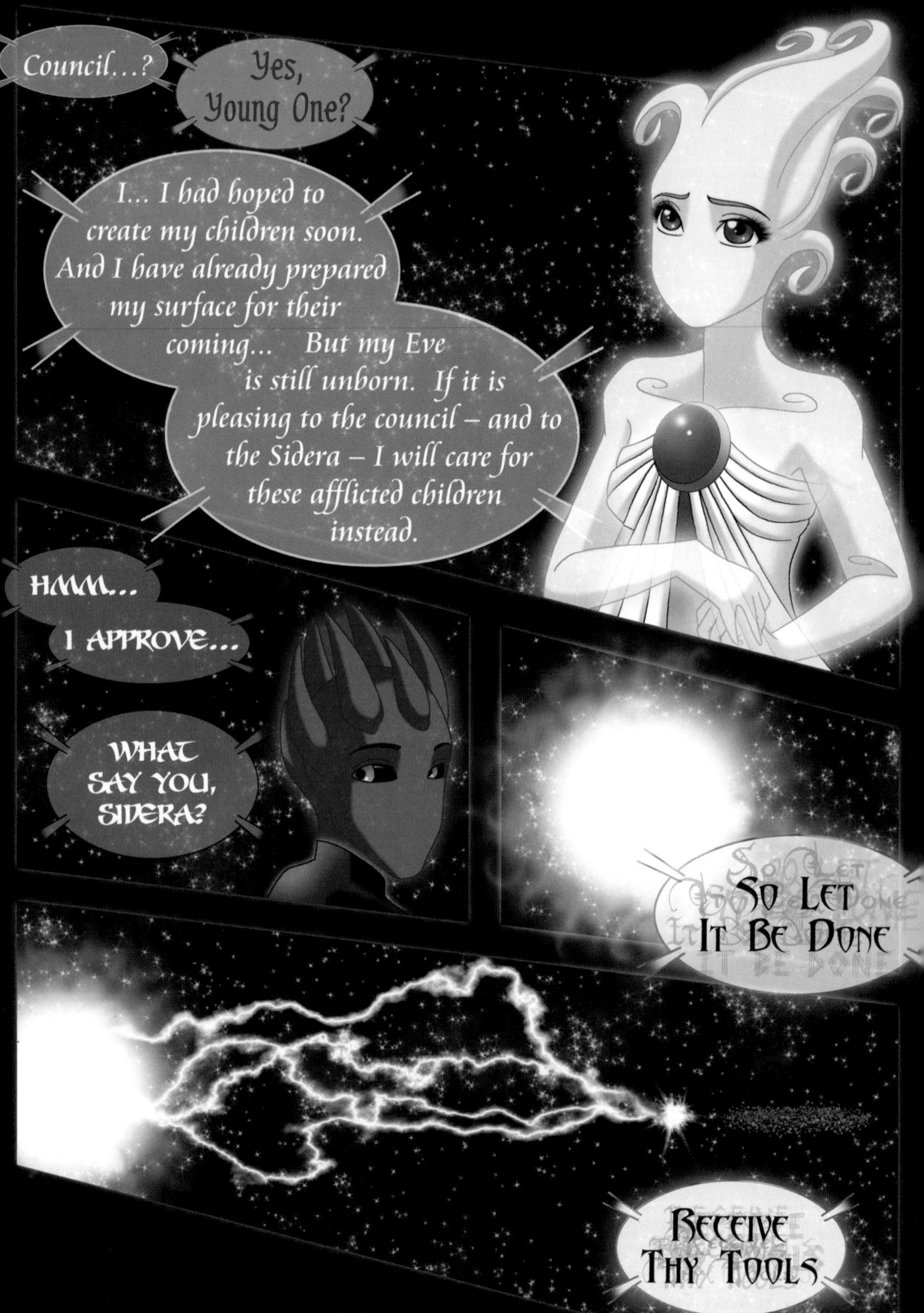
Council...?
Yes, Young One?
I... I had hoped to create my children soon. And I have already prepared my surface for their coming... But my Eve is still unborn. If it is pleasing to the council – and to the Sidera – I will care for these afflicted children instead.
HMM...
I APPROVE...
WHAT SAY YOU, SIDERA?
So Let It Be Done
Receive Thy Tools

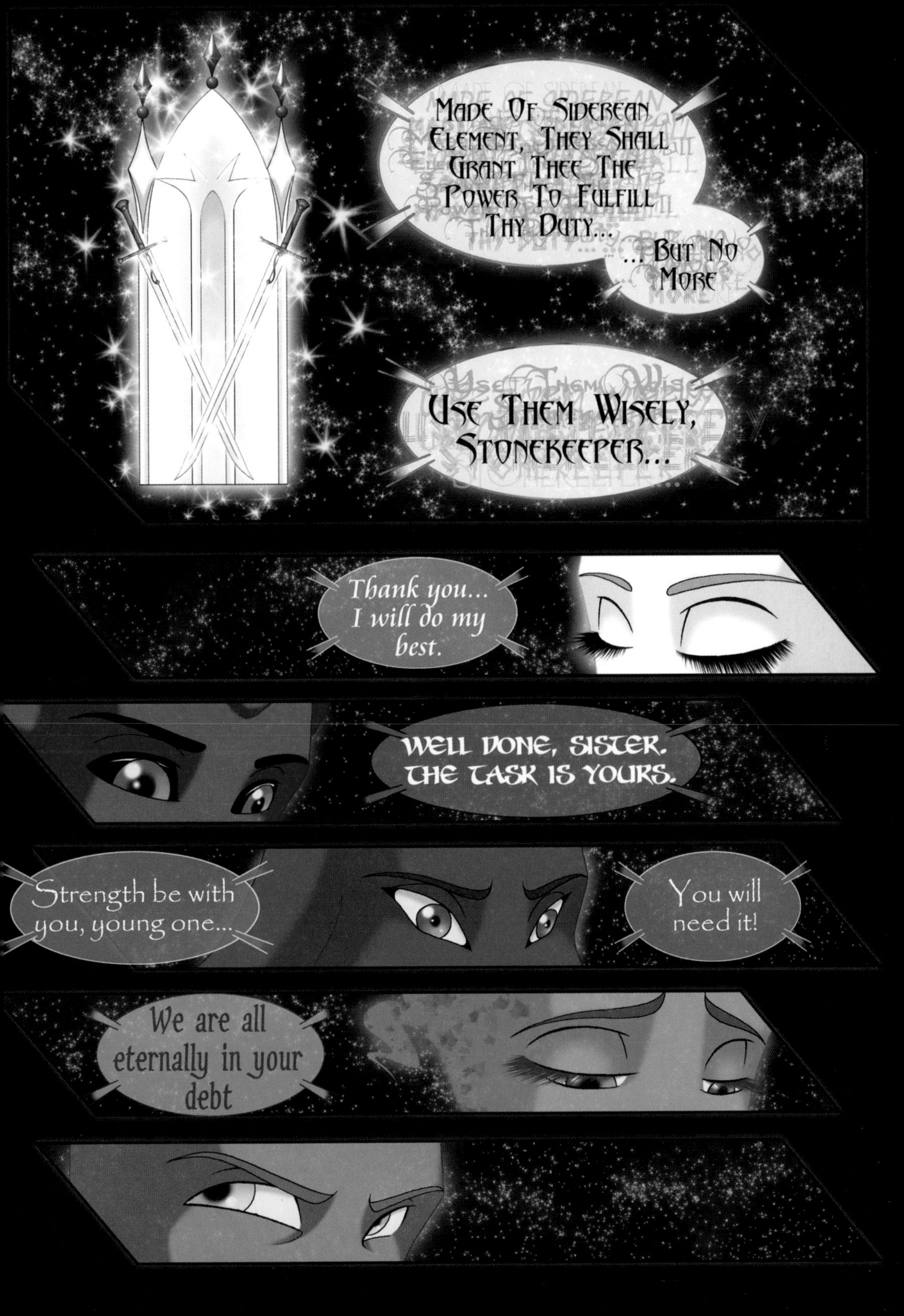

Made Of Siderean Element, They Shall Grant Thee The Power To Fulfill Thy Duty...
...But No More
Use Them Wisely, Stonekeeper...
Thank you... I will do my best.
Well done, sister. The task is yours.
Strength be with you, young one...
You will need it!
We are all eternally in your debt

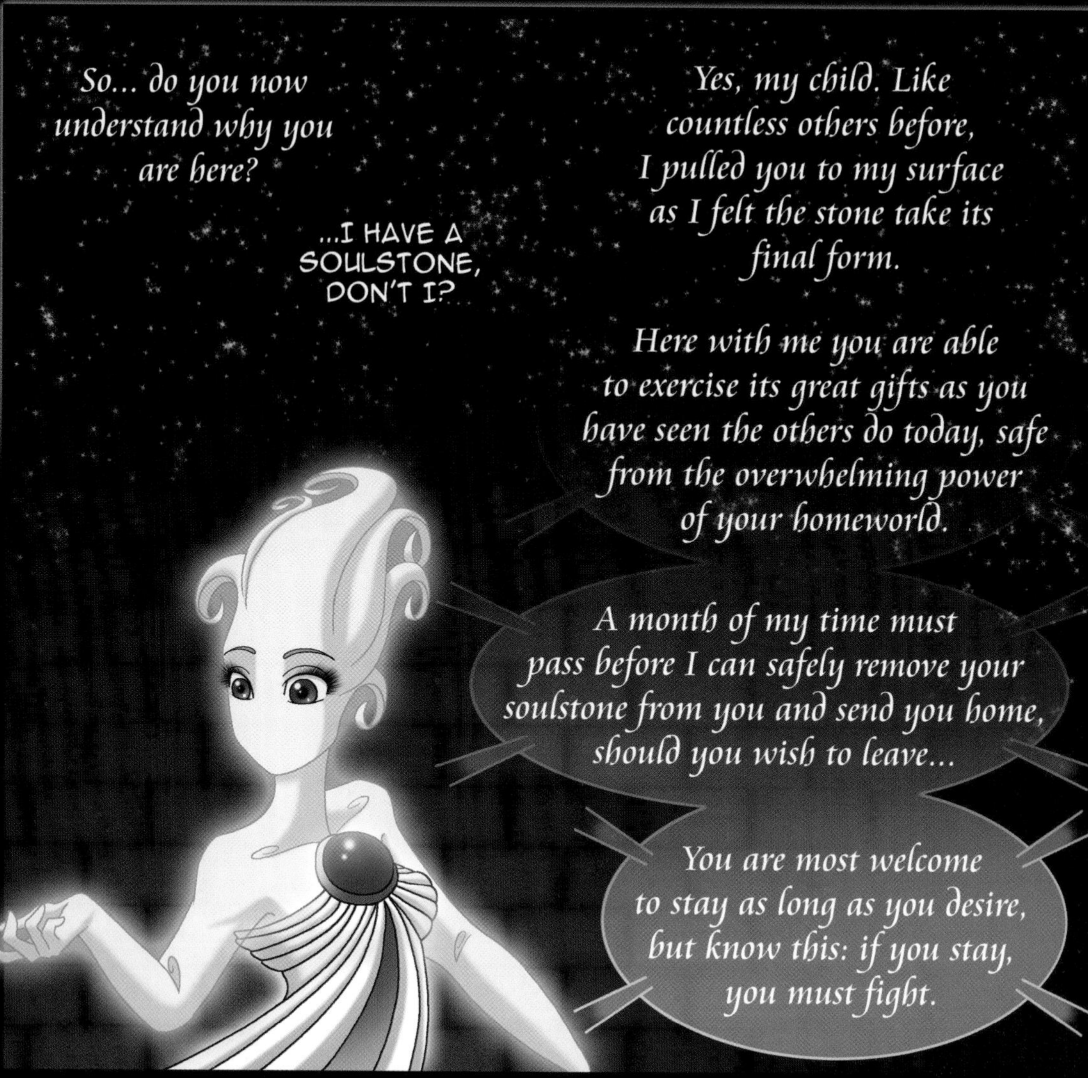

So... do you now understand why you are here?
...I HAVE A SOULSTONE, DON'T I?
Yes, my child. Like countless others before, I pulled you to my surface as I felt the stone take its final form.
Here with me you are able to exercise its great gifts as you have seen the others do today, safe from the overwhelming power of your homeworld.
A month of my time must pass before I can safely remove your soulstone from you and send you home, should you wish to leave...
You are most welcome to stay as long as you desire, but know this: if you stay, you must fight.

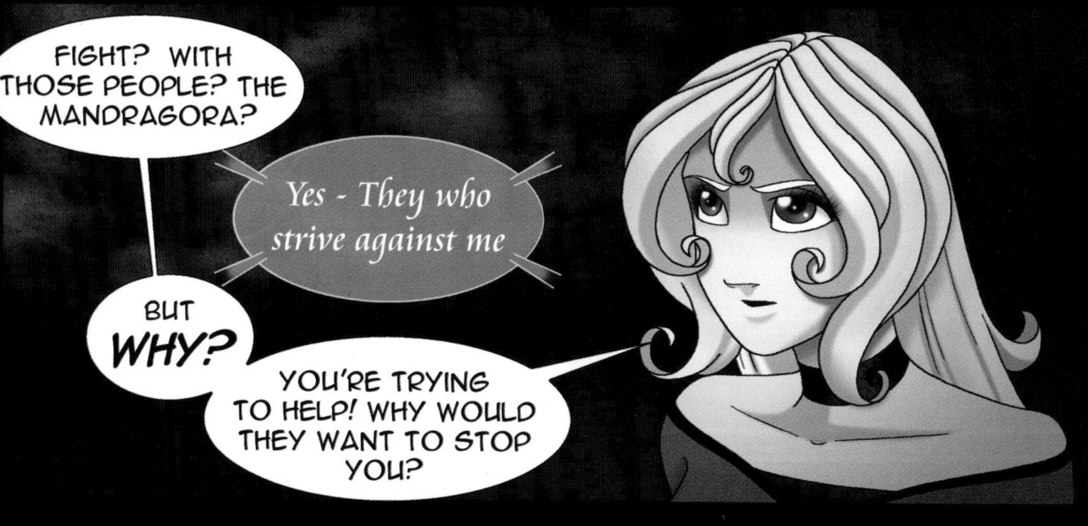

FIGHT? WITH THOSE PEOPLE? THE MANDRAGORA?
Yes - They who strive against me
BUT WHY?
YOU'RE TRYING TO HELP! WHY WOULD THEY WANT TO STOP YOU?

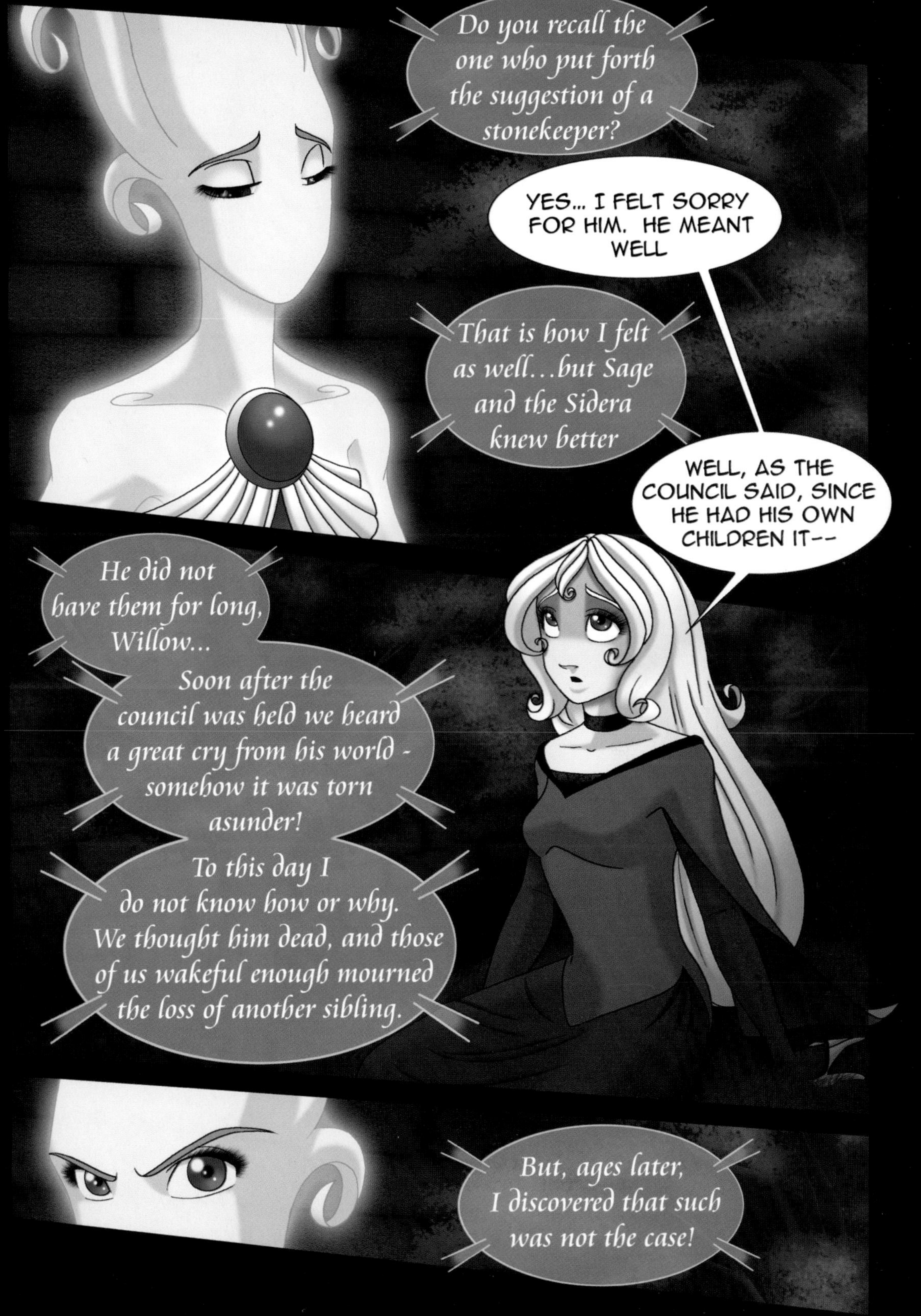
Do you recall the one who put forth the suggestion of a stonekeeper?
YES... I FELT SORRY FOR HIM. HE MEANT WELL
That is how I felt as well...but Sage and the Sidera knew better
WELL, AS THE COUNCIL SAID, SINCE HE HAD HIS OWN CHILDREN IT--
He did not have them for long, Willow...
Soon after the council was held we heard a great cry from his world - somehow it was torn asunder!
To this day I do not know how or why. We thought him dead, and those of us wakeful enough mourned the loss of another sibling.
But, ages later, I discovered that such was not the case!

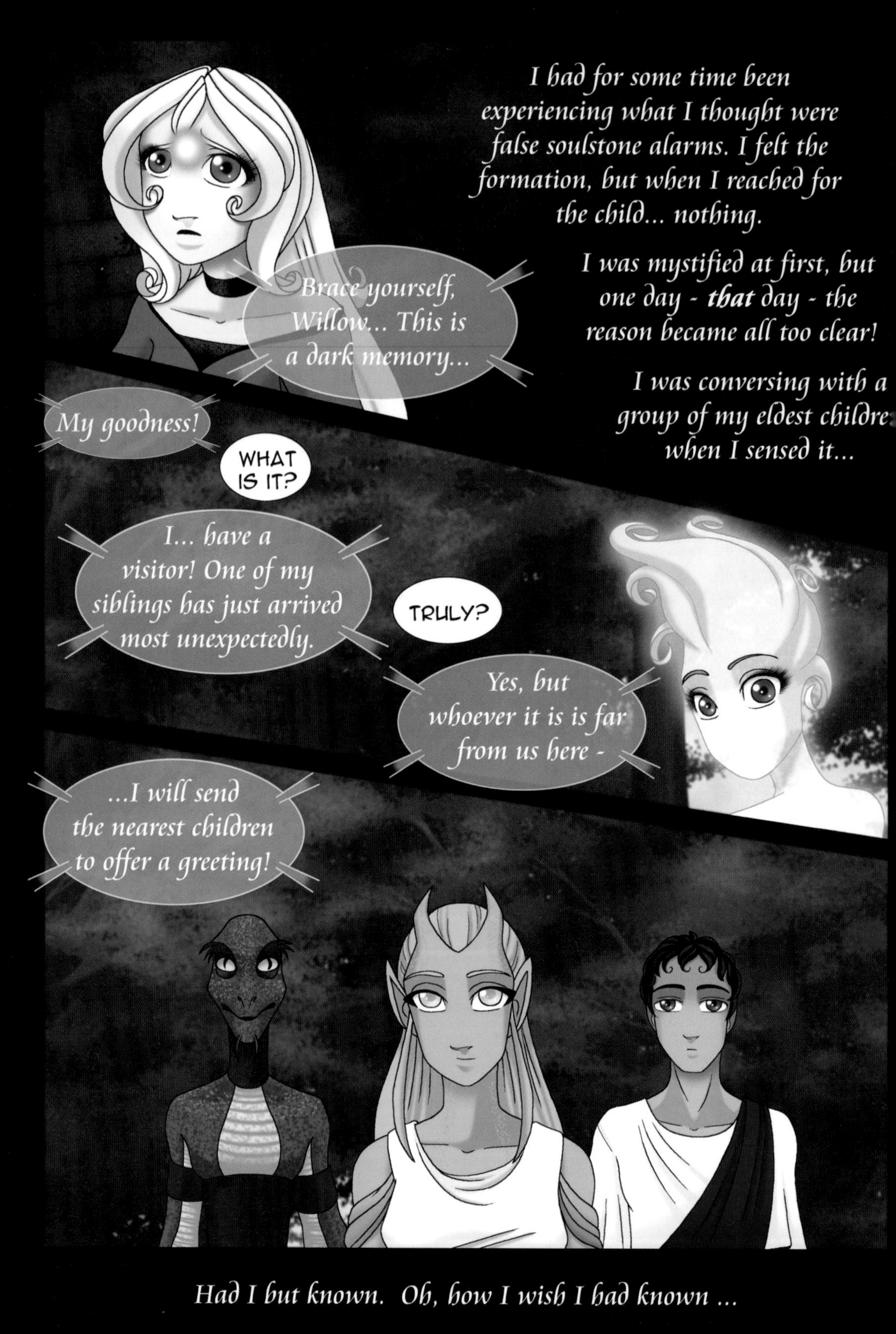
Brace yourself, Willow... This is a dark memory...
I had for some time been experiencing what I thought were false soulstone alarms. I felt the formation, but when I reached for the child... nothing.
I was mystified at first, but one day - ***that*** day - the reason became all too clear!
I was conversing with a group of my eldest childre when I sensed it...
My goodness!
WHAT IS IT?
I... have a visitor! One of my siblings has just arrived most unexpectedly.
TRULY?
Yes, but whoever it is is far from us here -
...I will send the nearest children to offer a greeting!
Had I but known. Oh, how I wish I had known ...

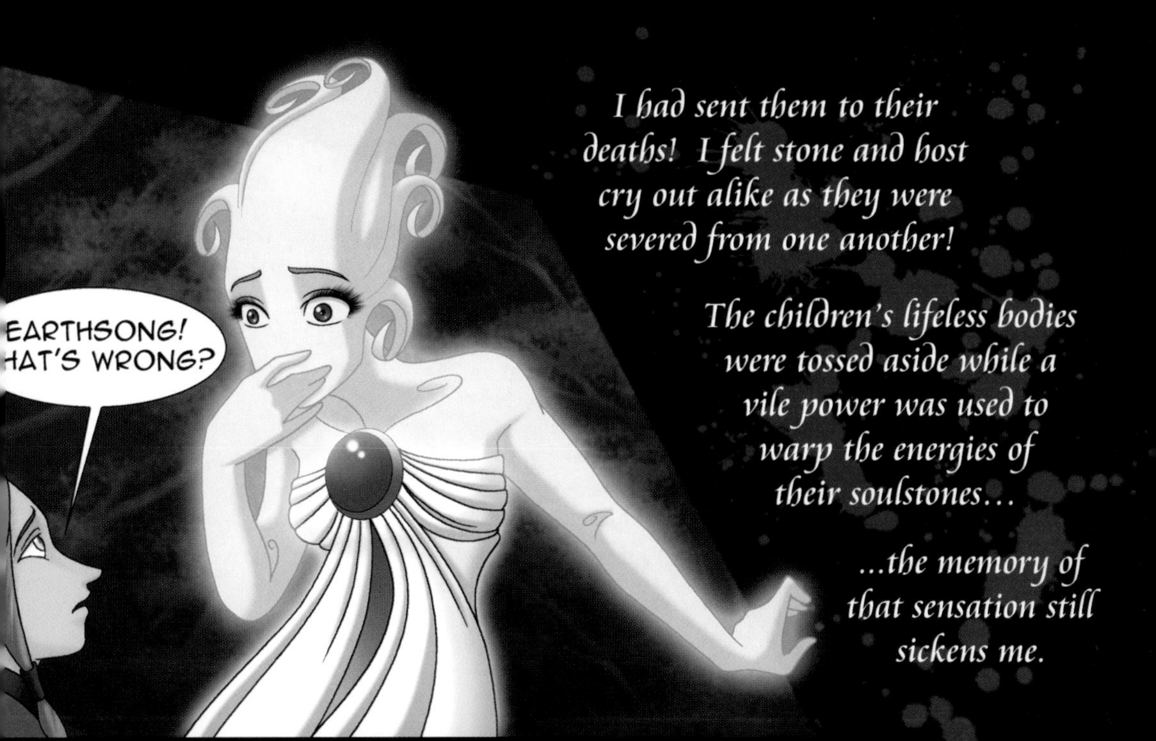
I had sent them to their deaths! I felt stone and host cry out alike as they were severed from one another!
EARTHSONG! HAT'S WRONG?
The children's lifeless bodies were tossed aside while a vile power was used to warp the energies of their soulstones…
...the memory of that sensation still sickens me.

I quickly explained to those around me what had just transpired...

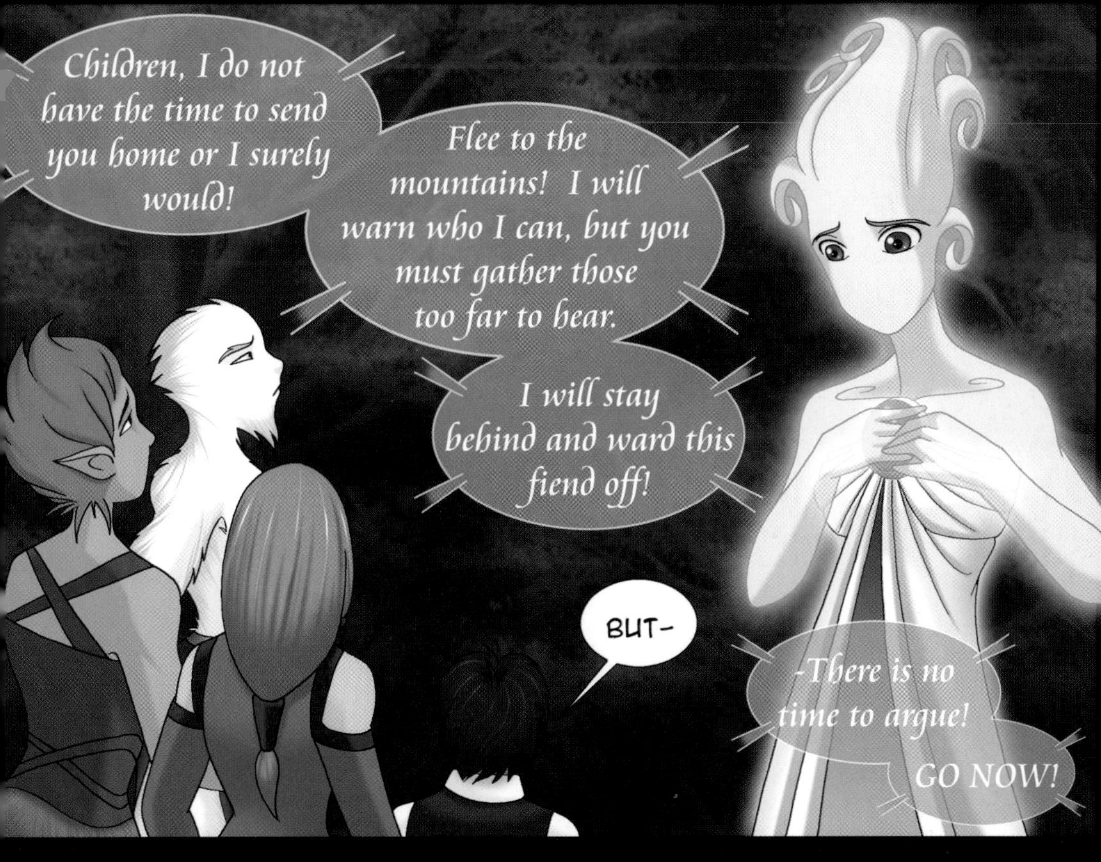
Children, I do not have the time to send you home or I surely would!
Flee to the mountains! I will warn who I can, but you must gather those too far to hear.
I will stay behind and ward this fiend off!
BUT-
-There is no time to argue!
GO NOW!

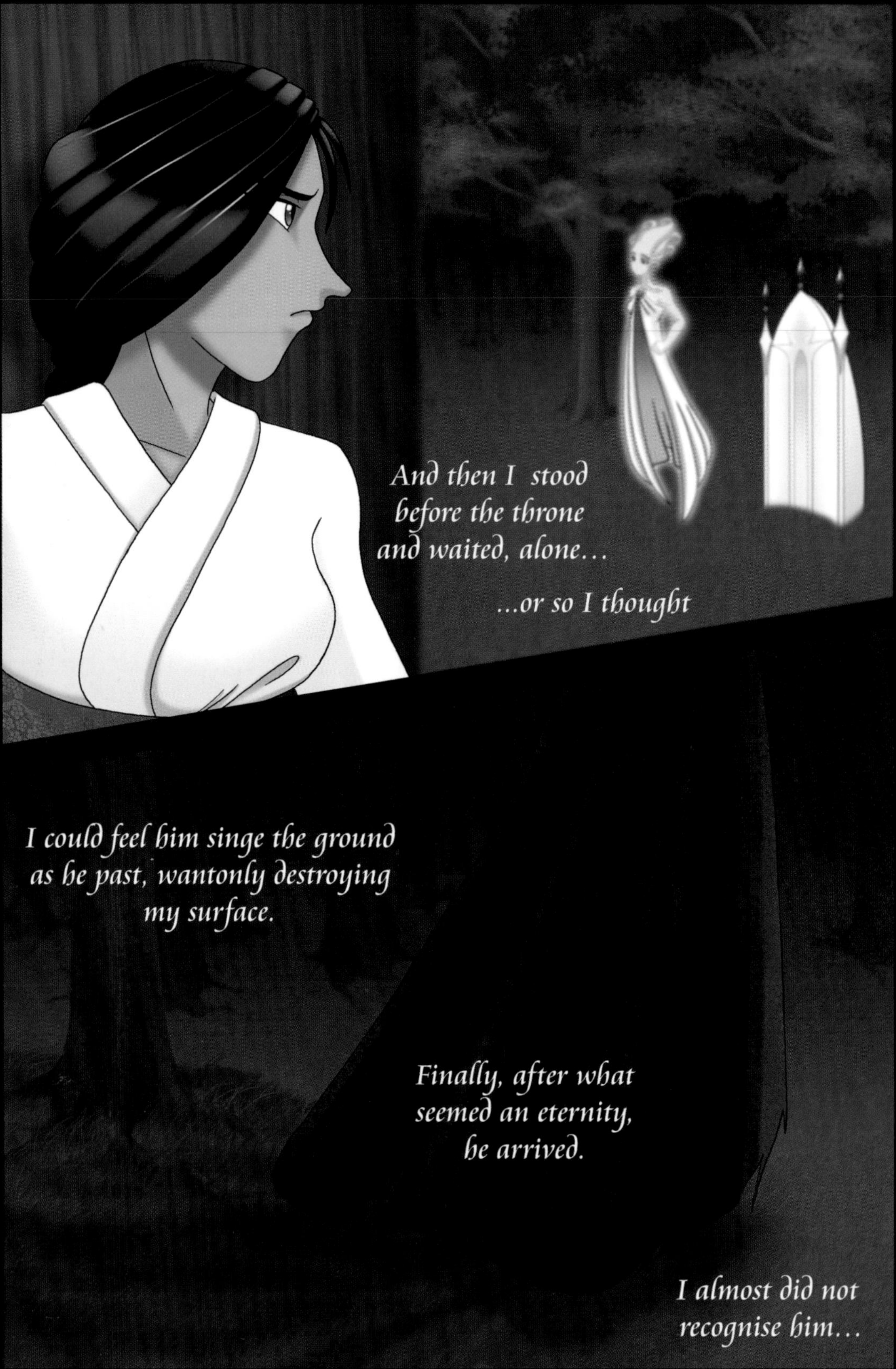
And then I stood
before the throne
and waited, alone…
…or so I thought
I could feel him singe the ground
as he past, wantonly destroying
my surface.
Finally, after what
seemed an eternity,
he arrived.
I almost did not
recognise him…

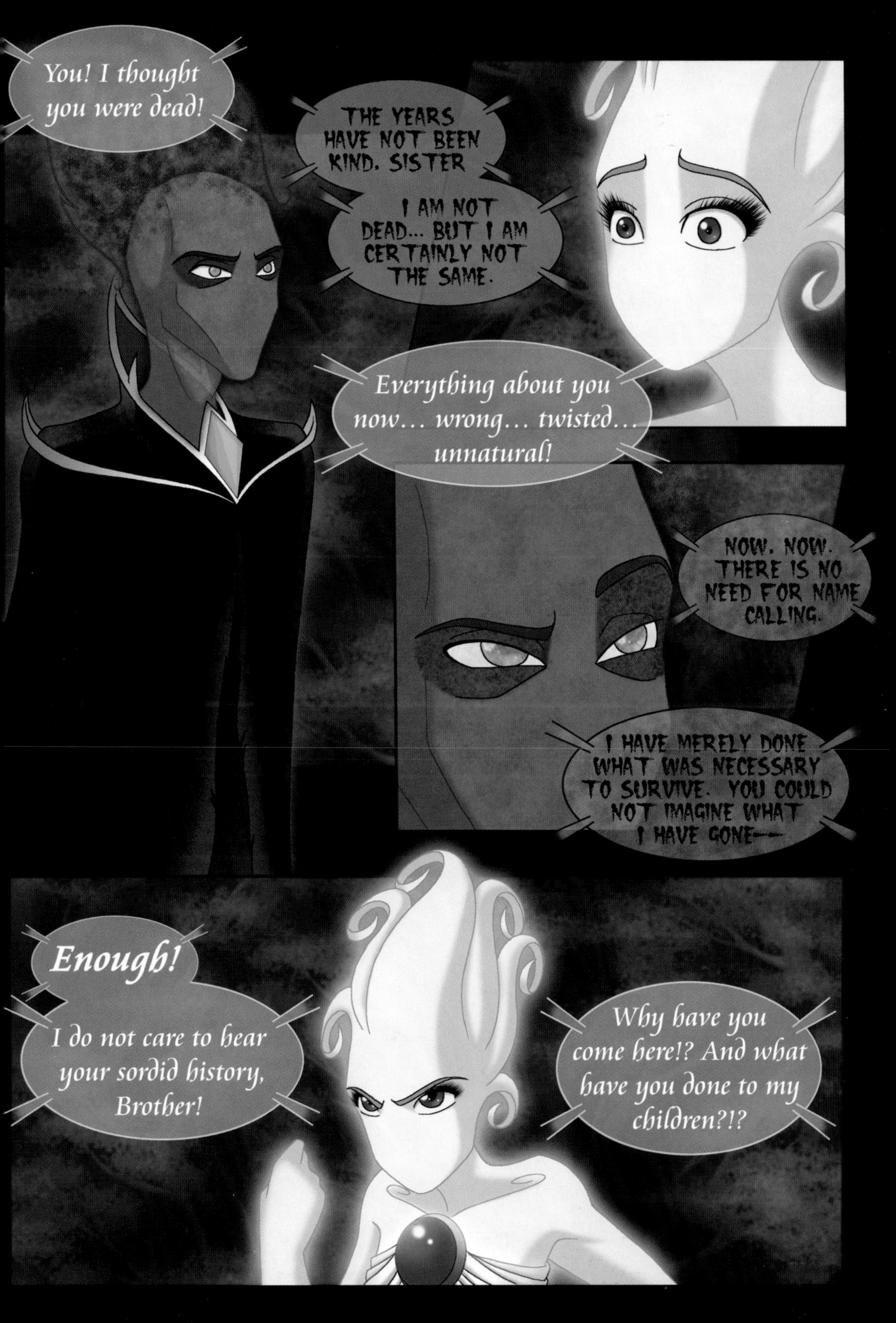
You! I thought you were dead!
THE YEARS HAVE NOT BEEN KIND. SISTER
I AM NOT DEAD... BUT I AM CERTAINLY NOT THE SAME.
Everything about you now... wrong... twisted... unnatural!
NOW. NOW. THERE IS NO NEED FOR NAME CALLING.
I HAVE MERELY DONE WHAT WAS NECESSARY TO SURVIVE. YOU COULD NOT IMAGINE WHAT I HAVE GONE—
Enough!
I do not care to hear your sordid history, Brother!
Why have you come here!? And what have you done to my children?!?

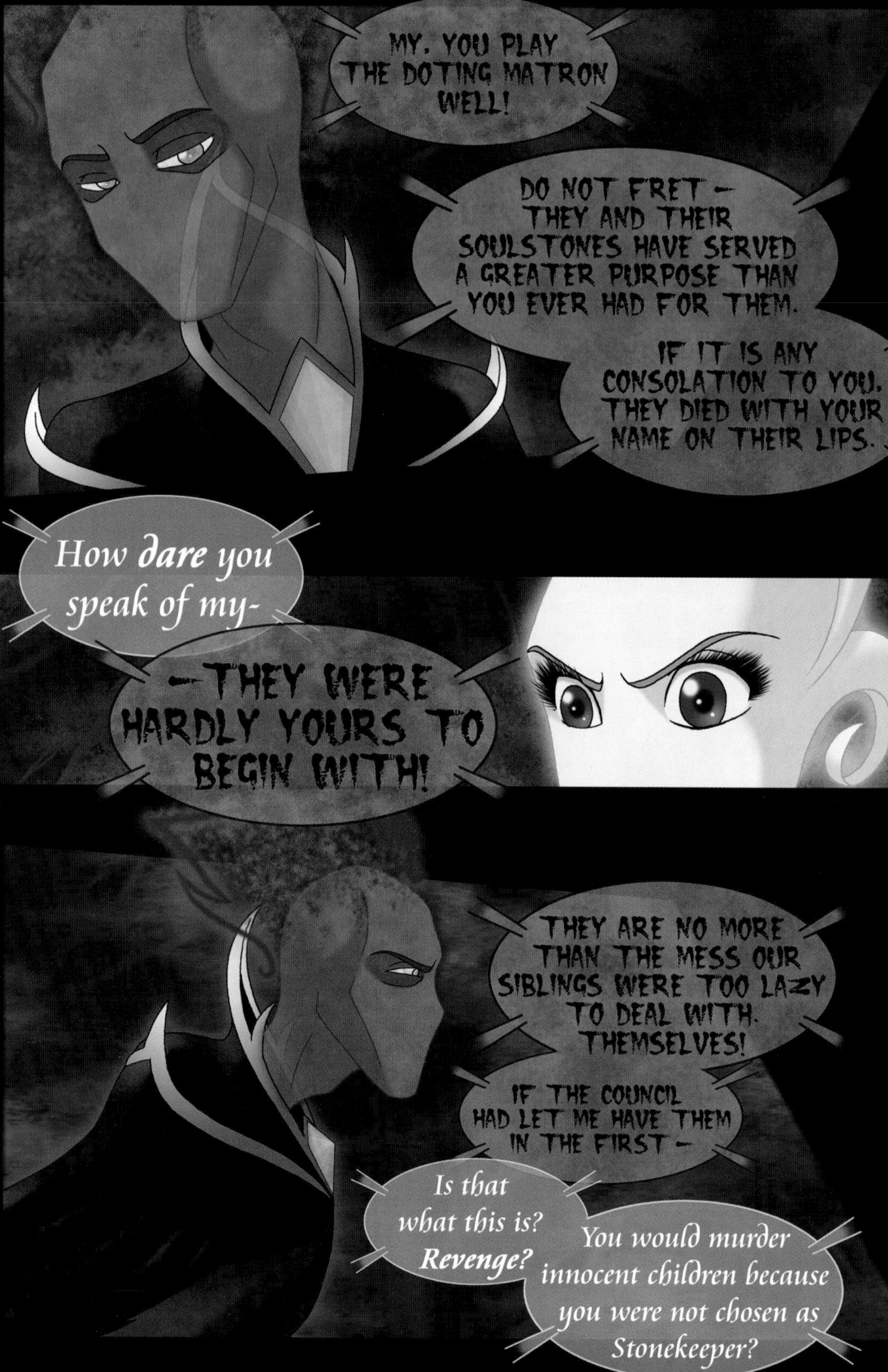
MY, YOU PLAY THE DOTING MATRON WELL!
DO NOT FRET - THEY AND THEIR SOULSTONES HAVE SERVED A GREATER PURPOSE THAN YOU EVER HAD FOR THEM.
IF IT IS ANY CONSOLATION TO YOU, THEY DIED WITH YOUR NAME ON THEIR LIPS.
How dare you speak of my-
-THEY WERE HARDLY YOURS TO BEGIN WITH!
THEY ARE NO MORE THAN THE MESS OUR SIBLINGS WERE TOO LAZY TO DEAL WITH THEMSELVES!
IF THE COUNCIL HAD LET ME HAVE THEM IN THE FIRST -
Is that what this is? Revenge?
You would murder innocent children because you were not chosen as Stonekeeper?

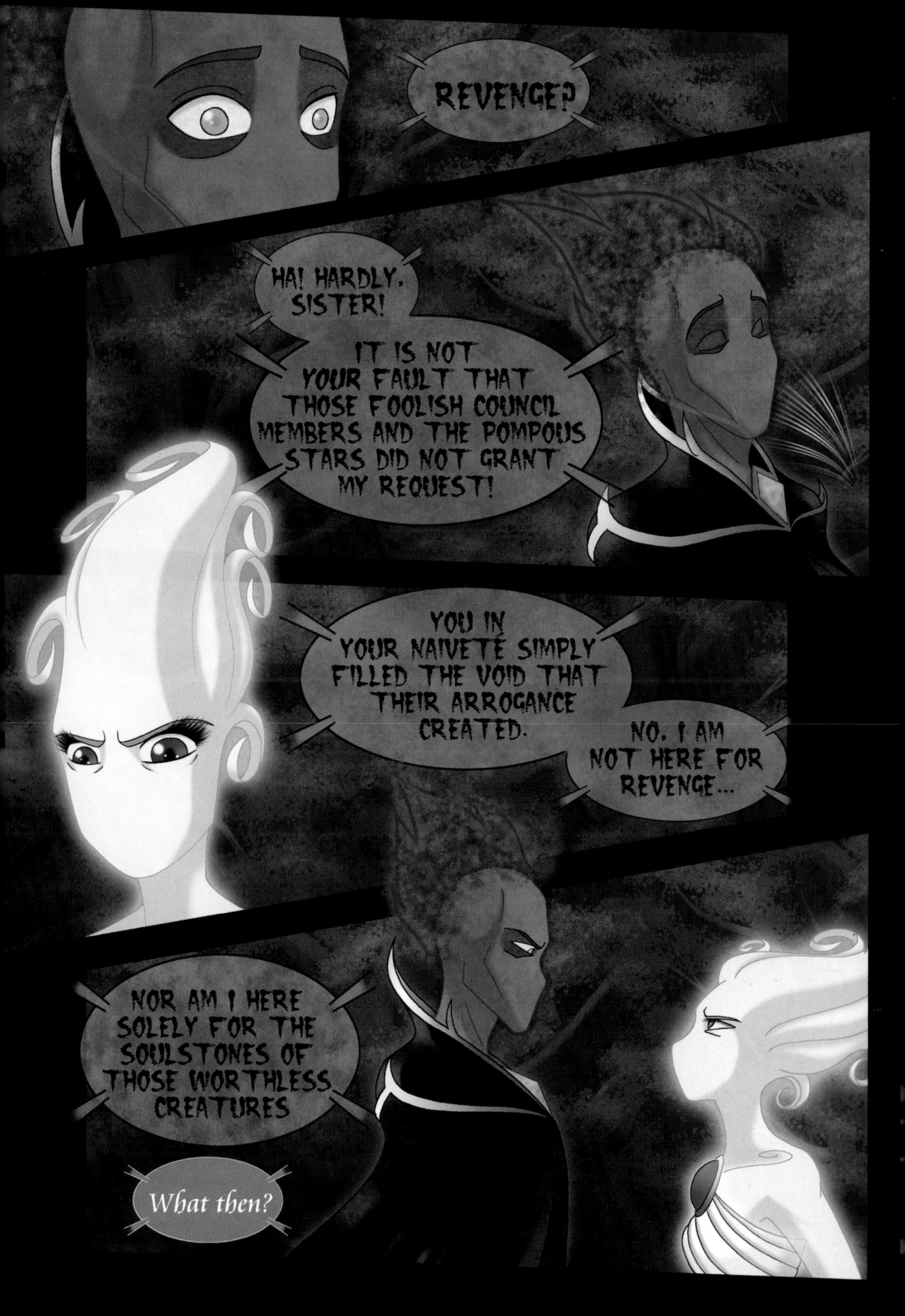
REVENGE?
HA! HARDLY, SISTER!
IT IS NOT YOUR FAULT THAT THOSE FOOLISH COUNCIL MEMBERS AND THE POMPOUS STARS DID NOT GRANT MY REQUEST!
YOU IN YOUR NAIVETÉ SIMPLY FILLED THE VOID THAT THEIR ARROGANCE CREATED.
NO. I AM NOT HERE FOR REVENGE...
NOR AM I HERE SOLELY FOR THE SOULSTONES OF THOSE WORTHLESS CREATURES
What then?

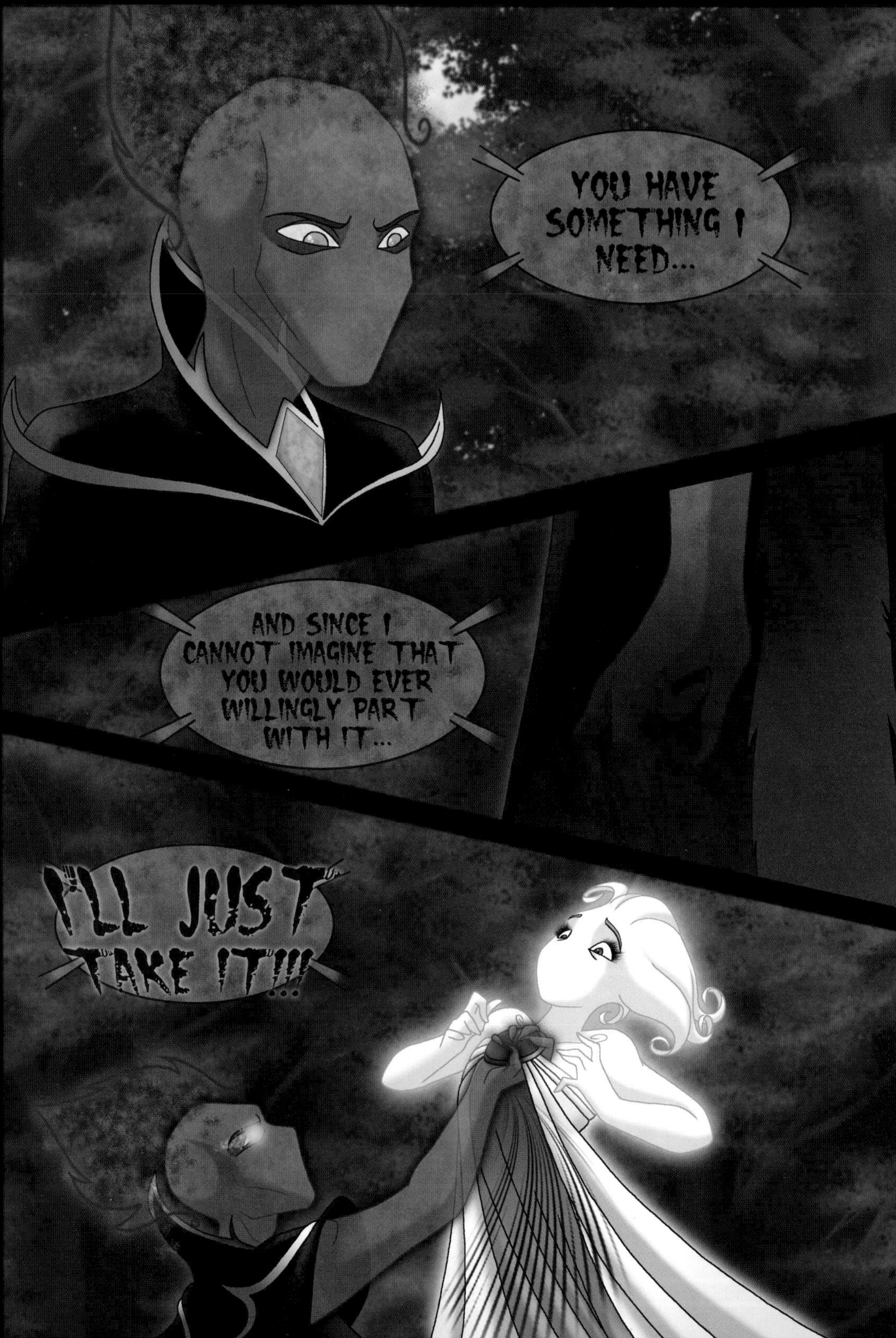
YOU HAVE SOMETHING I NEED...
AND SINCE I CANNOT IMAGINE THAT YOU WOULD EVER WILLINGLY PART WITH IT...
I'LL JUST TAKE IT!!!

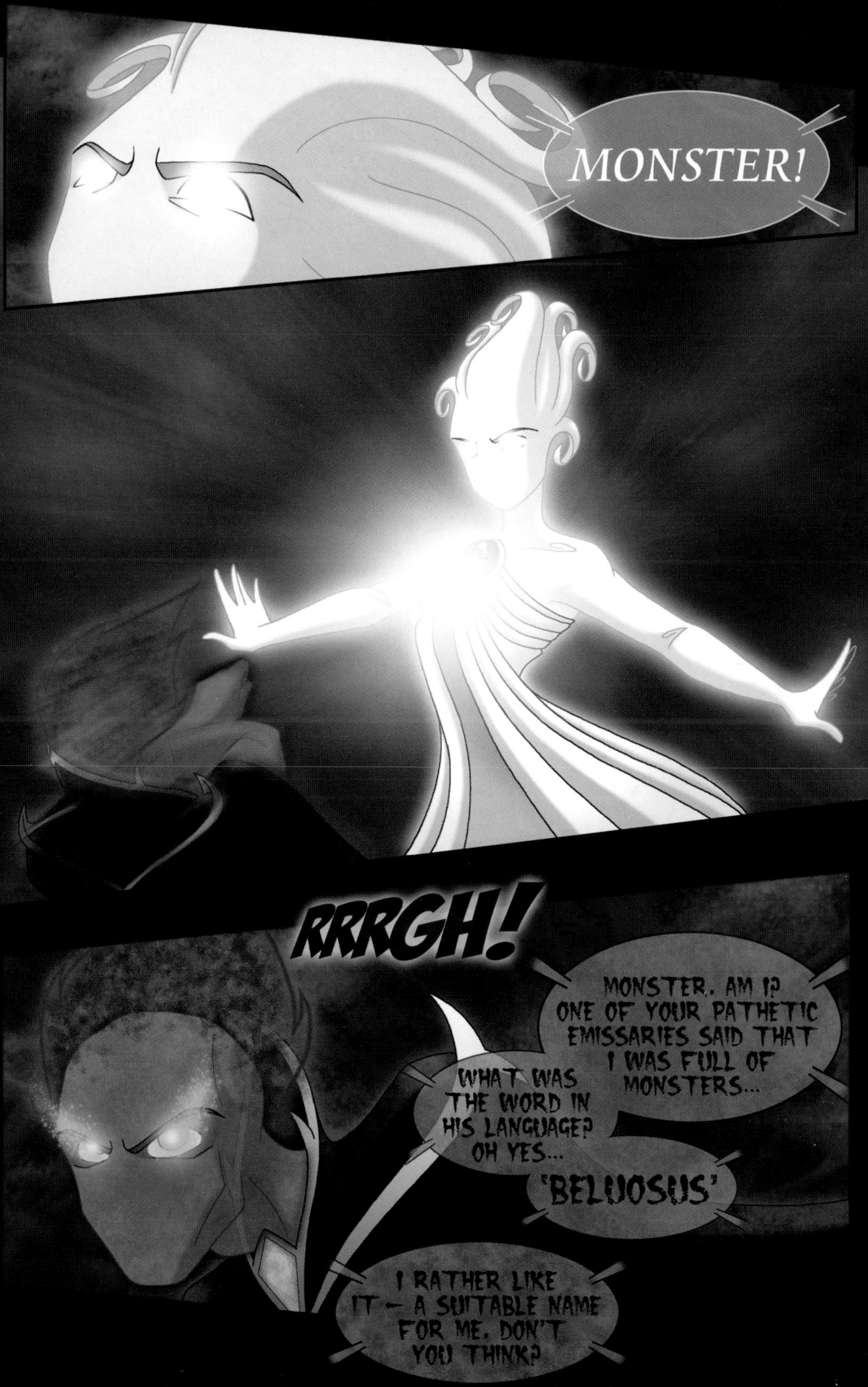
MONSTER!
RRRGH!
MONSTER, AM I? ONE OF YOUR PATHETIC EMISSARIES SAID THAT I WAS FULL OF MONSTERS...
WHAT WAS THE WORD IN HIS LANGUAGE? OH YES...
'BELUOSUS'
I RATHER LIKE IT – A SUITABLE NAME FOR ME, DON'T YOU THINK?

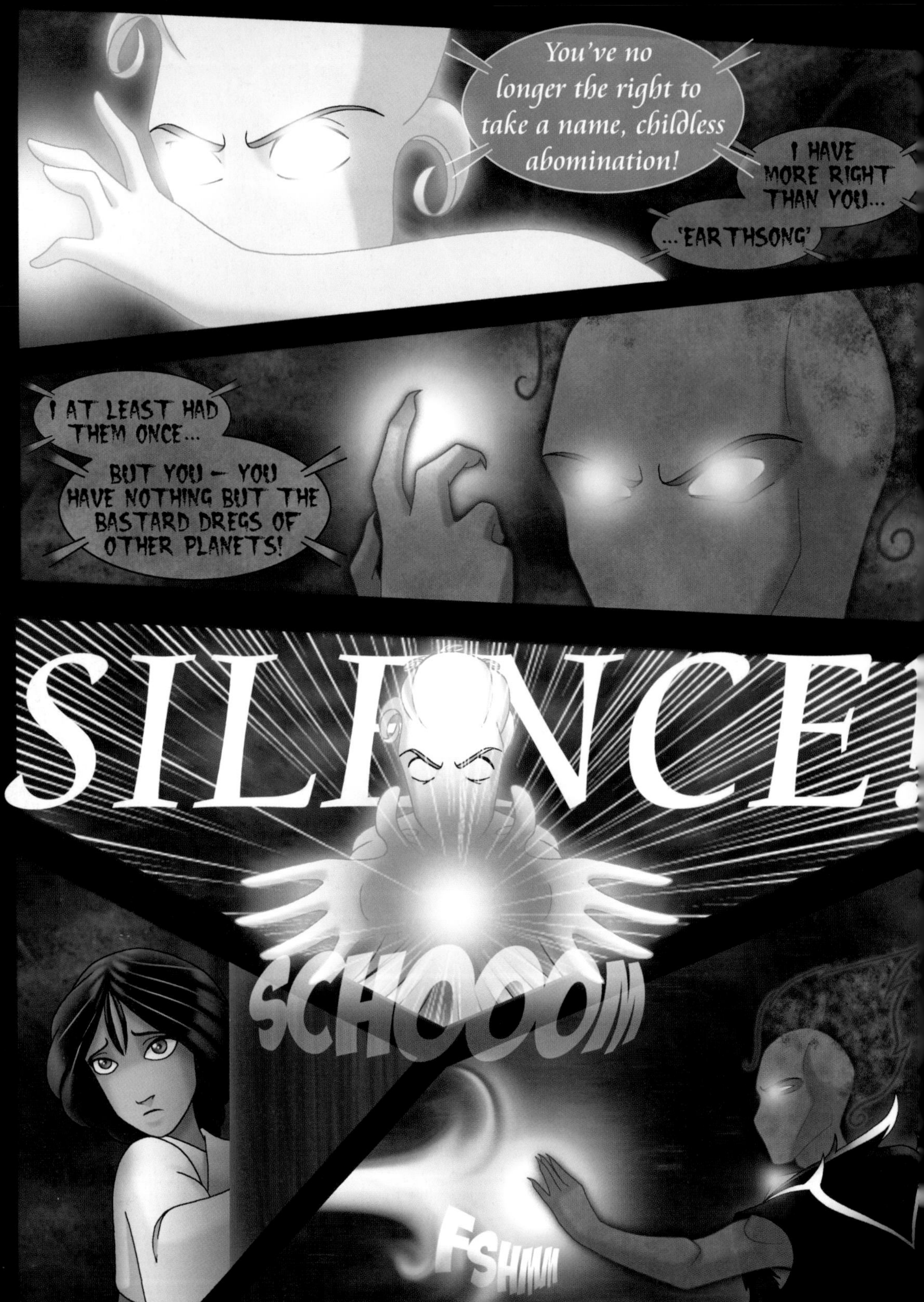

You've no longer the right to take a name, childless abomination!
I HAVE MORE RIGHT THAN YOU...
...'EARTHSONG'
I AT LEAST HAD THEM ONCE...
BUT YOU – YOU HAVE NOTHING BUT THE BASTARD DREGS OF OTHER PLANETS!
SILENCE!
SCHOOOM
FSHMM

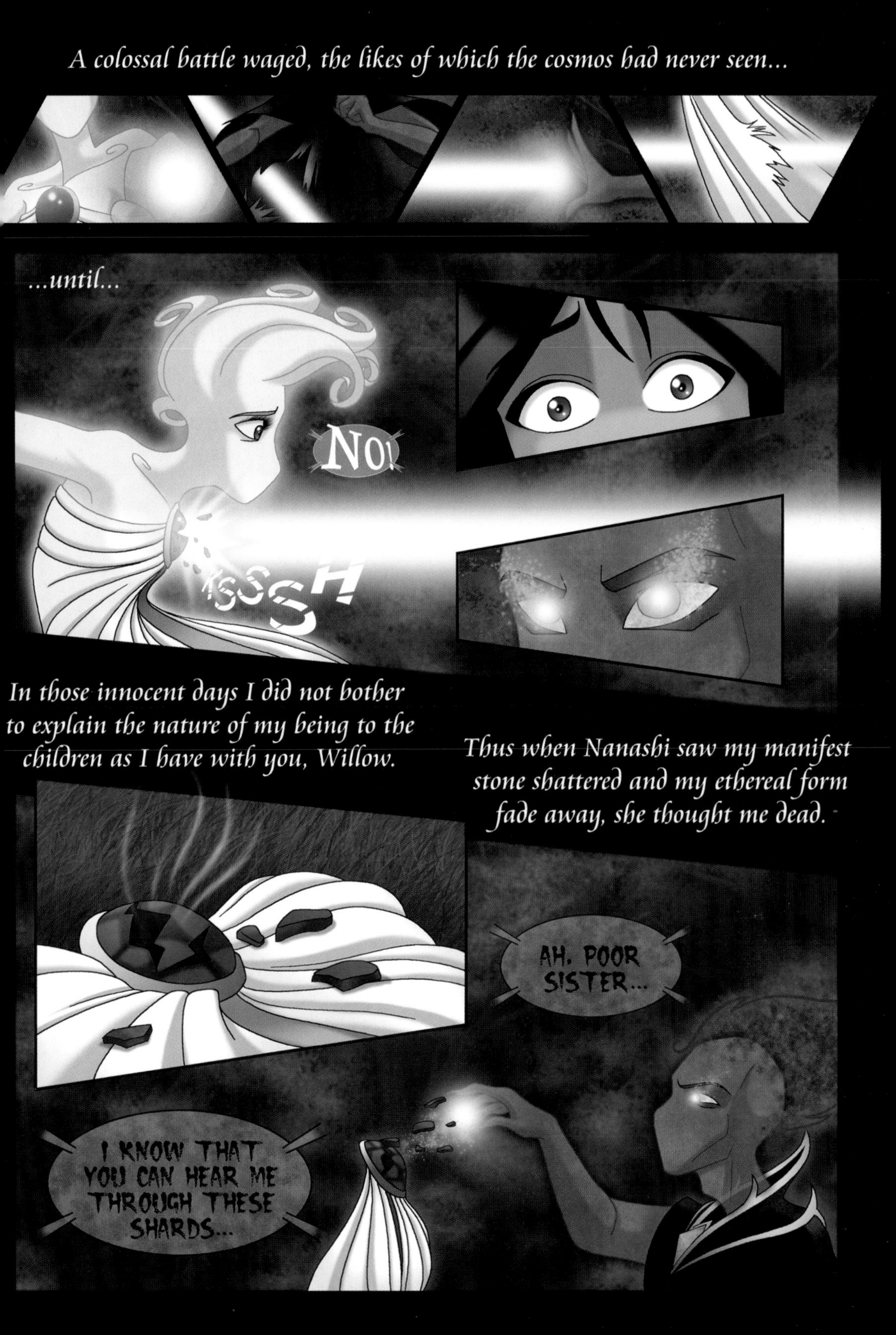

A colossal battle waged, the likes of which the cosmos had never seen...
...until...
NO!
KSSSSH!
In those innocent days I did not bother to explain the nature of my being to the children as I have with you, Willow.
Thus when Nanashi saw my manifest stone shattered and my ethereal form fade away, she thought me dead.
AH, POOR SISTER...
I KNOW THAT YOU CAN HEAR ME THROUGH THESE SHARDS...

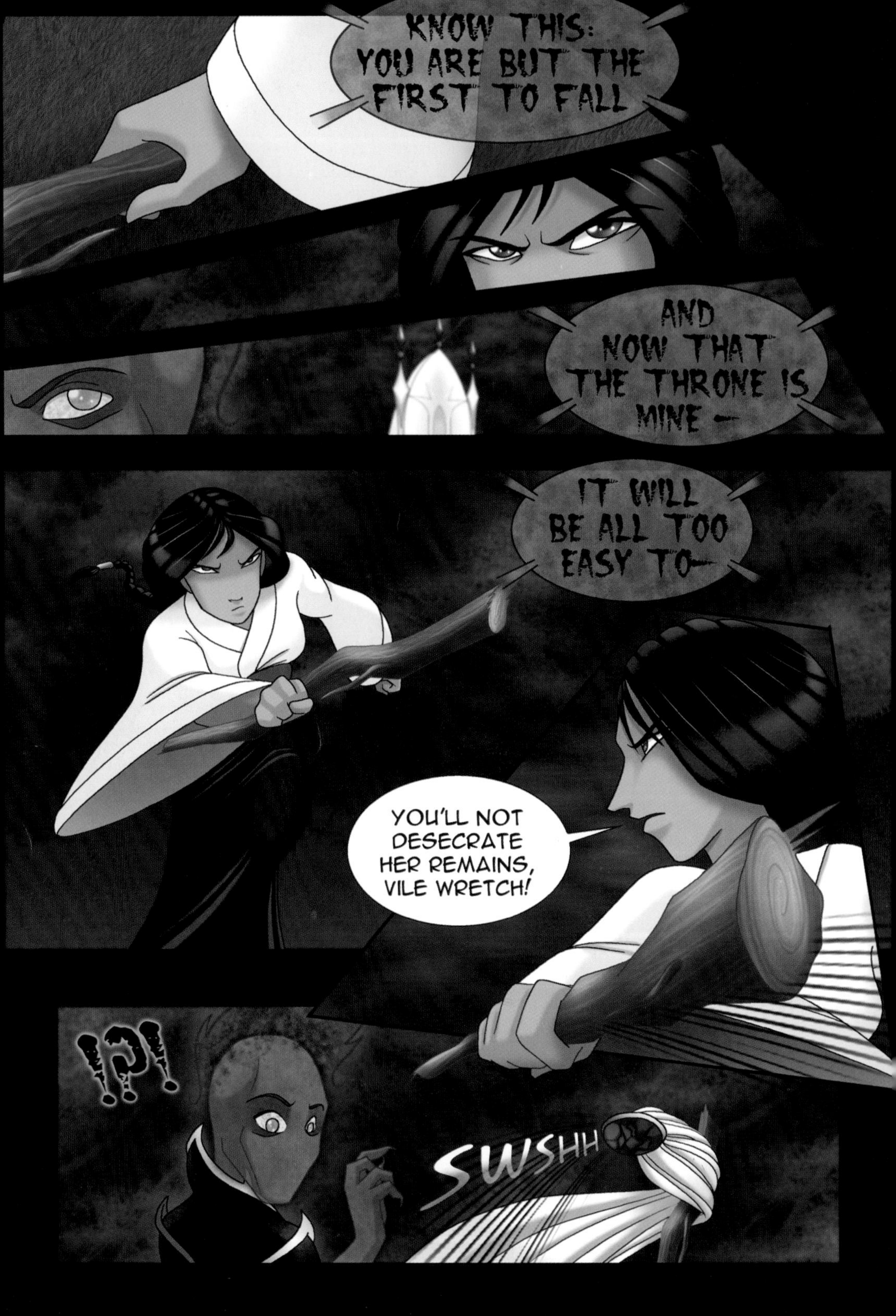
KNOW THIS: YOU ARE BUT THE FIRST TO FALL
AND NOW THAT THE THRONE IS MINE –
IT WILL BE ALL TOO EASY TO–
YOU'LL NOT DESECRATE HER REMAINS, VILE WRETCH!
!?!
SWSHH

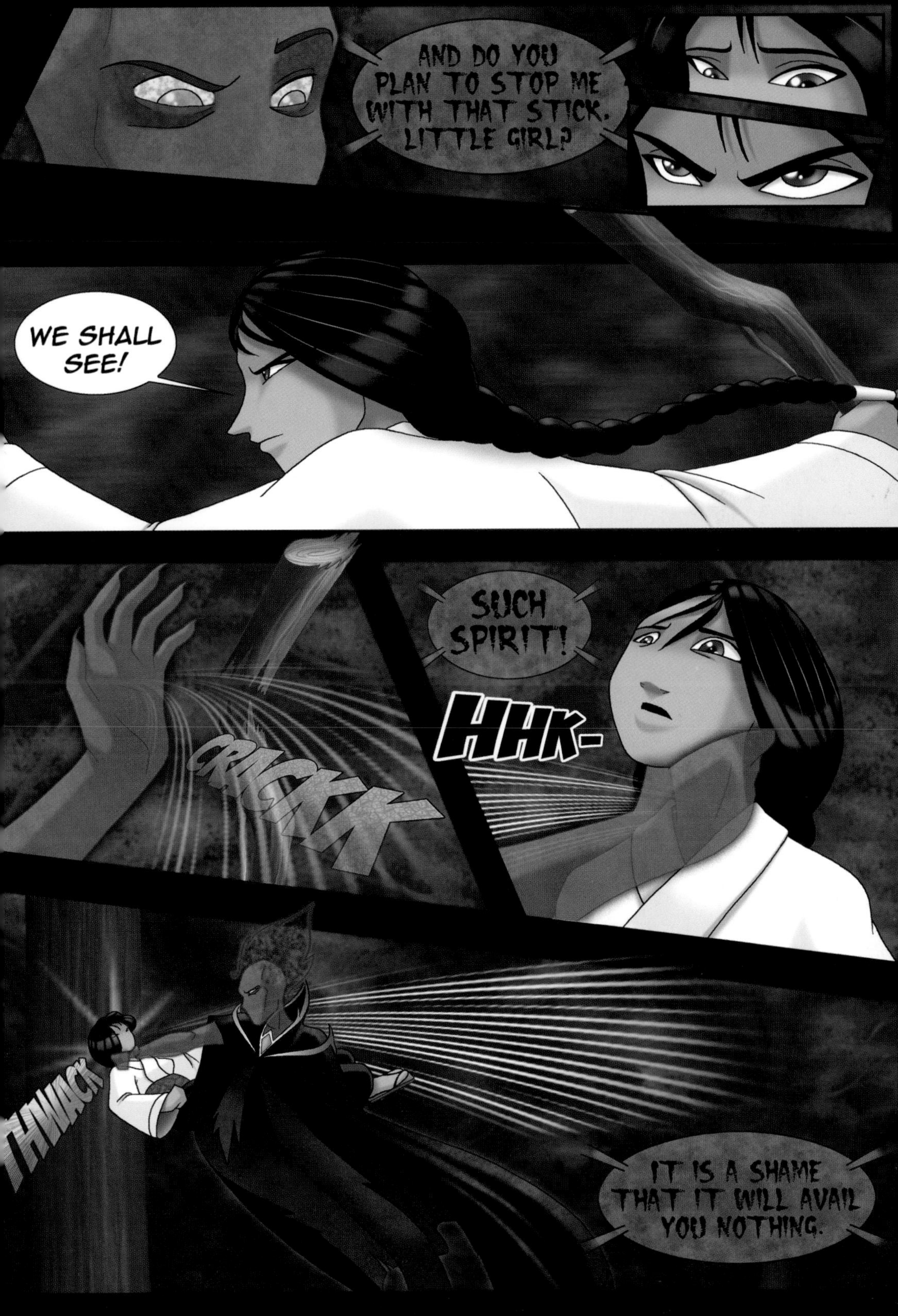
AND DO YOU PLAN TO STOP ME WITH THAT STICK, LITTLE GIRL?
WE SHALL SEE!
CRACKK
SUCH SPIRIT!
HHK-
THWACK
IT IS A SHAME THAT IT WILL AVAIL YOU NOTHING.

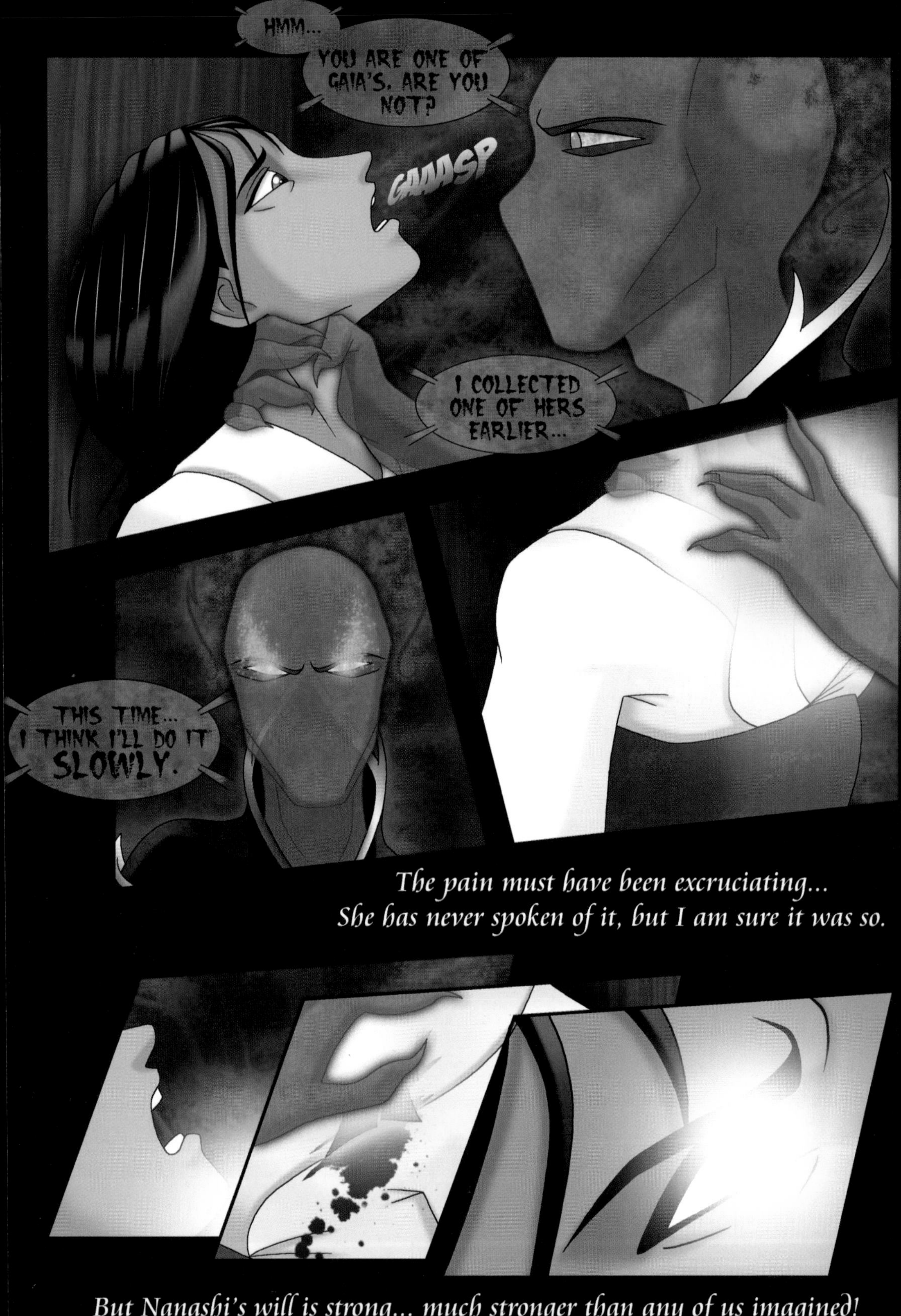
HMM...
YOU ARE ONE OF GAIA'S, ARE YOU NOT?
GAAASP
I COLLECTED ONE OF HERS EARLIER...
THIS TIME... I THINK I'LL DO IT SLOWLY.
The pain must have been excruciating...
She has never spoken of it, but I am sure it was so.
But Nanashi's will is strong... much stronger than any of us imagined!

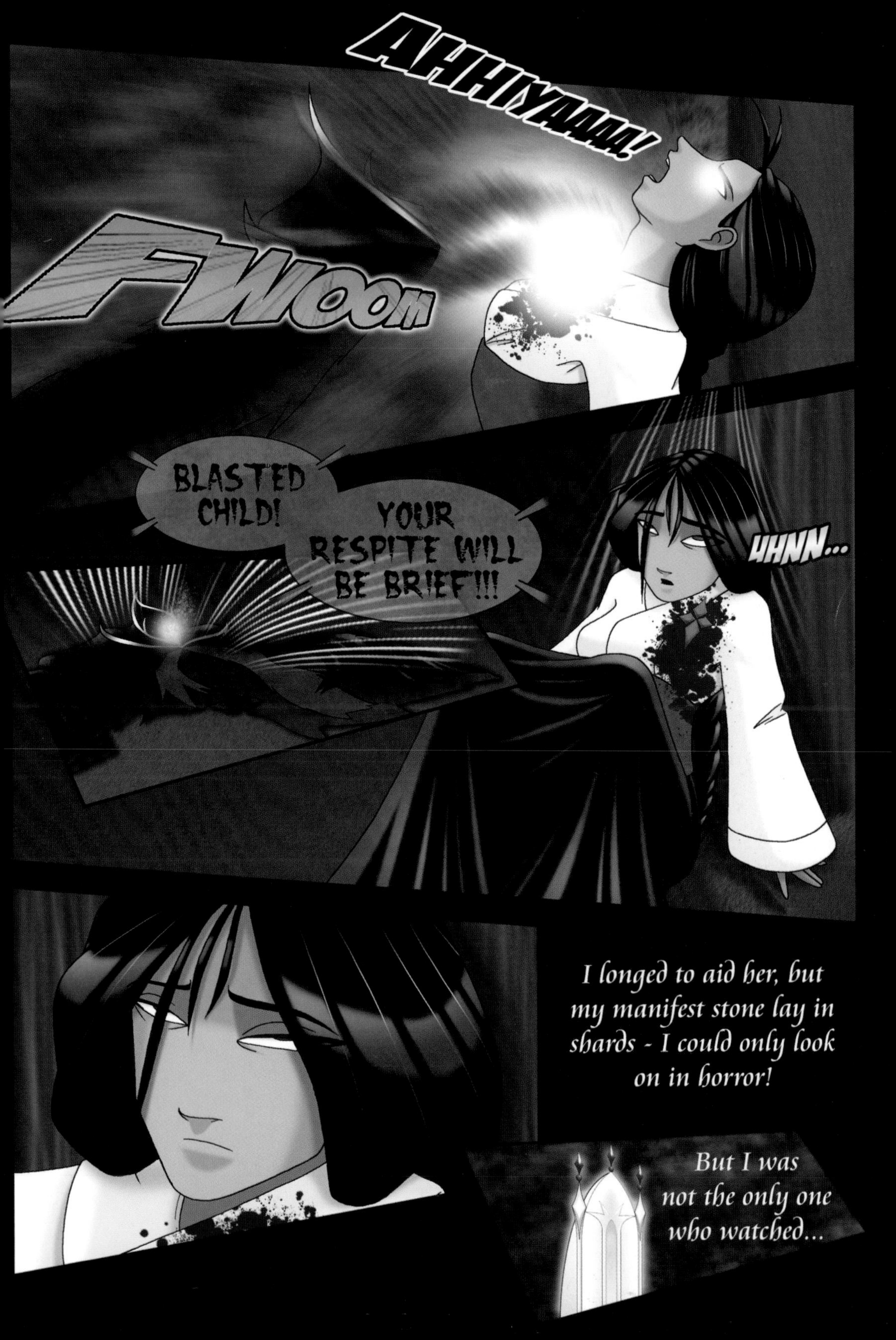
AHHIYAAAA!
FWOOM
BLASTED CHILD!
YOUR RESPITE WILL BE BRIEF!!!
UHNN...
I longed to aid her, but my manifest stone lay in shards - I could only look on in horror!
But I was not the only one who watched...

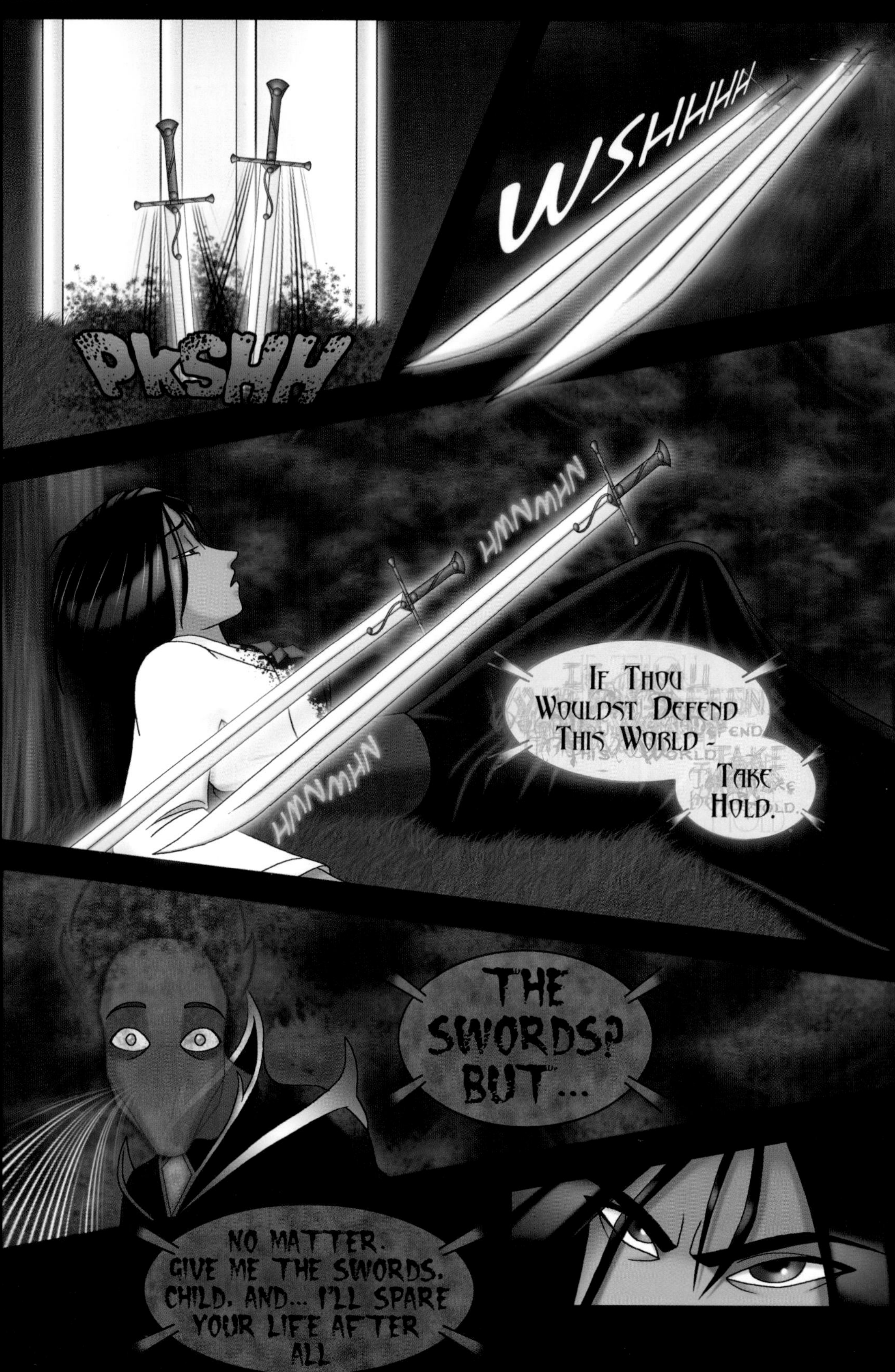
PKSHH
WSHHHH
HMNMHN
HMNMHN
HMNMHN
If Thou Wouldst Defend This World -
Take Hold.
THE SWORDS? BUT...
NO MATTER. GIVE ME THE SWORDS, CHILD, AND... I'LL SPARE YOUR LIFE AFTER ALL

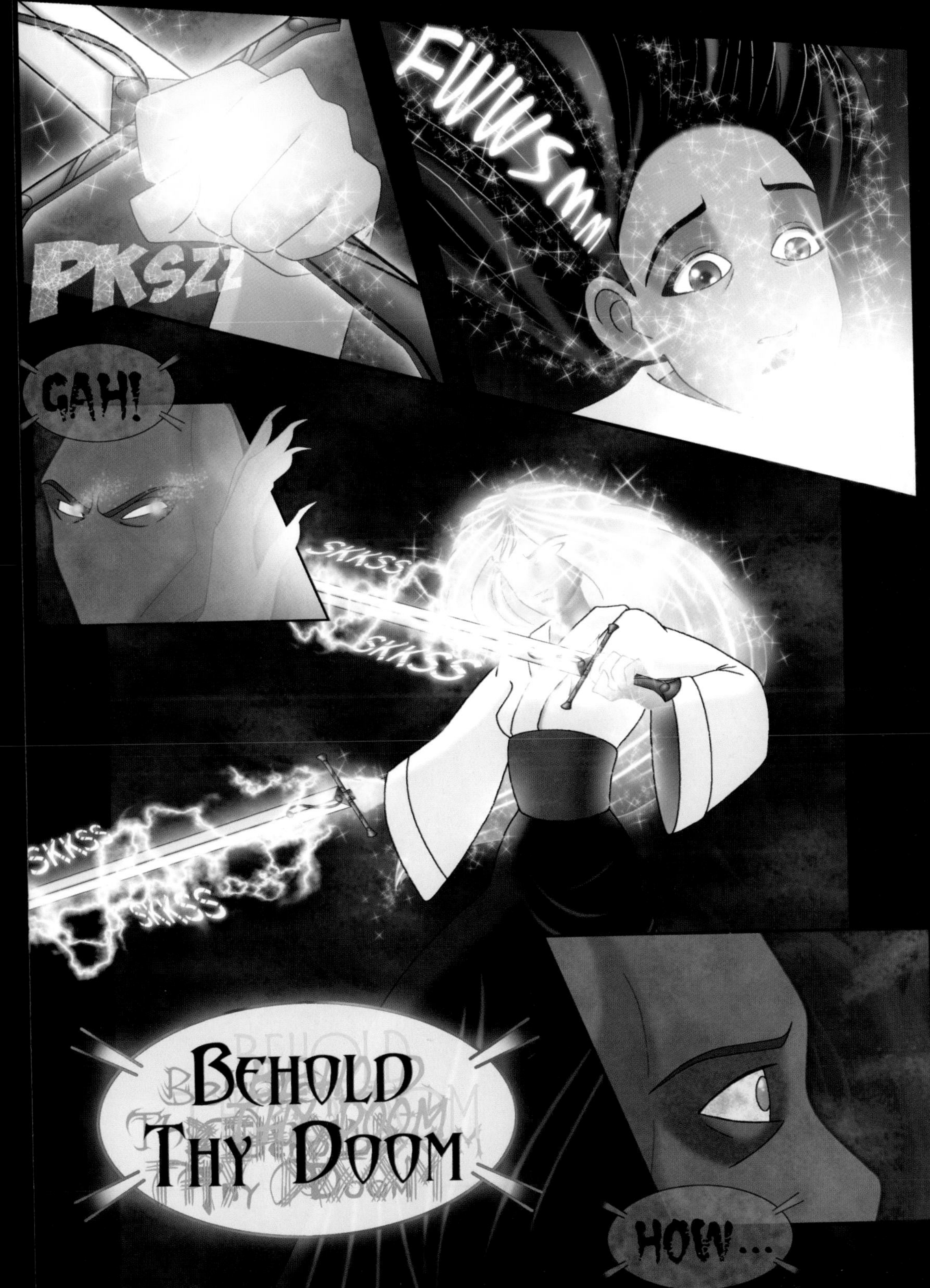
PKSZZ
FWWSMM
GAH!
SKKSS
SKKSS
SKKSS
SKKSS
BEHOLD THY DOOM
HOW...

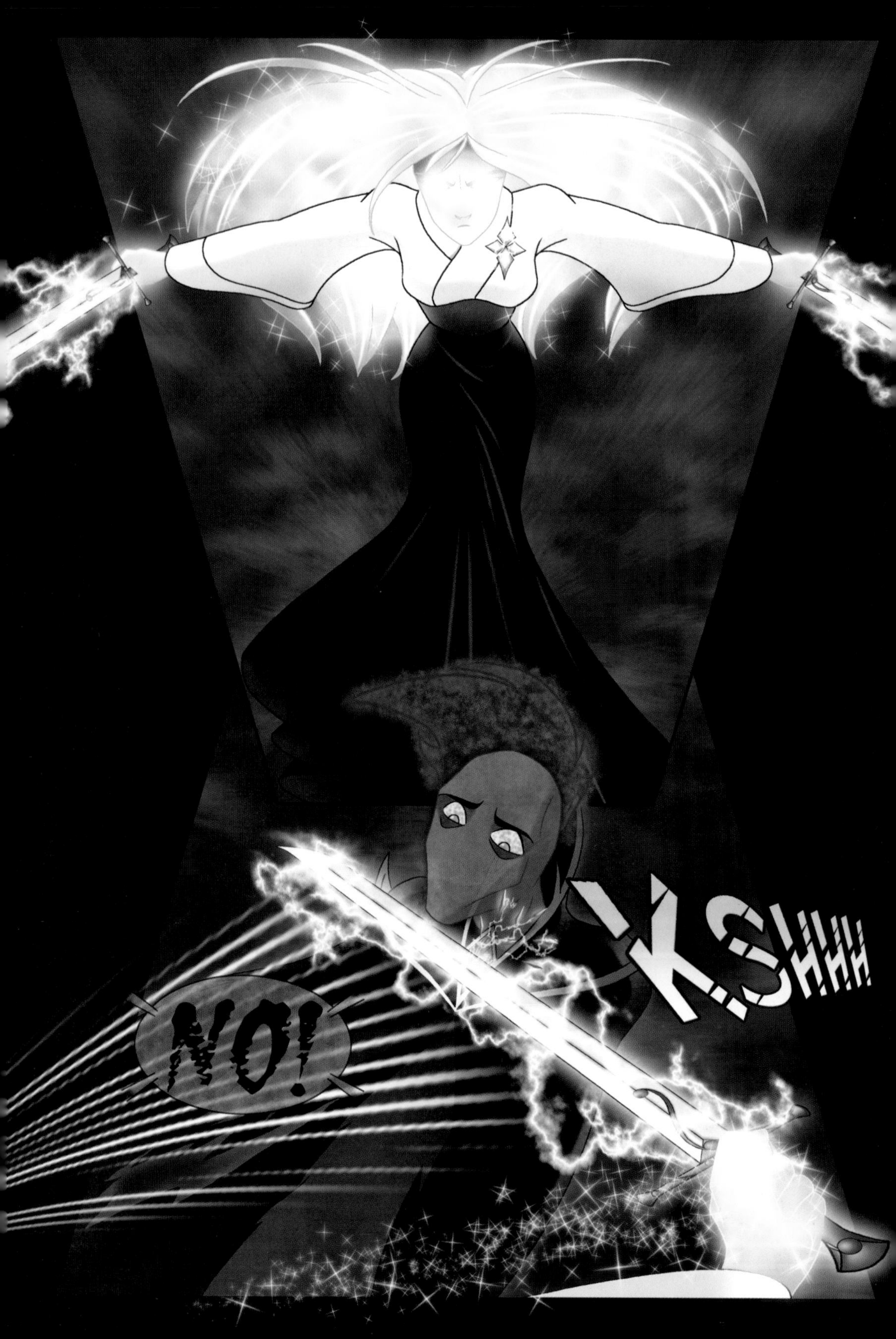
NO!
KSHHHH

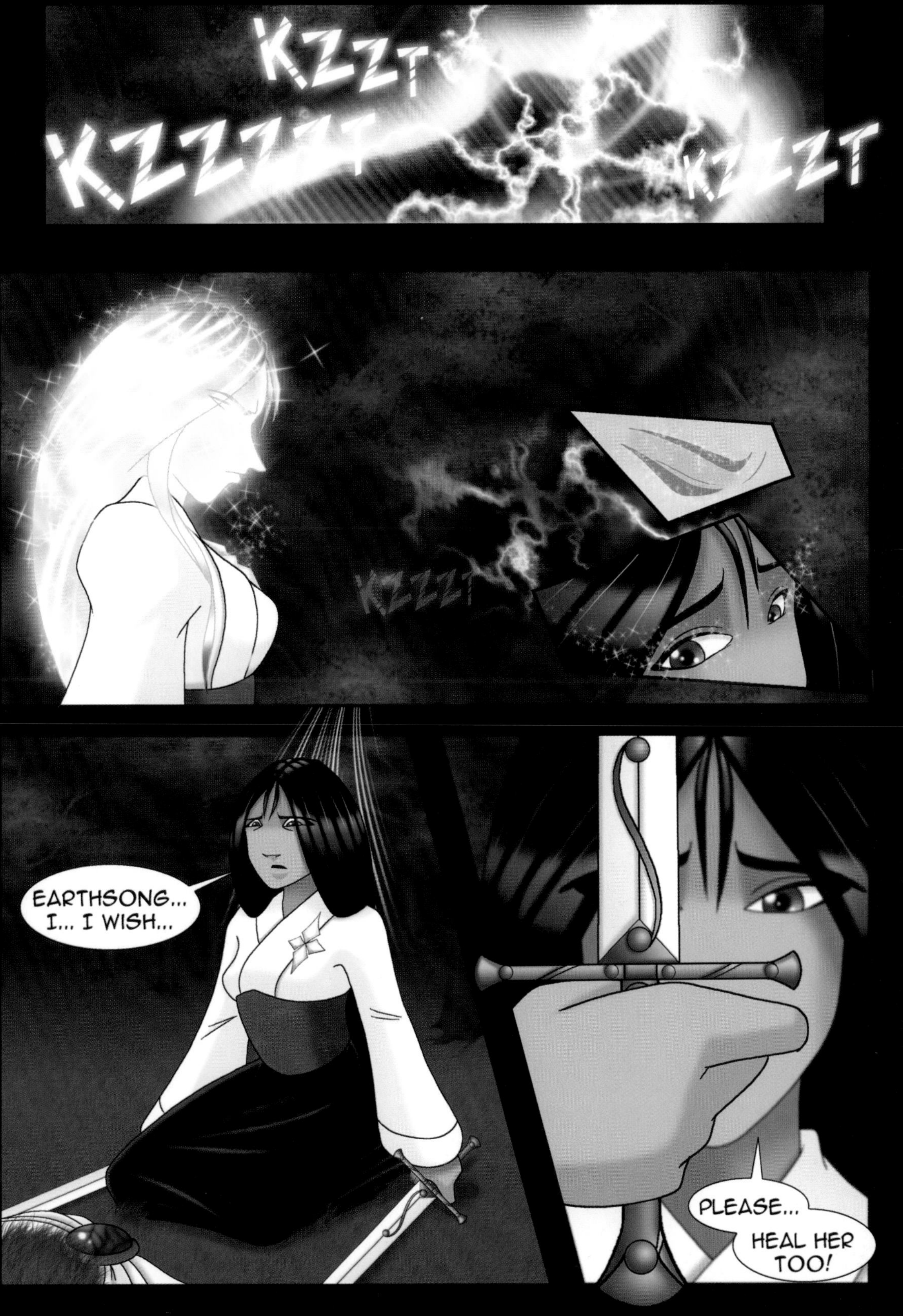
KZZZT
KZZZZZT
KZZZZT
KZZZT
EARTHSONG... I... I WISH...
PLEASE... HEAL HER TOO!

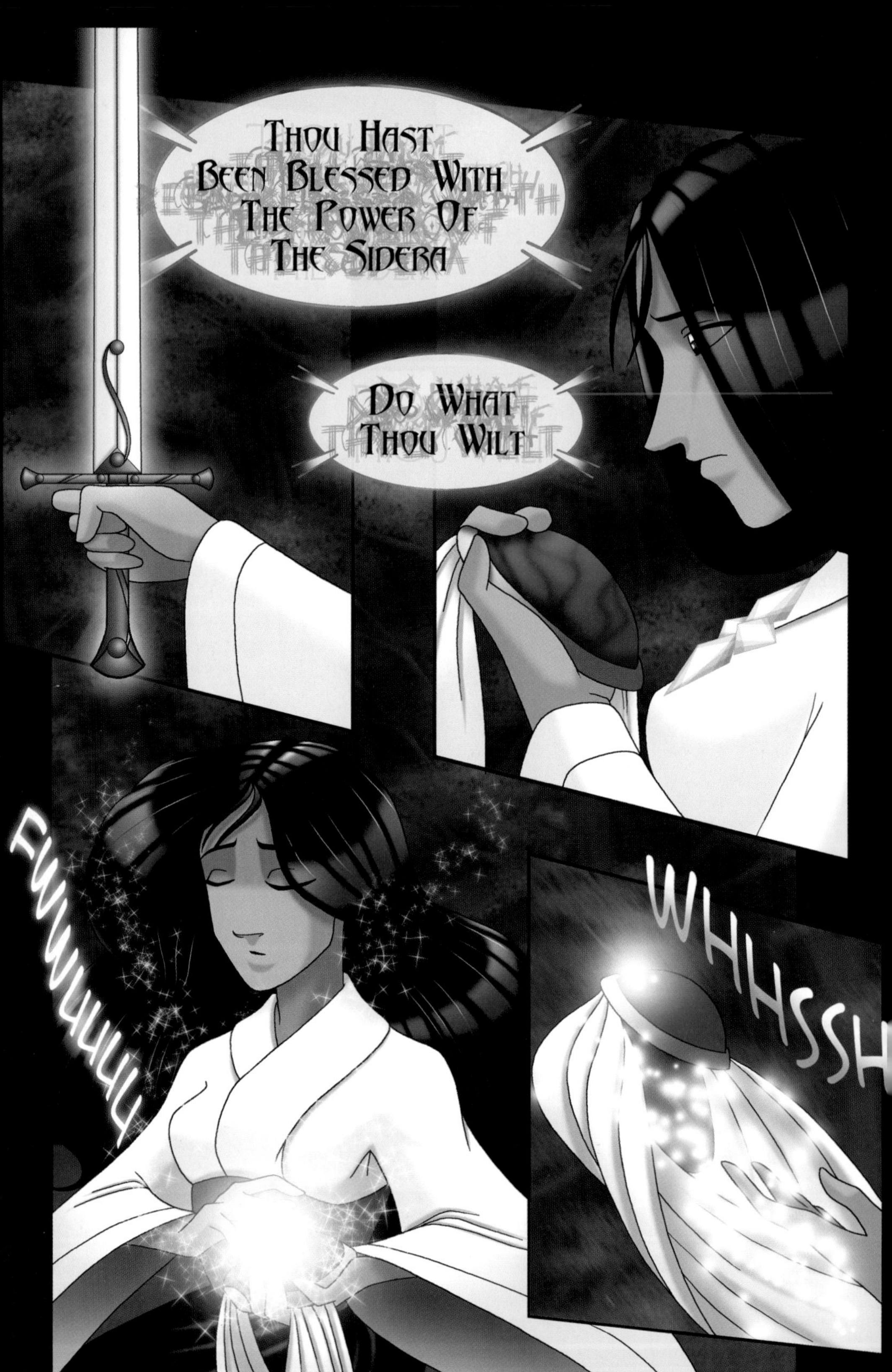
Thou Hast Been Blessed With The Power Of The Sidera
Do What Thou Wilt
FWUUUUU
WHHSSH

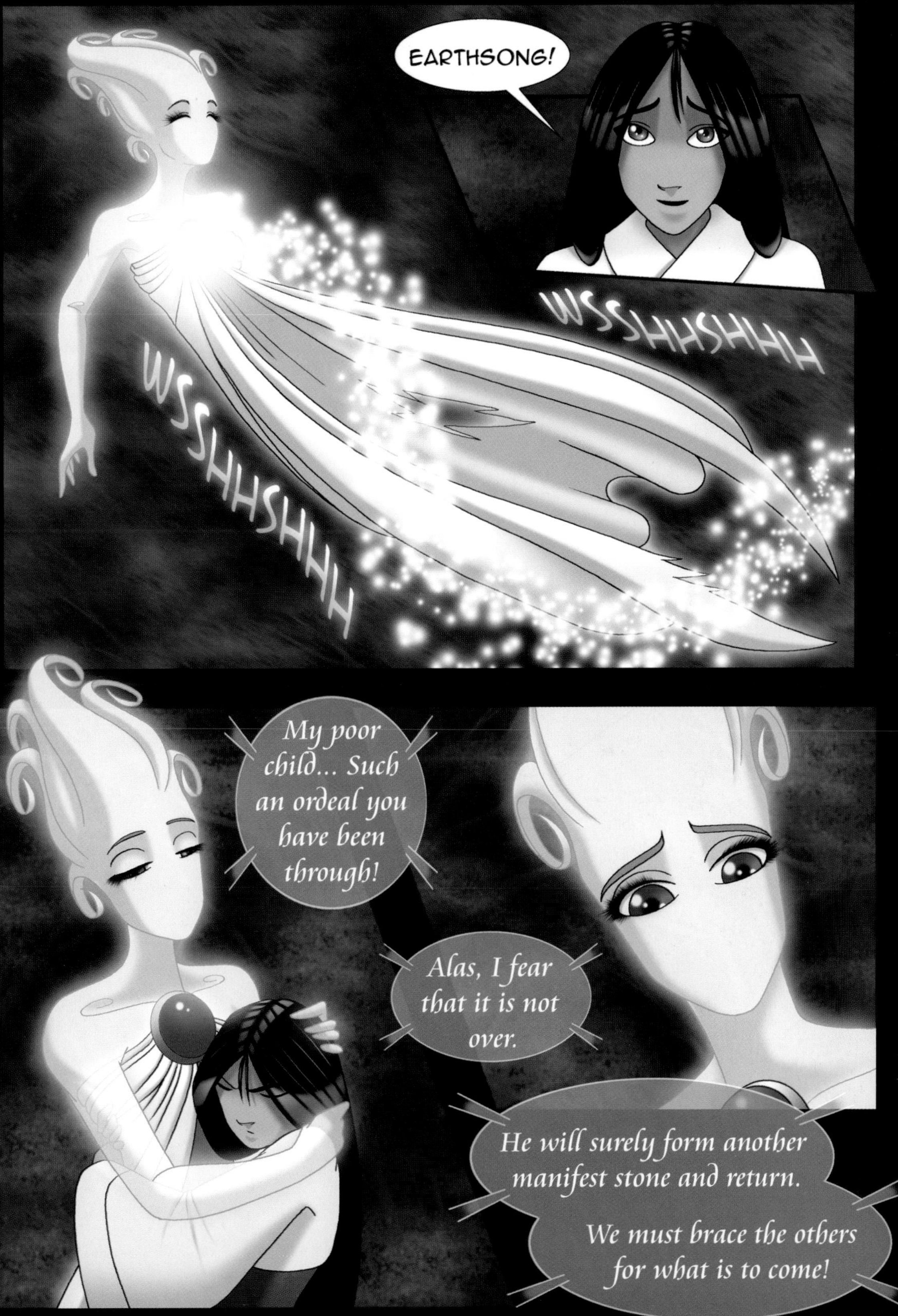
EARTHSONG!
WSSHHSHHH
WSSHHSHHH
My poor child... Such an ordeal you have been through!
Alas, I fear that it is not over.
He will surely form another manifest stone and return.
We must brace the others for what is to come!

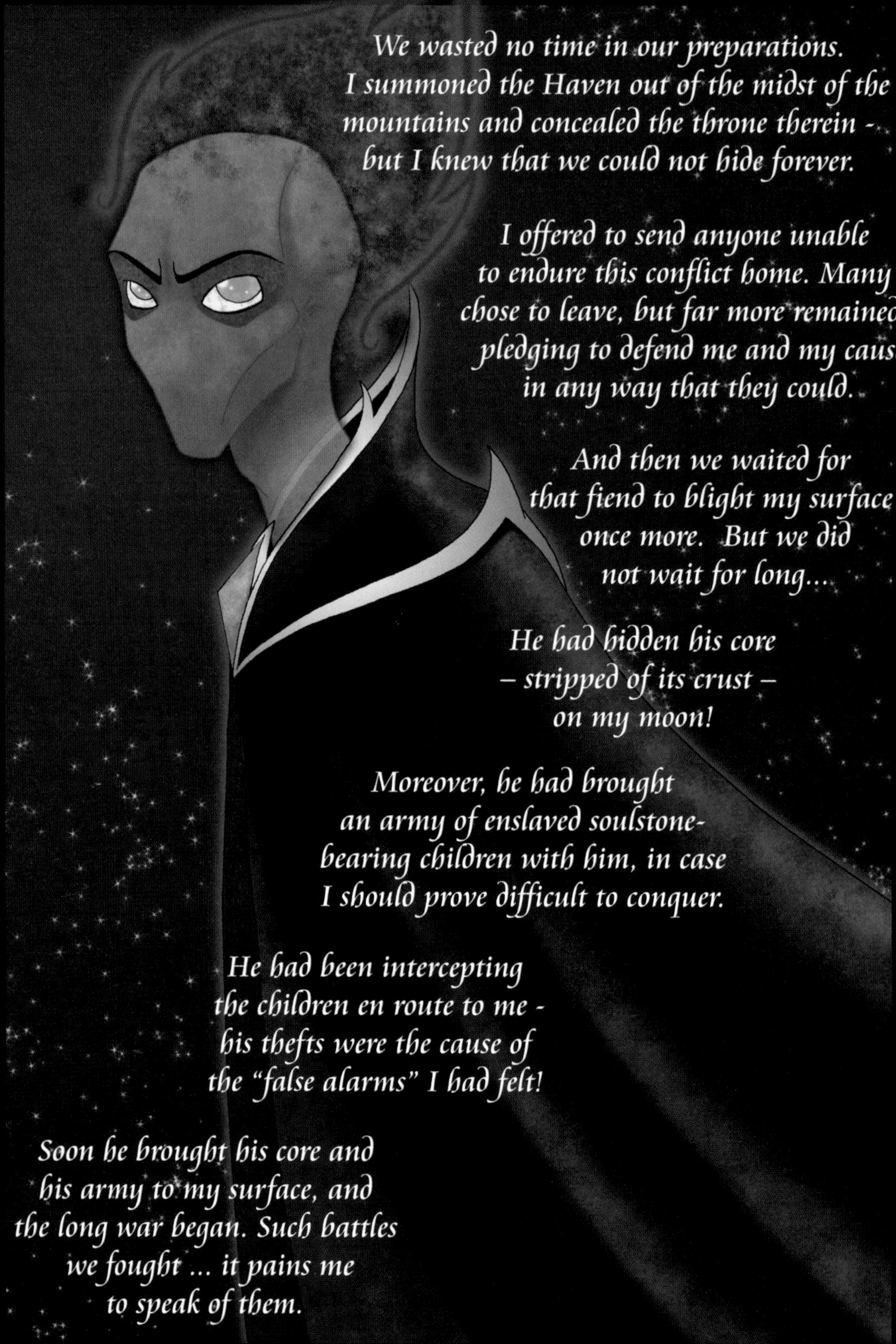

We wasted no time in our preparations.
I summoned the Haven out of the midst of the mountains and concealed the throne therein - but I knew that we could not hide forever.

I offered to send anyone unable to endure this conflict home. Many chose to leave, but far more remained, pledging to defend me and my cause in any way that they could.

And then we waited for that fiend to blight my surface once more. But we did not wait for long...

He had hidden his core – stripped of its crust – on my moon!

Moreover, he had brought an army of enslaved soulstone-bearing children with him, in case I should prove difficult to conquer.

He had been intercepting the children en route to me - his thefts were the cause of the "false alarms" I had felt!

Soon he brought his core and his army to my surface, and the long war began. Such battles we fought ... it pains me to speak of them.

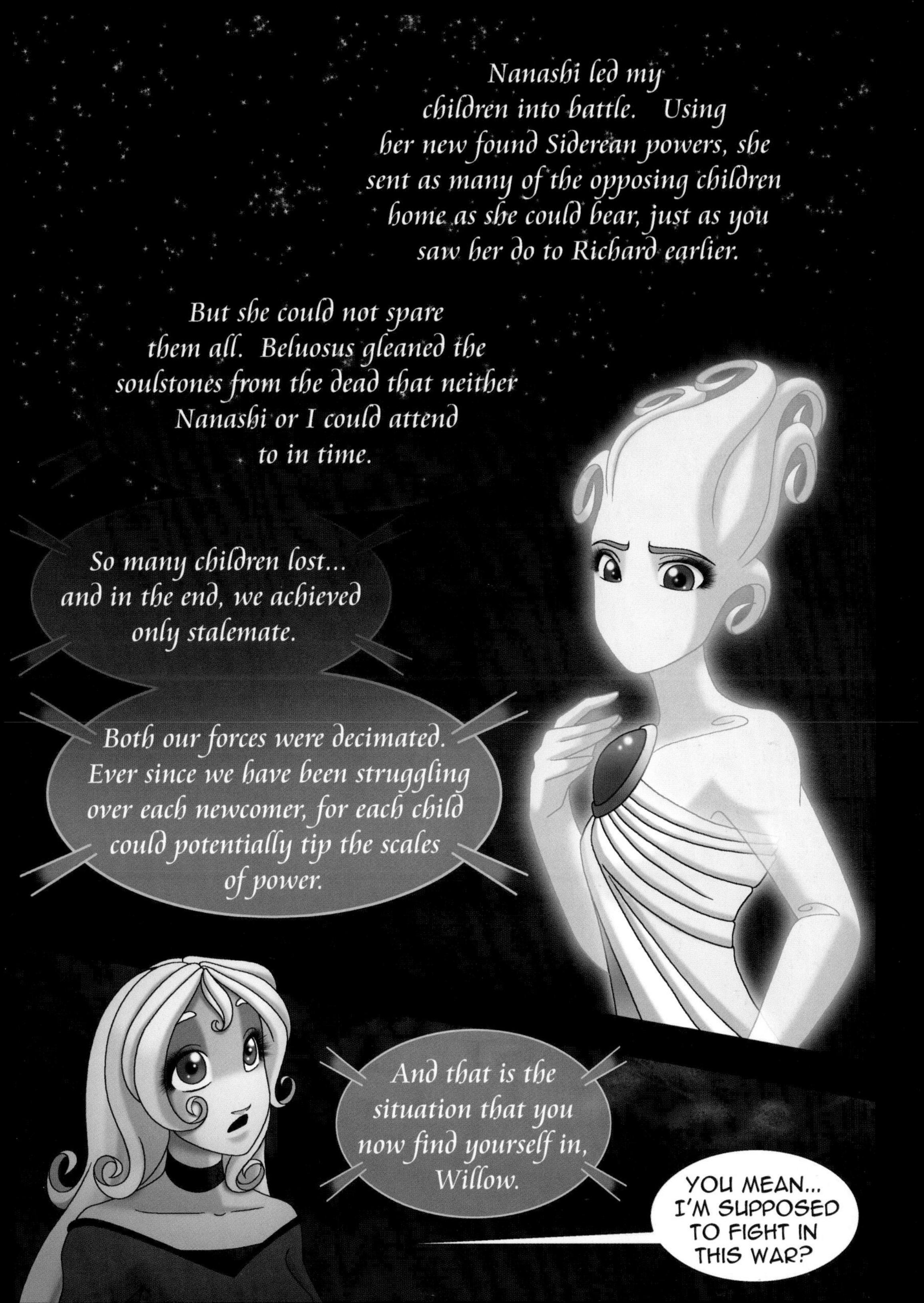
Nanashi led my children into battle. Using her new found Siderean powers, she sent as many of the opposing children home as she could bear, just as you saw her do to Richard earlier.
But she could not spare them all. Beluosus gleaned the soulstones from the dead that neither Nanashi or I could attend to in time.
So many children lost... and in the end, we achieved only stalemate.
Both our forces were decimated. Ever since we have been struggling over each newcomer, for each child could potentially tip the scales of power.
And that is the situation that you now find yourself in, Willow.
YOU MEAN... I'M SUPPOSED TO FIGHT IN THIS WAR?

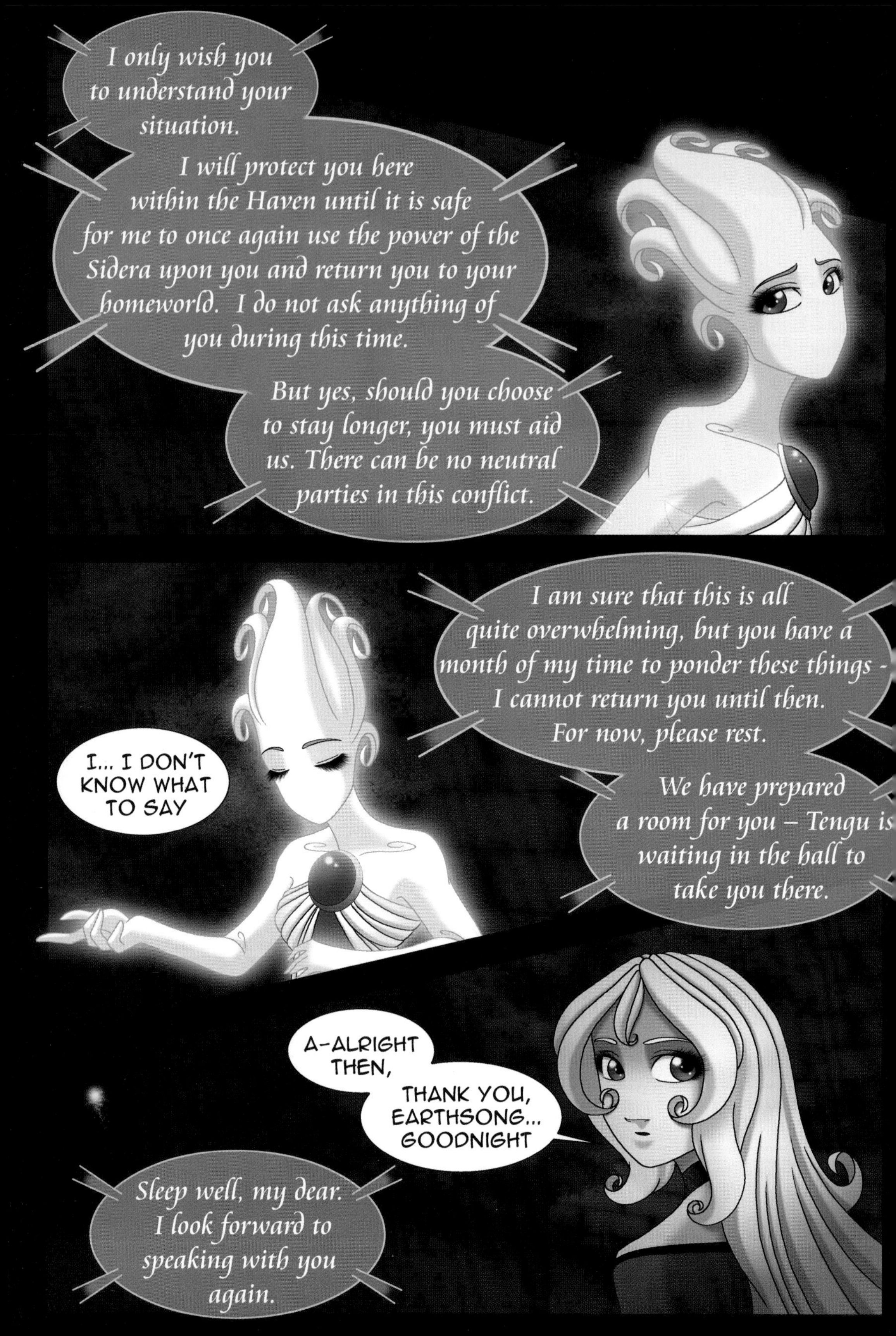
I only wish you to understand your situation.
I will protect you here within the Haven until it is safe for me to once again use the power of the Sidera upon you and return you to your homeworld. I do not ask anything of you during this time.
But yes, should you choose to stay longer, you must aid us. There can be no neutral parties in this conflict.
I am sure that this is all quite overwhelming, but you have a month of my time to ponder these things - I cannot return you until then. For now, please rest.
I... I DON'T KNOW WHAT TO SAY
We have prepared a room for you – Tengu is waiting in the hall to take you there.
A-ALRIGHT THEN,
THANK YOU, EARTHSONG... GOODNIGHT
Sleep well, my dear. I look forward to speaking with you again.

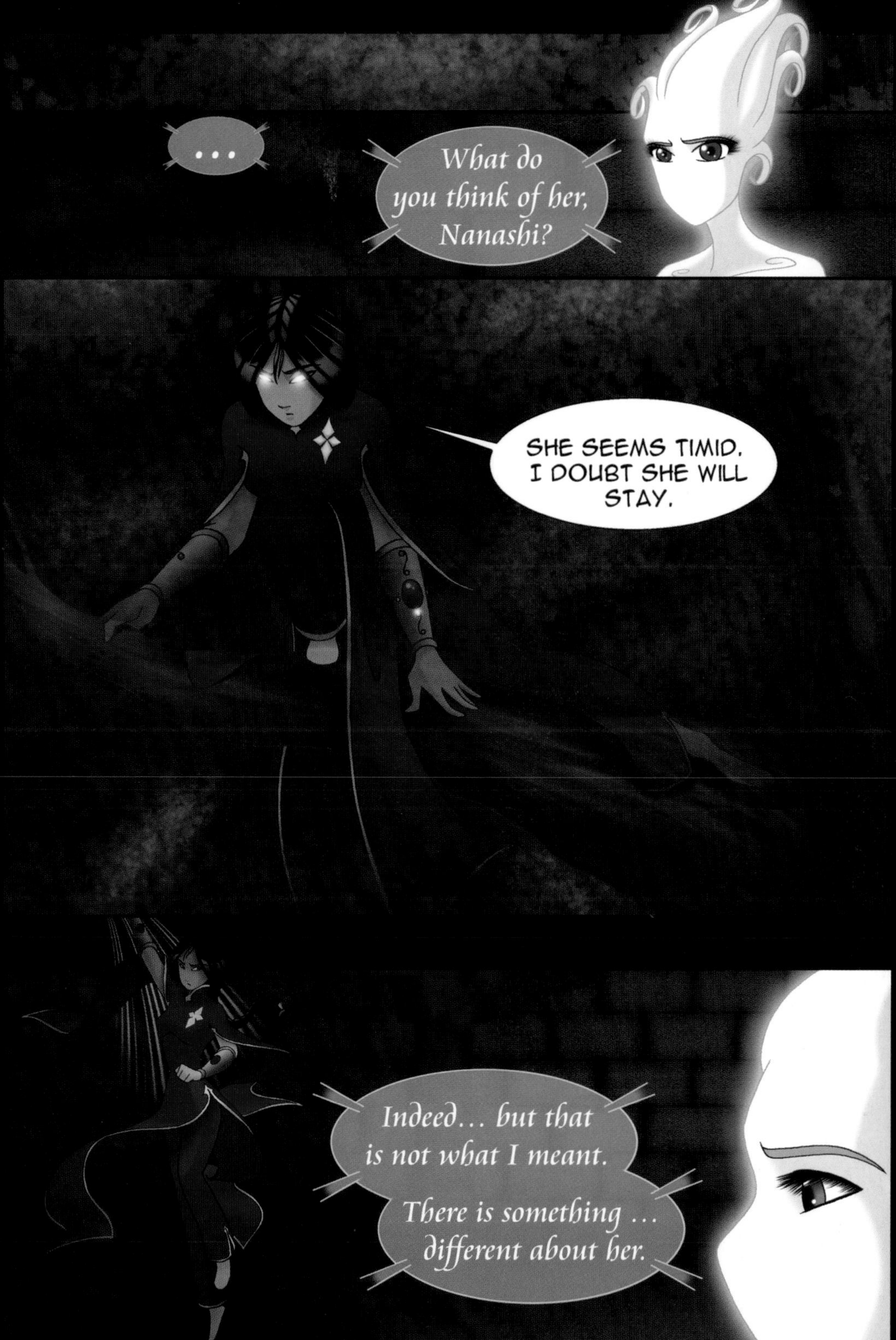
...
What do you think of her, Nanashi?
SHE SEEMS TIMID. I DOUBT SHE WILL STAY.
Indeed... but that is not what I meant.
There is something ... different about her.

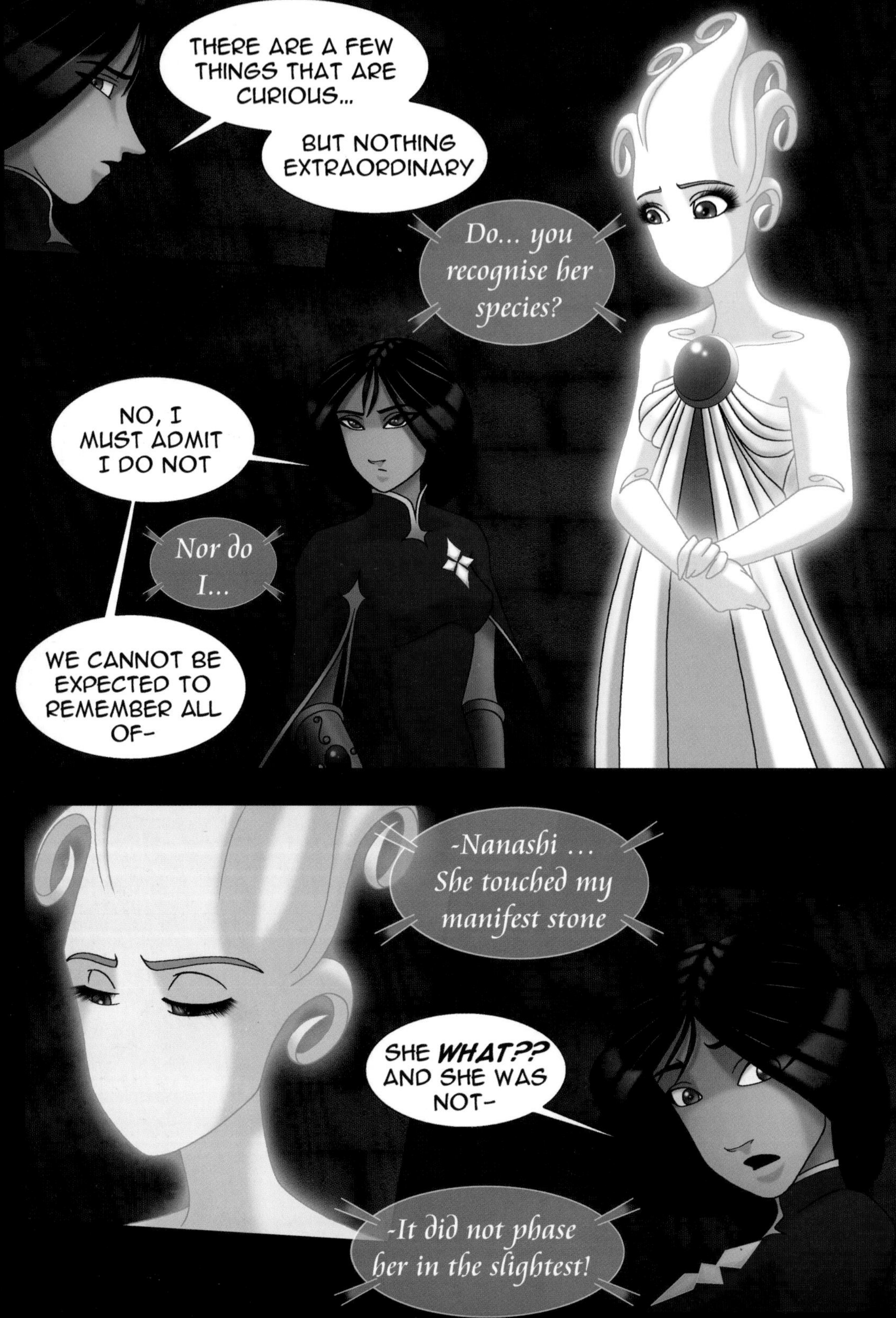
THERE ARE A FEW THINGS THAT ARE CURIOUS...
BUT NOTHING EXTRAORDINARY
Do... you recognise her species?
NO, I MUST ADMIT I DO NOT
Nor do I...
WE CANNOT BE EXPECTED TO REMEMBER ALL OF-
-Nanashi ... She touched my manifest stone
SHE *WHAT??* AND SHE WAS NOT-
-It did not phase her in the slightest!

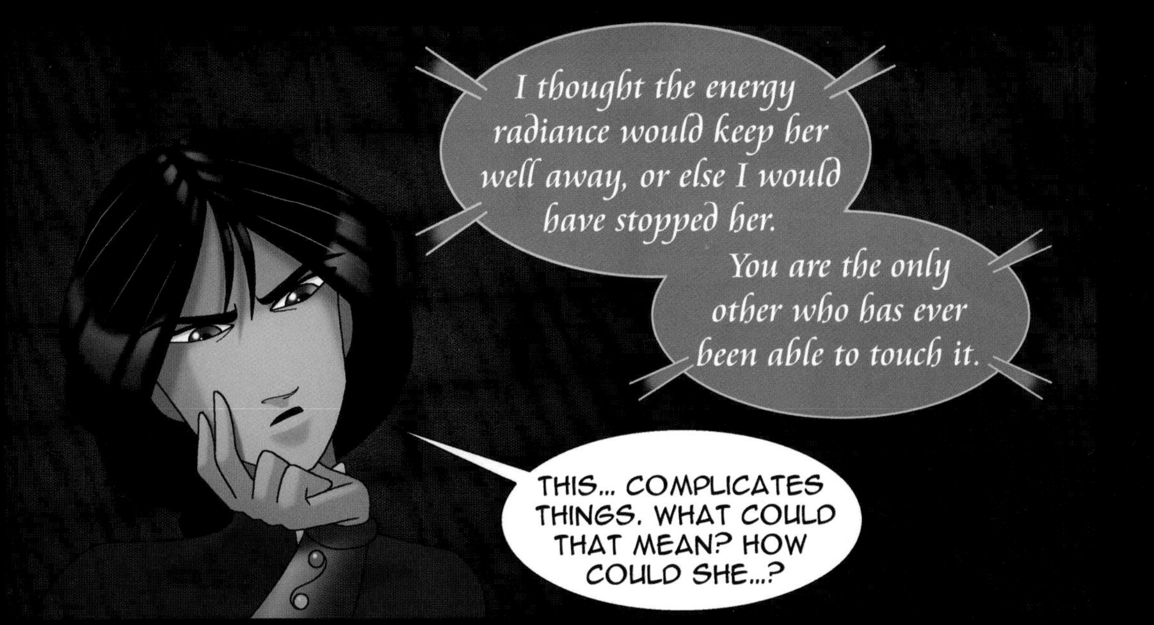
I thought the energy radiance would keep her well away, or else I would have stopped her.
You are the only other who has ever been able to touch it.
THIS... COMPLICATES THINGS. WHAT COULD THAT MEAN? HOW COULD SHE...?

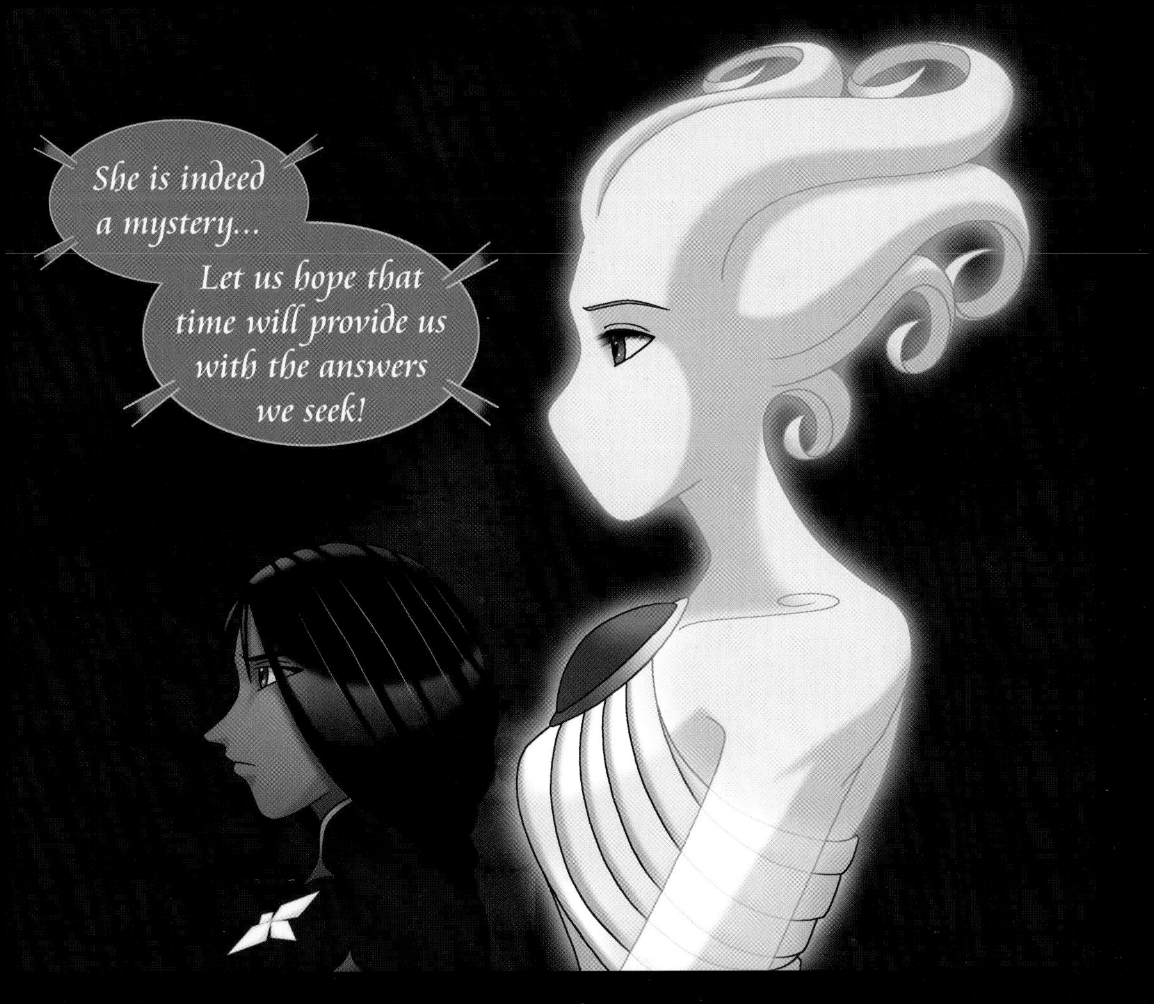
She is indeed a mystery...
Let us hope that time will provide us with the answers we seek!

Next Time In

EARTHSONG

Volume II

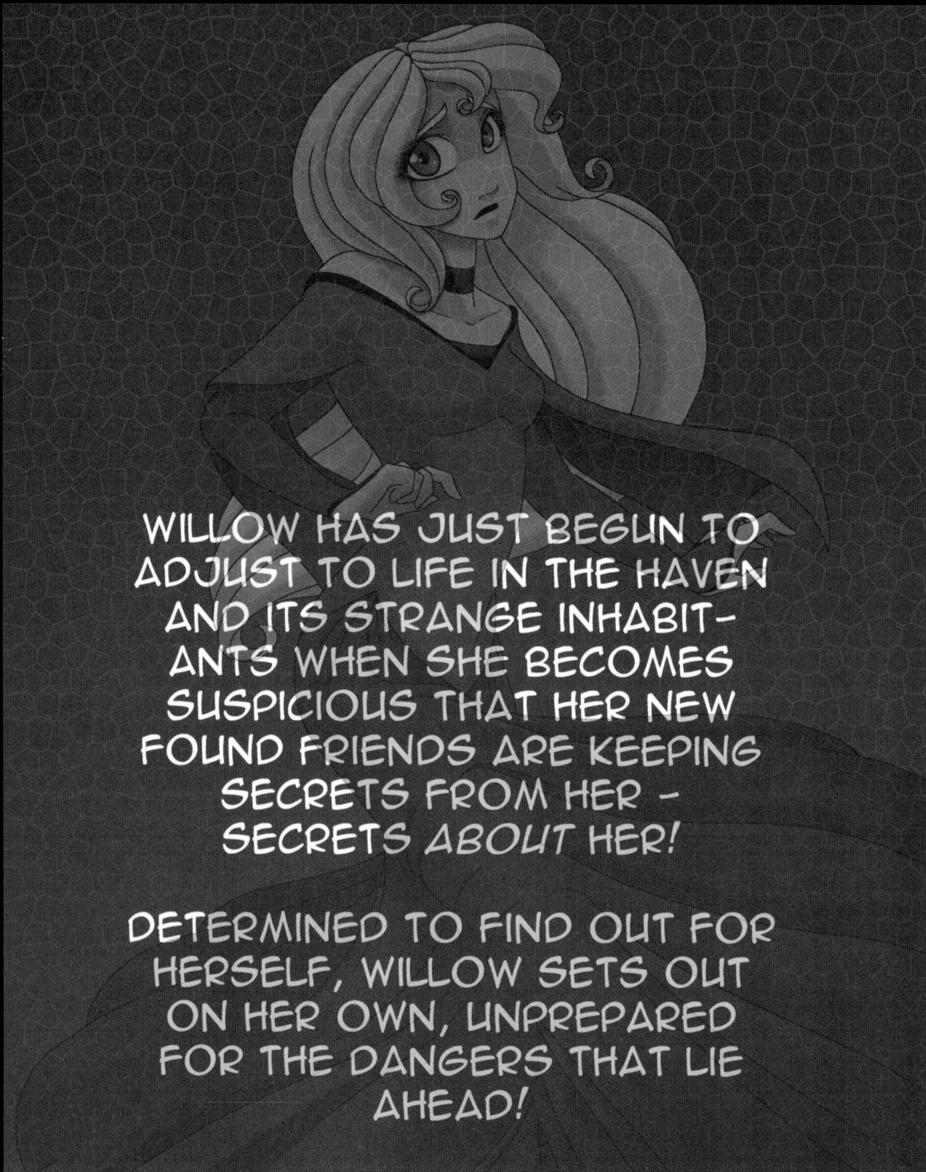
WILLOW HAS JUST BEGUN TO ADJUST TO LIFE IN THE HAVEN AND ITS STRANGE INHABIT-ANTS WHEN SHE BECOMES SUSPICIOUS THAT HER NEW FOUND FRIENDS ARE KEEPING SECRETS FROM HER - SECRETS *ABOUT* HER!
DETERMINED TO FIND OUT FOR HERSELF, WILLOW SETS OUT ON HER OWN, UNPREPARED FOR THE DANGERS THAT LIE AHEAD!

EARTHSONG

CHARACTER GALLERY

CHECK OUT THE STATS ON YOUR FAVOURITE CHARACTERS!

EARTHSONG

STATUS: STONEKEEPER, CHILDLESS
FUN FACT: EARTHSONG MODELED HER MANIFEST FORM AFTER GAIA'S – SHE WAS ALSO NAMED BY ONE OF GAIA'S VISITING CHILDREN

BELUOSUS

PRONOUNCED: BEL-OOO-**OH**-SUS
STATUS: THOUGHT DEAD, CHILDREN LOST, CORE CURRENTLY RESIDES ON EARTHSONG'S SURFACE
FUN FACT: "BELUOSUS" IS NOT HIS ORIGINAL NAME...

NANASHI

PRONOUNCED: NA-NASH-EEE
AGE: UNKNOWN
HEIGHT: 5'6"
SOULSTONE ABILITY: SIDEREAN
FUN FACT: HER FATHER WAS A SAMURAI AND TAUGHT HER HOW TO FIGHT

WILLOW

AGE: 21
HEIGHT: 5'6"
SOULSTONE ABILITY: UNTESTED
FUN FACT: LADY YATES HAS BEEN DRAWING WILLOW EVER SINCE SHE WAS 16 YEARS OLD!

K'thonna

PRONOUNCED: KUH-THON-YAH
AGE: 25
HEIGHT: 5'11"
SOULSTONE ABILITY: METAL CRAFTING
FUN FACT: K'THONYA'S HAIR WAS INSPIRED BY ALICIA KEYS

TENGU

PRONOUNCED: TENG-OOO
AGE: 3
HEIGHT: 8"
SOULSTONE ABILITY: ELECTRICITY
FUN FACT: "FAIRY DUST" ISN'T DUST AT ALL – IT'S SPARKS!

SKOGUL

PRONOUNCED: SKOH-GULL
AGE: 24
HEIGHT: 6'1"
SOULSTONE ABILITY: WIND/AIR
FUN FACT: IN THE FIRST VERSION OF EARTHSONG, SKOGUL'S HAIR WAS MORE BIRD-LIKE, MAKING HER HEAD LOOK LIKE A BLUEJAY'S!

ulkurz

PRONOUNCED: ULL-KURZ
AGE: 34
HEIGHT: USUALLY CROUCHES AT ABOUT 4'6"
SOULSTONE ABILITY: PHASING
FUN FACT: ULKURZ IS THE OLDEST MEMBER OF THE MANDGRAGORA

SAGE

STATUS: NO SOULSTONES FORMING
FUN FACT: SAGE IS THE ELDEST OF THE ALPHA PLANETS. HE REFUSED AT FIRST TO TAKE A NAME WHEN HE CREATED HIS CHILDREN. WHEN THE OTHER PLANETS BEGAN TO REFER TO HIM AS "THE SAGEST OF THE PLANETS", HE EVENTUALLY RELENTED AND ALLOWED THEM TO SIMPLY CALL HIM "SAGE"

GAIA

STATUS: SUFFERING FROM THE SOULSTONE PHENOMENON
FUN FACT: GAIA IS EARTH'S MANIFEST!

OLIBLISH

STATUS: SUCCOMBED TO THE SOULSTONE PHENOMENON SEVERAL MILLENNIA AGO
FUN FACT: OLIBLISH'S CHARACTER DESIGN IS INSPIRED BY THE GODS OF ANCIENT EGYPTIAN MYTHOLOGY

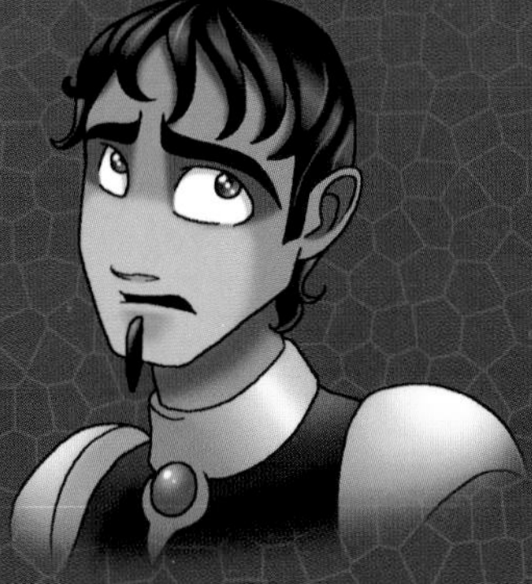

RICHARD

AGE: 28
HEIGHT: 6'2"
SOULSTONE ABILITY: LIMB PROJECTION
FUN FACT: RICHARD'S APPEARANCE IS ROUGHLY BASED ON ONE OF MY OLD BOSSES! HE NAGGED ME TO DRAW HIM AS A COMIC CHARACTER, SO I OBLIGED BY PUTTING HIM INTO THE COMIC AND PROMPTLY KNOCKING HIM OFF! >:D

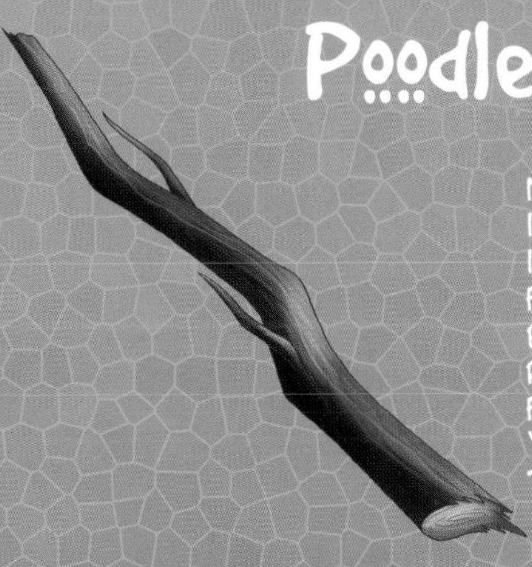

Poodle The Beating Stick

NANASHI'S WEAPON OF CIRCUMSTANCE IN THE *GENESIS* FLASHBACK EARNED ITS ILLUSTRIOUS TITLE COURTESY OF MY FELLOW WEBCOMIC CREATOR AND FRIEND, BLIX! EVER SINCE IT HAS BECOME A LONG RUNNING JOKE AMONGST *EARTHSONG* FANS WHO ROUTINELY THREATEN TO "POODLE" ANY WHO WOULD STAND IN THEIR WAY.

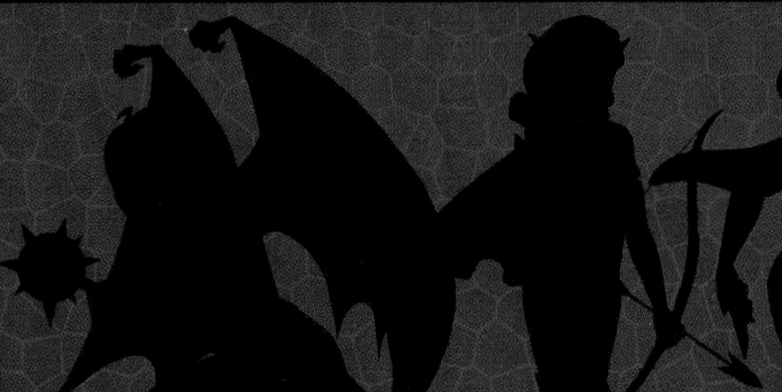

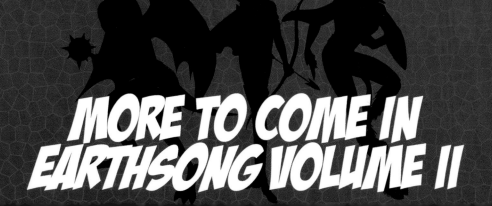

MORE TO COME IN EARTHSONG VOLUME II

GLOSSARY

THERE'S A GREAT DEAL OF UNIQUE
TERMINOLOGY IN EARTHSONG –
THIS GLOSSARY SHOULD HELP YOU
KEEP IT ALL STRAIGHT!

ABDITE STONE – CREATED BY EARTHSONG SPECIFICALLY TO
HIDE THE HAVEN, THIS ROCK APPEARS SOLID ON ONE SIDE AND
CLEAR ON THE OTHER.

ALPHA PLANETS – THE FIRST THREE PLANETS CREATED BY THE
SIDERA: SAGE, GAIA, AND OLIBLISH. THEIR ELEMENT IS THE MOST
POTENT OF ALL THE PLANETS.

AMETHYST TREE – SIMILAR TO A WILLOW, THESE TREES
FEATURE A BRIGHT SILVER BARK AND TRANSPARENT LAVENDER
LEAVES.

FUN FACT: IN THE ORIGINAL EARTHSONG, WILLOW WOKE UP
UNDER A TREE THAT HAD HANGING BRANCHES LIKE A WILLOW BUT
LEAVES LIKE A MAPLE. ACCORDINGLY IT WAS DUBBED THE "WIPLE"
TREE. UNFORTUNATELY THOUGH, MANY PEOPLE THOUGHT THAT I
DIDN'T KNOW WHAT A REAL WILLOW LOOKED LIKE AND HAD MADE A
MISTAKE. SUCH WAS NOT THE CASE, BUT MY CREATIVITY WAS
BEING INTERPRETED AS IGNORANCE NONETHELESS! REGARDLESS,
I RESOLVED THAT SHOULD I EVER START OVER AGAIN, THE WIPLE
TREE WOULD BE THE FIRST THING I CHANGED... AND SO I DID!

AUGMENT STONE – EVERY PLANET'S SURFACE CONTAINS SCAT-
TERED TRACES OF OTHER PLANETS' ELEMENTS (WHAT WE CALL
JEWELS). WHEN A STONE MADE OF AN MATCHING ELEMENT IS
WORN BY A SOULSTONE HOST, IT SERVES TO AUGMENT, OR HELP
FOCUS, THE POWERS OF THAT CHILD.

BADLANDS – THE REGION AROUND BELLIOSUS' LANDED CORE,
WHICH HE HAS TWISTED AND SCARRED PURPOSEFULLY IN SPITE OF
EARTHSONG.

CHILD – THE SENTIENT LIFEFORCE CREATED BY A PLANET.
FORMED OF THE PLANET'S OWN CONSCIOUSNESS, EACH CHILD
HAS A DEGREE OF A PLANET'S ELEMENT NATURALLY PRESENT IN
THEIR BLOOD.

CORE – THE MAIN COLLECTION OF A PLANET'S ELEMENT, FOUND
DEEP BELOW THE SURFACE AT CENTRE OF THE WORLD.

GLOSSARY

ELEMENT – THE CONSCIOUS MATTER THAT CONSTITUTES THE CORE OF A PLANET

EVE – A PLANET'S FIRST CHILD IS REFERRED TO AS AN EVE. EVES ARE IMMORTAL AND POSSESS ONE UNIQUE POWER THAT THEY PASS ON, THOUGH IN A DIMINISHED FORM, TO SUBSEQUENT GENERATIONS OF CHILDREN.

HAVEN – FORMED OUT OF THE MOUNTAIN AND HIDDEN BY ABDITE STONE, THIS BUILDING PROTECTS EARTHSONG, HER THRONE, AND HER VISITING CHILDREN.

HOMEWORLD – A VISITING CHILD'S PLANET OF ORIGIN.

HOST/BEARER – THE UNLUCKY CHILD THAT LOOSE ELEMENT CHOOSES TO FORM A SOULSTONE IN.

MANDRAGORA – THE NAME OF BELUOSZUS' FOLLOWERS.

MANIFEST – THE FORM PROJECTED BY THE MANIFEST STONE.

MANIFEST STONE – COMPOSED OF A VERY DENSE COLLECTION OF A PLANET'S ELEMENT, THIS STONE ALLOWS THE PLANET TO FOCUS THEIR CONSCIOUSNESS AND THEIR POWERS ABOVE THEIR SURFACE. WITHOUT IT, THEY CANNOT CREATE OR COMMUNICATE WITH THEIR CHILDREN.

PLANETARY COUNCIL – A GATHERING OF ALL THE PLANETS' MANIFEST STONES. THIS IS A RARE OCCURRENCE AS IT TAKES SAGE QUITE A BIT OF ENERGY TO GATHER THEM ALL FROM THE FAR CORNERS OF THE UNIVERSE AND MOST OF THE PLANETS ARE UNINTERESTED IN ATTENDING ANYHOW!

GLOSSARY

POWERS – SOULSTONES GRANT THEIR BEARERS SPECIAL ABILITIES, AKIN TO THOSE THEY HAD WHEN THE GENERATIONS WERE CLOSER TO THEIR EVE.

REMNANT – THE LAST FEW MOMENTS OF A CHILD'S PRE-EARTHSONG LIFE. THE MOST THEY CAN REMEMBER *CLEARLY* IS THE EVENT THAT TRIGGERED THEIR SOULSTONE'S FORMATION.

SIDERA – THE STARS, MADE UP OF A SINGLE CONSCIOUSNESS, ARE COMPOSED OF PURE ELEMENT AND ARE RESPONSIBLE FOR GIVING LIFE TO THE PLANETS.

SIDEREAN POWERS – THE SIDERA HAVE ACCESS TO ALL TYPES OF POWERS, BUT THIS SPECIFICALLY REFERS TO THE POWER TO SEPARATE HOST FROM STONE AND RETURN BOTH TO THEIR HOMEWORLD.

SOULSTONE – WHEN A PLANET'S ELEMENT SEEPS AWAY FROM THE CORE, IT SEEKS A CHILD AS HOST IN LIEU OF THE CORE. WHEN ENOUGH ELEMENT HAS BUILT UP IN A HOST, IT HAS ONLY TO WAIT FOR THE CHILD TO EXPERIENCE A POWERFUL EMOTION TO TRIGGER ITS FINAL FORMATION INTO A SOULSTONE. SOULSTONES ARE VERY DANGEROUS TO A CHILD ON ITS HOMEWORLD, AS THE RESONANCE FROM THE PLANET WILL OVERLOAD IT AND ANNIHILATE BOTH STONE AND HOST. BUT FAR AWAY, ON EARTHSONG'S SURFACE, THEY ARE SAFE AND THE SOULSTONES GRANT INCREDIBLE POWERS TO THEIR BEARERS. SOULSTONES TYPICALLY FORM NEAR A CHILD'S HEART.

STONEKEEPER – THE TITLE FOR EARTHSONG'S DUTIES.

NOW THAT WAS A MOUTHFUL!
HOPE YOU FOUND IT HANDY!

FANART

I'VE GOTTEN A LOT OF GREAT FANART OVER THE YEARS - MY FANS ARE AS TALENTED AS THEY ARE GENEROUS! SO I WANTED TO INCLUDE A FEW OF MY FAVOURITES IN THE BOOK TOO!

IF YOU WOULD LIKE TO SEND ME FANART, EMAIL IT TO
FANART@EARTHSONGSAGA.COM

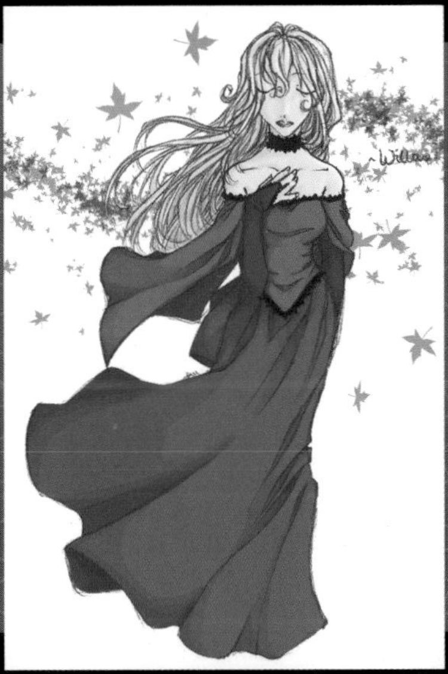

WILLOW
BY BLU-CHAN

BLU-CHAN'S GALLERY:
HTTP://LUNA-KITSUNE-BLU.DEVIANTART.COM/

WILLOW
BY REED BOND

REED'S GALLERY:
HTTP://REED682.DEVIANTART.COM

REED'S COMIC:
WWW.NORMAL.BONDINGPLACE.COM

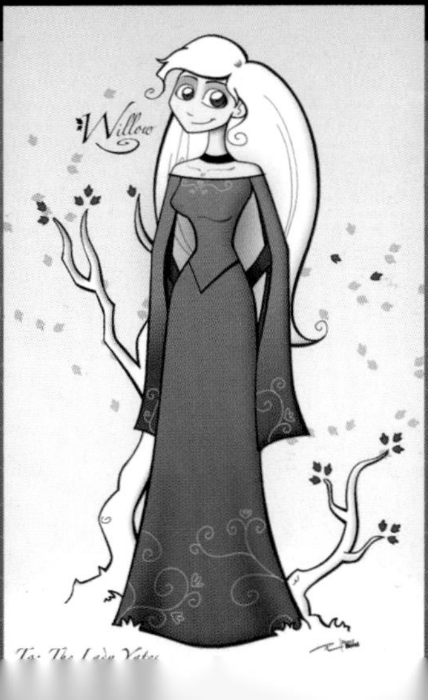
Willow

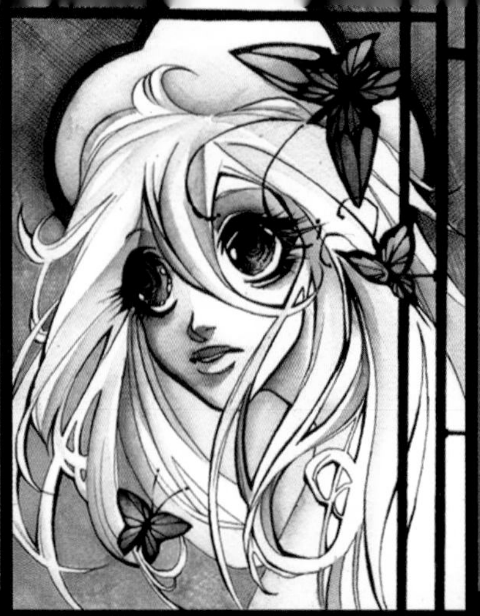

WILLOW
BY BLIX

BLIX'S GALLERY:
HTTP://BLIX-IT.DEVIANTART.COM/

BLIX'S COMIC:
WWW.EATKITTIES.COM

WILLOW AND EARTHSONG
BY KARLA GROTH

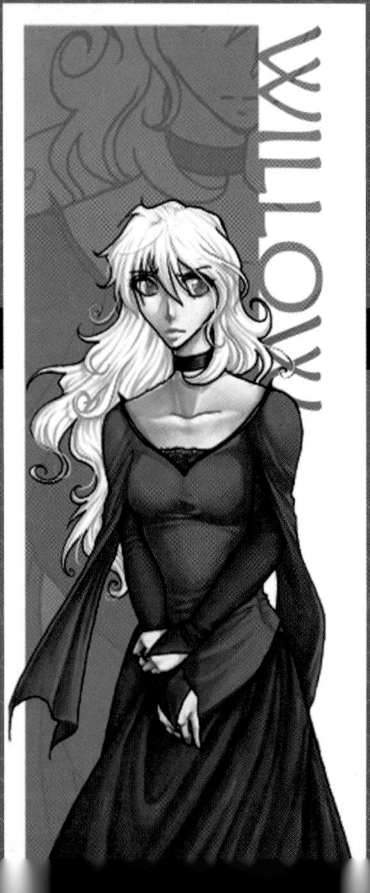
WILLOW

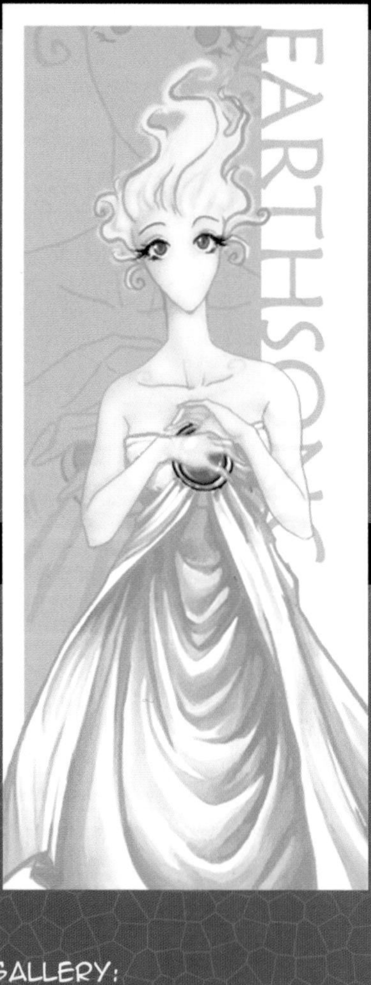
EARTHSONG

KARLA'S GALLERY:
HTTP://FENOMENA.DEVIANTART.COM/

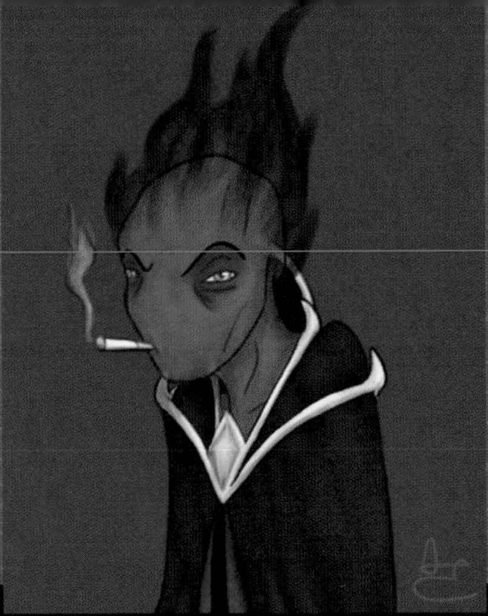

BELUOSUS THE ADDICT
BY CAT

CAT'S GALLERY:
HTTP://CATWINGS.DEVIANTART.COM/

ULKURZ INSPIRED
BY CAT

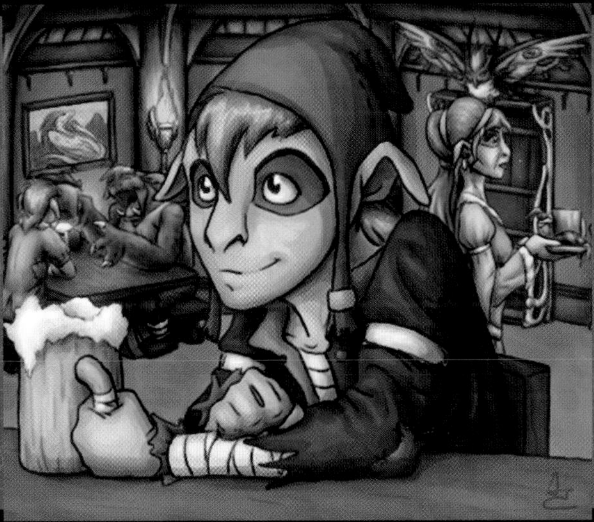

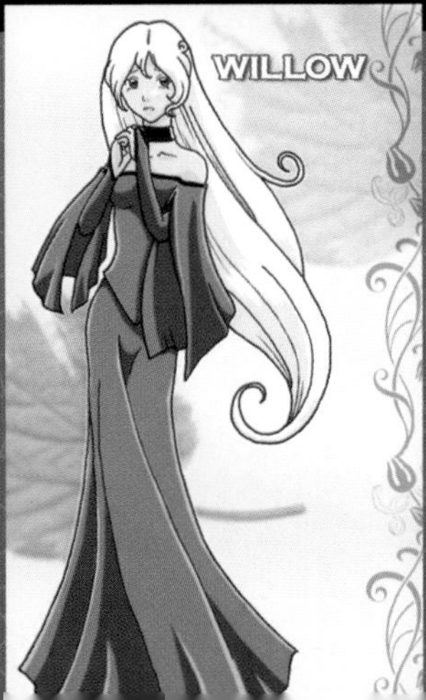
WILLOW

WILLOW
BY SHIRU04

SHIRU04'S GALLERY:
HTTP://SHIRU04.DEVIANTART.COM/

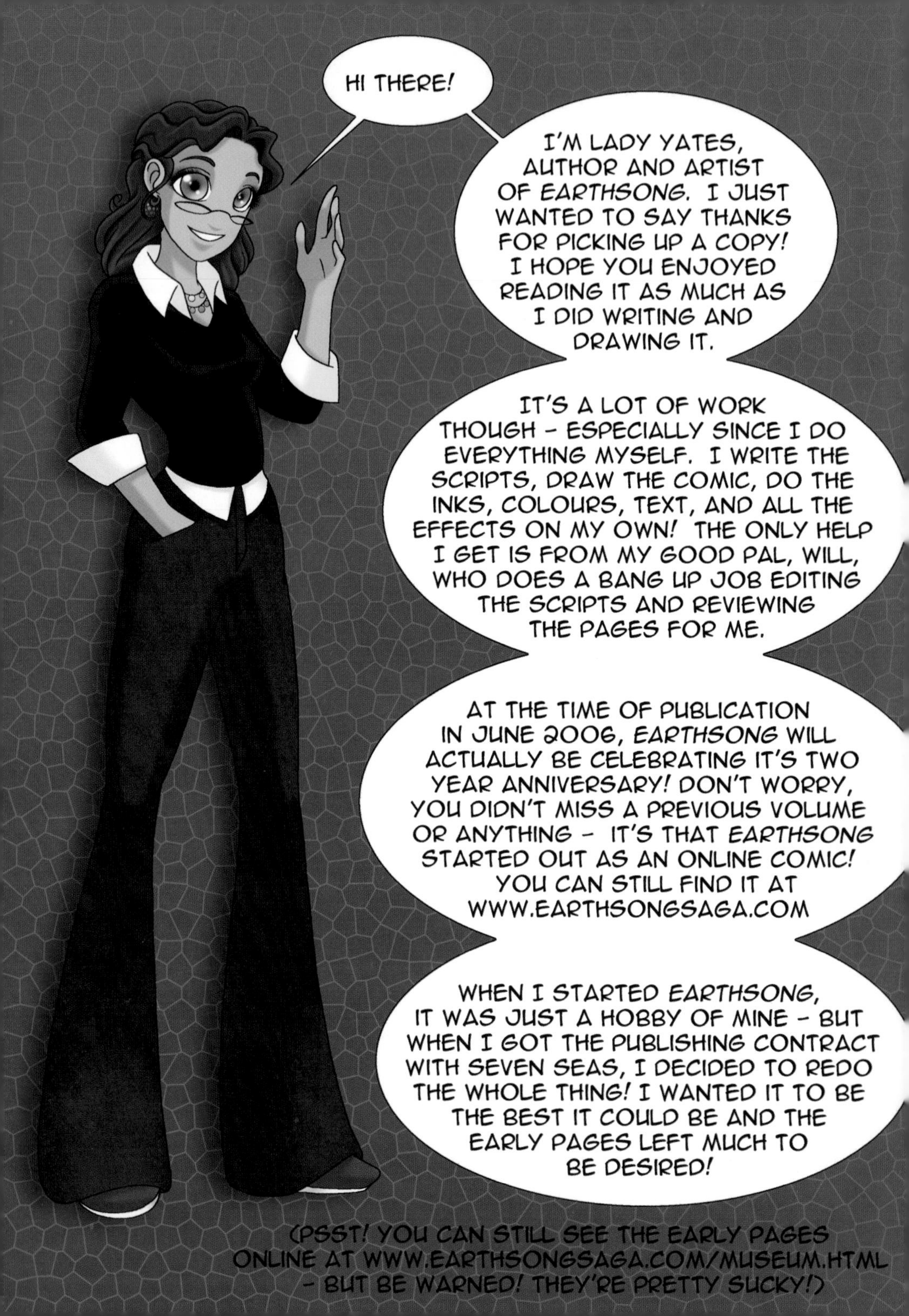
HI THERE!
I'M LADY YATES, AUTHOR AND ARTIST OF EARTHSONG. I JUST WANTED TO SAY THANKS FOR PICKING UP A COPY! I HOPE YOU ENJOYED READING IT AS MUCH AS I DID WRITING AND DRAWING IT.
IT'S A LOT OF WORK THOUGH - ESPECIALLY SINCE I DO EVERYTHING MYSELF. I WRITE THE SCRIPTS, DRAW THE COMIC, DO THE INKS, COLOURS, TEXT, AND ALL THE EFFECTS ON MY OWN! THE ONLY HELP I GET IS FROM MY GOOD PAL, WILL, WHO DOES A BANG UP JOB EDITING THE SCRIPTS AND REVIEWING THE PAGES FOR ME.
AT THE TIME OF PUBLICATION IN JUNE 2006, EARTHSONG WILL ACTUALLY BE CELEBRATING IT'S TWO YEAR ANNIVERSARY! DON'T WORRY, YOU DIDN'T MISS A PREVIOUS VOLUME OR ANYTHING - IT'S THAT EARTHSONG STARTED OUT AS AN ONLINE COMIC! YOU CAN STILL FIND IT AT WWW.EARTHSONGSAGA.COM
WHEN I STARTED EARTHSONG, IT WAS JUST A HOBBY OF MINE - BUT WHEN I GOT THE PUBLISHING CONTRACT WITH SEVEN SEAS, I DECIDED TO REDO THE WHOLE THING! I WANTED IT TO BE THE BEST IT COULD BE AND THE EARLY PAGES LEFT MUCH TO BE DESIRED!
(PSST! YOU CAN STILL SEE THE EARLY PAGES ONLINE AT WWW.EARTHSONGSAGA.COM/MUSEUM.HTML - BUT BE WARNED! THEY'RE PRETTY SUCKY!)

SO WITH ONLY THREE MONTHS UNTIL MY DEADLINE, I PRETTY MUCH HAD TO BURY MYSELF IN THE COMIC IN ORDER TO GET IT DONE!

IT TAKES 4 TO 6 HOURS AT LEAST TO DO EACH PAGE AND I HAD TO DO 2 OR 3 PAGES A DAY FOR THE LAST TWO MONTHS! IT WAS REALLY TIRING, BUT DEFINITELY WORTH IT! I'M VERY PROUD OF THIS EDITION OF EARTHSONG – I'VE COME A LONG WAY SINCE I STARTED IN 2004.

AS A BONUS TO ALL YOU GREAT PEOPLE WHO BOUGHT THE BOOK, I'VE CREATED A SPECIAL SECTION OF MY WEBSITE JUST FOR YOU!

GO TO WWW.EARTHSONGSAGA.COM/VOLUME1.HTML TO GET EXCLUSIVE DESKTOP WALLPAPERS, INSIGHTFUL TUTORIALS, AND OTHER NEAT STUFF!

SEE YA LATER, GATORS!

P.S. HERE'S A LITTLE INFO ABOUT ME IF YOU'RE INTERESTED!

LADY STATS:

AGE: 25
LOCATION: ONTARIO, CANADA

LIKES: DRAWING, PLAYING GUITAR, READING, FLEA MARKETS, MYTHOLOGY AND FOLKLORE, COMICS AND CARTOONS (JAPANESE AND AMERICAN!), LIVE MUSIC, MOVIES, COCONUT, HEIROGLYPHS, STRATEGY GAMES, AND COLLECTING FONTS!

DISLIKES: TEAM SPORTS, CHICK FLICKS, CAULIFLOWER, PINK

CONTACT ME AT LADYYATES@EARTHSONGSAGA.COM

THANK YOU!

MANY GRATEFUL THANKS GO OUT TO:

JASON AND KURT – YOU TWO MADE MY DREAM COME TRUE! IT MEANS THE WORLD TO ME THAT YOU TRUSTED AND BELIEVED IN ME. THANK YOU FOR THIS WONDERFUL OPPORTUNITY.

MOM AND DAD – FOR GIVING ME A HERITAGE OF ARTISTIC TALENT, A LOVE OF CARTOONS AND COMICS, AND A LIFETIME OF LOVE AND SUPPORT

MEL AND BILL – WITHOUT YOU GUYS, EARTHSONG NEVER WOULD HAVE MADE IT ONLINE!

WILL – MY TRUSTY TINMAN, WITHOUT WHOM THE WORLD OF EARTHSONG WOULD BE THAT MUCH DIMMER.

MY FORUM MEMBERS – I LOVE YOU GUYS. IT BLOWS MY MIND HOW INVOLVED AND INTERESTED YOU ARE IN THE COMIC AND IN EACH OTHER – *MAD HUGGLES FOR MY ONLINE FAMILY*

MY FORUM MODS – BRINGERS OF SANITY TO THE CHAOS THAT IS THE FORUM! I COULD NEVER REPAY YOU ALL FOR THE WORK THAT YOU PUT INTO IT.

MY COMIC PALS – THE WEBCOMIC WORLD'S ONE COLD AND LONELY PLACE IF YOU AIN'T GOT FRIENDS – THANKS FOR ALWAYS BEING THERE FOR ME, WHETHER IT BE THROUGH FANART, A GUEST-STRIP, OR JUST AN EMAIL.

ANYONE WHO HAS EVER VOTED FOR MY COMIC ON TWC, BUZZ, OR ONLINE COMICS! – YOU HELPED ME GET WHERE I AM TODAY!

FANART SUBMITTERS – I'VE ALWAYS BEEN DEEPLY HONOURED BY THE GIGANTIC AMOUNT OF BEAUTIFUL FANART THAT I GET. AS AN ARTIST IT MEANS SO MUCH TO ME THAT SOMEONE ELSE LOVES MY CHARACTERS ENOUGH TO DRAW THEM.

JAIME SEENS – I WISH YOU COULD HAVE SEEN THIS... I HOPE IT WOULD HAVE MADE YOU PROUD.

AND LAST, BUT NOT LEAST...

MY HUSBAND – FOR DILIGENTLY SLEEPING ON THE BED WHILST I SLAVED AWAY ON THE COMIC

OH! AND THANK *YOU* FOR BUYING
THIS COPY OF EARTHSONG!!!

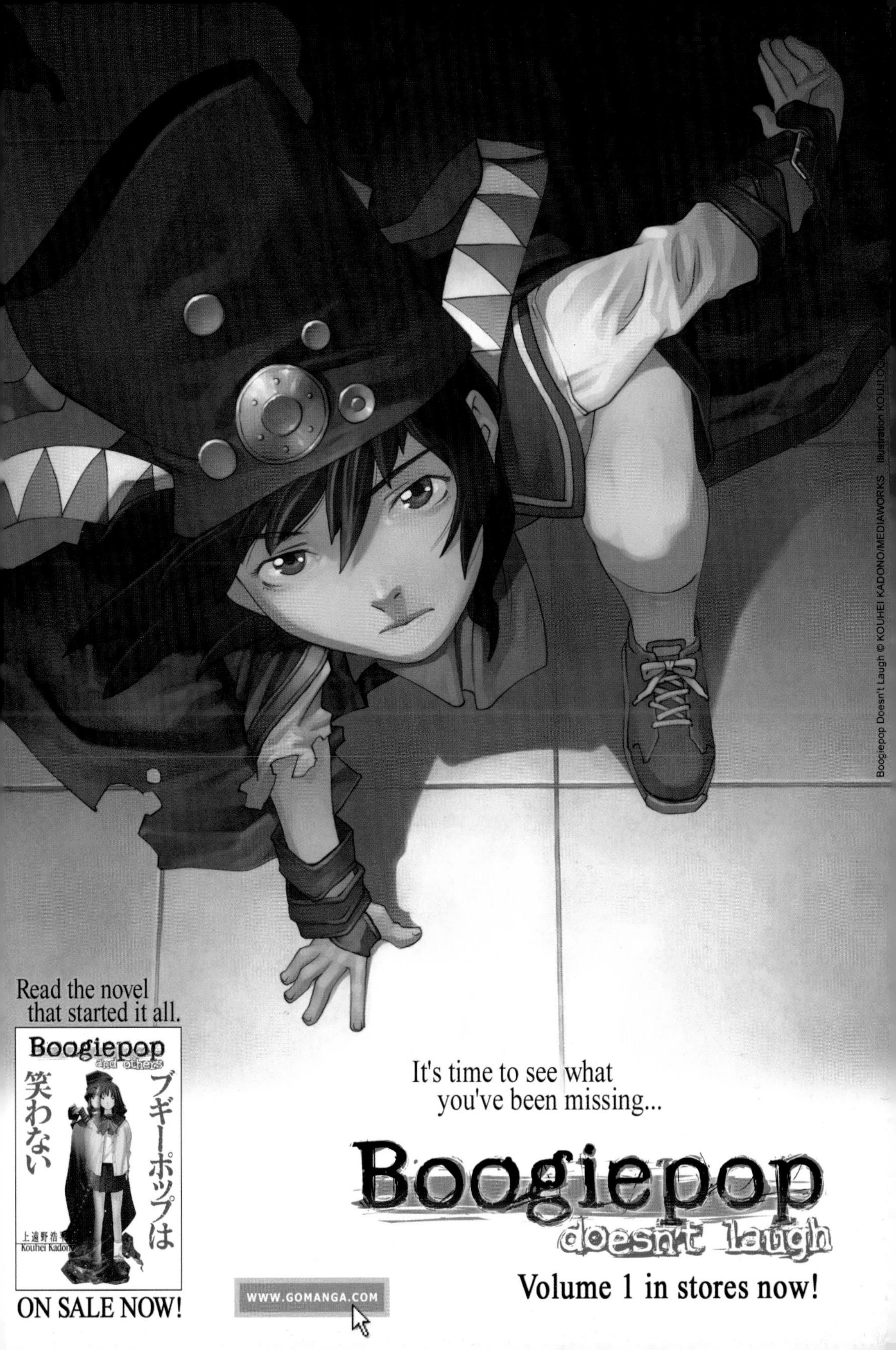
Boogiepop Doesn't Laugh © KOUHEI KADONO/MEDIAWORKS Illustration KOUJI OG
Read the novel that started it all.
Boogiepop and others
ブギーポップは笑わない
上遠野浩平
Kouhei Kadon
ON SALE NOW!
WWW.GOMANGA.COM
It's time to see what you've been missing...
Boogiepop doesn't laugh
Volume 1 in stores now!

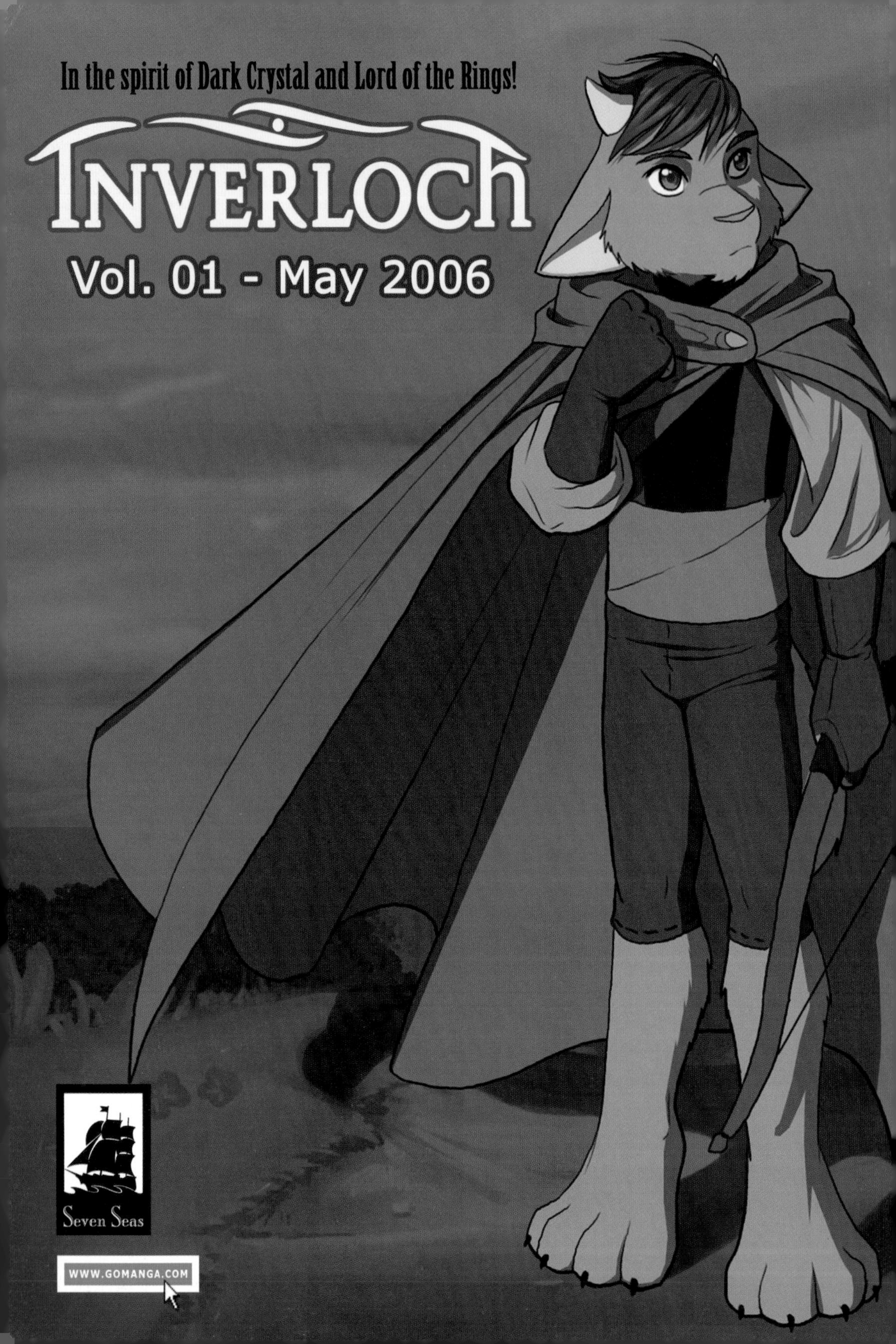
In the spirit of Dark Crystal and Lord of the Rings!
INVERLOCH
Vol. 01 - May 2006
Seven Seas
WWW.GOMANGA.COM

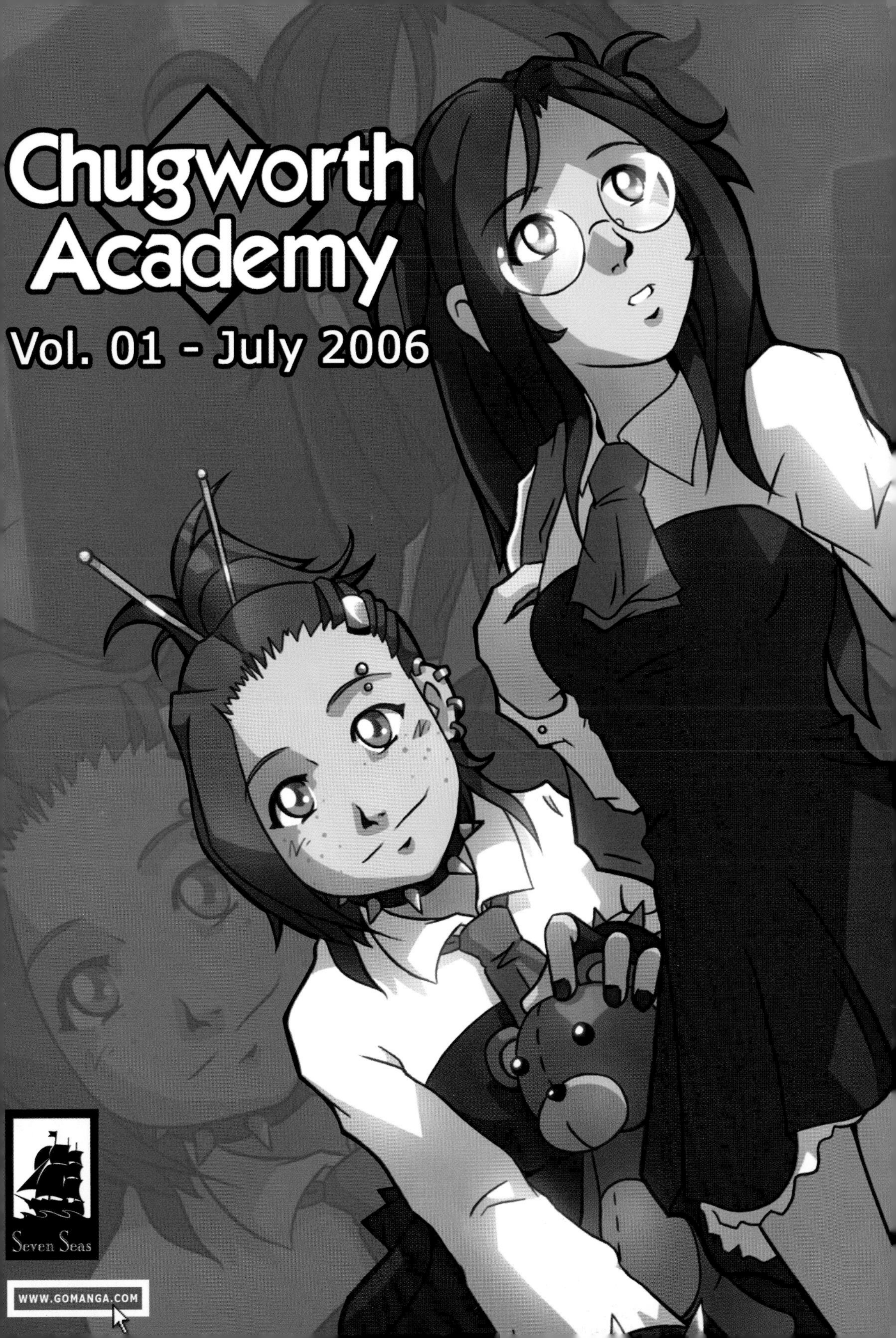
Chugworth Academy
Vol. 01 - July 2006
Seven Seas
WWW.GOMANGA.COM

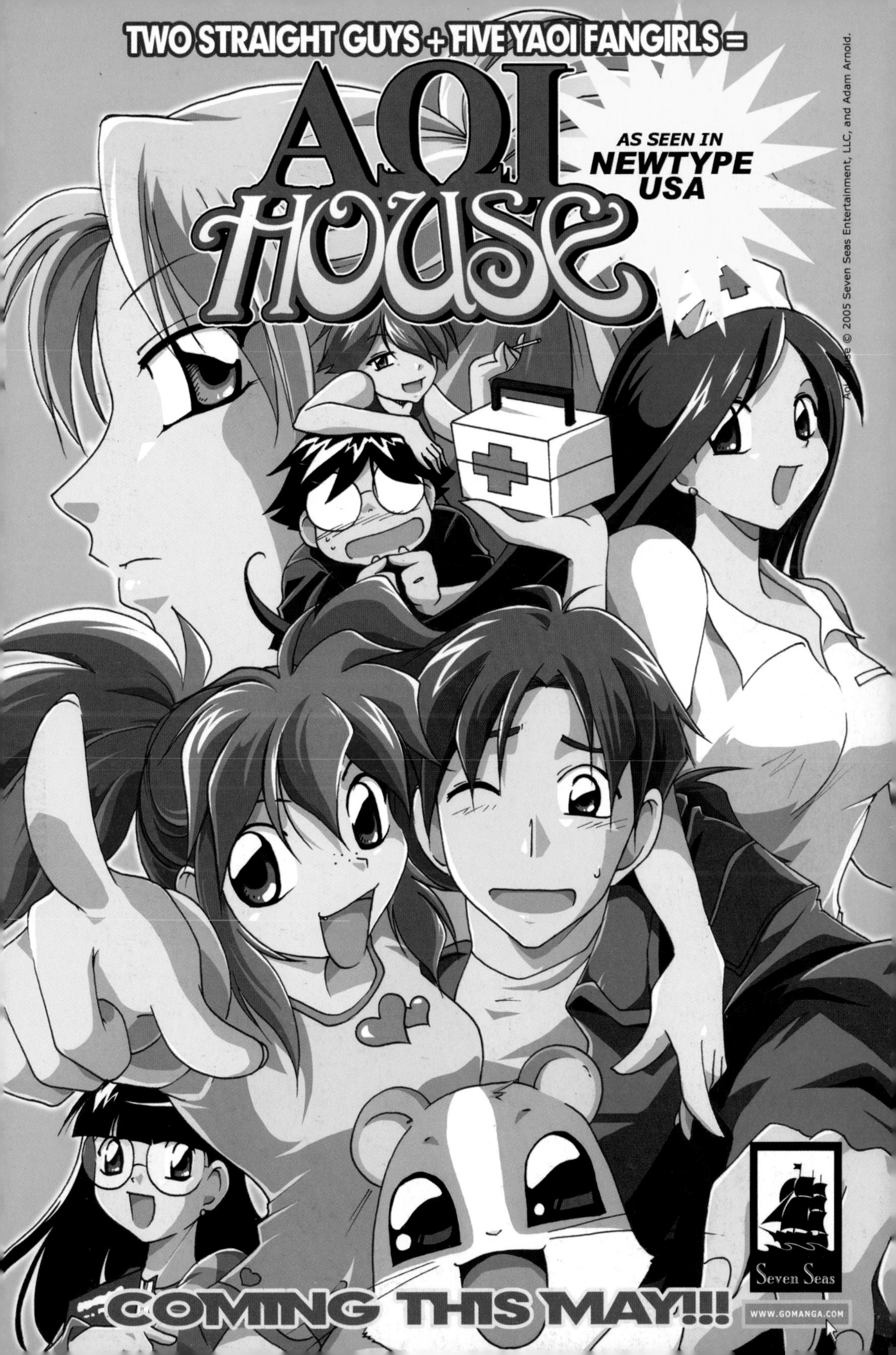
TWO STRAIGHT GUYS + FIVE YAOI FANGIRLS =
AOI HOUSE
AS SEEN IN
NEWTYPE
USA
Aoi House © 2005 Seven Seas Entertainment, LLC, and Adam Arnold.
Seven Seas
COMING THIS MAY!!!
WWW.GOMANGA.COM

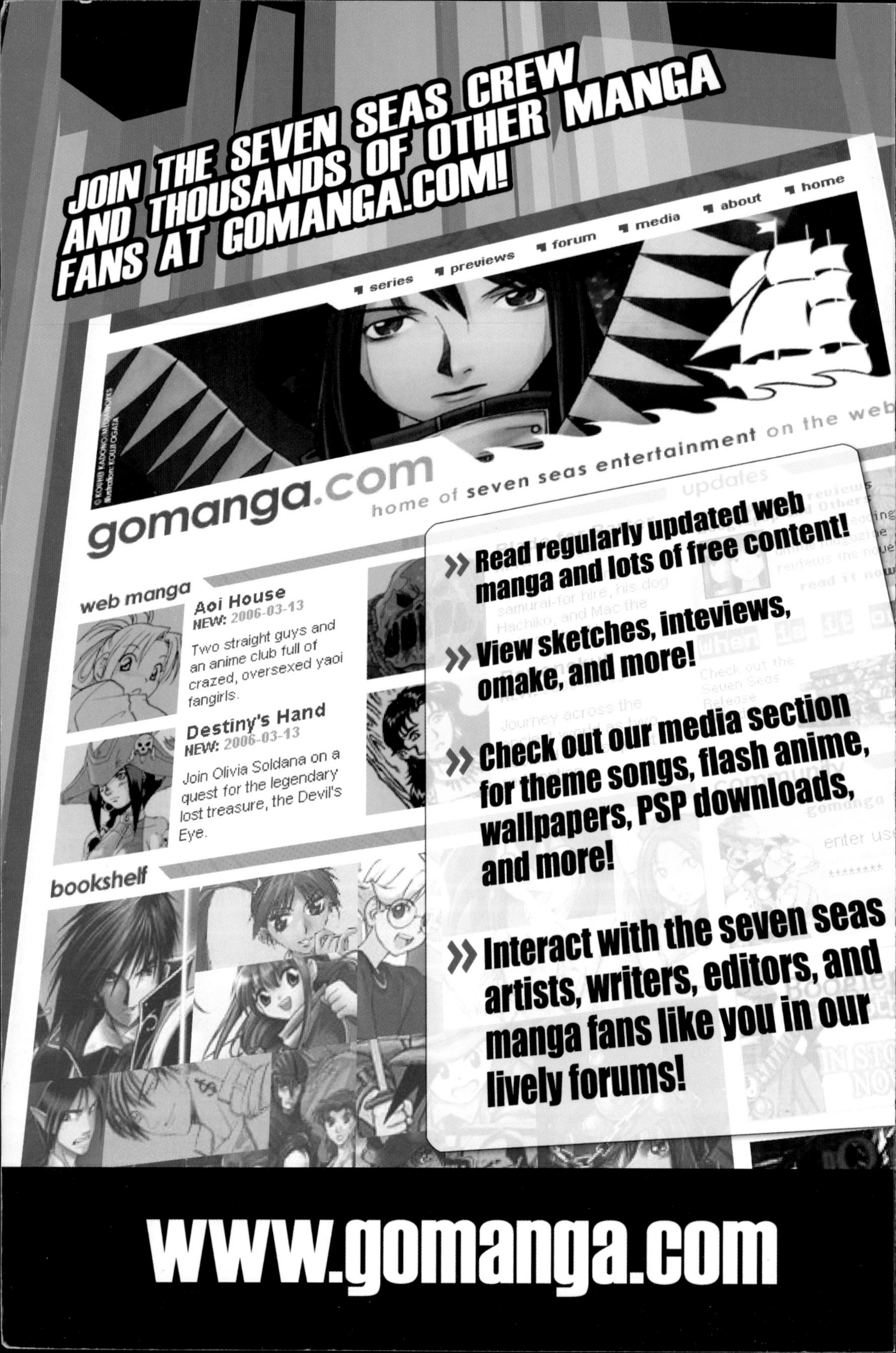
JOIN THE SEVEN SEAS CREW AND THOUSANDS OF OTHER MANGA FANS AT GOMANGA.COM!
series
previews
forum
media
about
home
gomanga.com
home of seven seas entertainment on the web
web manga
Aoi House
NEW: 2006-03-13
Two straight guys and an anime club full of crazed, oversexed yaoi fangirls.
Destiny's Hand
NEW: 2006-03-13
Join Olivia Soldana on a quest for the legendary lost treasure, the Devil's Eye.
bookshelf
» Read regularly updated web manga and lots of free content!
» View sketches, inteviews, omake, and more!
» Check out our media section for theme songs, flash anime, wallpapers, PSP downloads, and more!
» Interact with the seven seas artists, writers, editors, and manga fans like you in our lively forums!
www.gomanga.com